Raith Rovers On This Day

Raith Rovers On This Day

David W. Potter

K&B

Kennedy & Boyd,
an imprint of
Zeticula Ltd,
Unit 13,
196 Rose Street,
Edinburgh,
EH2 4AT,
Scotland.

http://www.kennedyandboyd.co.uk
admin@kennedyandboyd.co.uk

First published in 2018
Copyright © David W. Potter 2018
Cover design © Zeticula Ltd 2018

Every effort has been made to trace copyright holders of images. Any omissions will be corrected in future editions.

Paperback ISBN 978-1-84921-172-7

All rights reserved. No part of this publication may be reproduced, stored in a retrieval system, or transmitted in any form or by any means, electronic, mechanical, photocopying, recording or otherwise, without the prior permission of the publishers.

Acknowledgements

Most of the photographs in this book are taken from 'Always Next Season: 125 Years of Raith Rovers Football Club', now out of print but available in PDF form from http://www.pmfc.co.uk/ans.html and I would like to thank John Litster for his permission to use the photographs. I would also like to thank Tony Fimister of Photogenix, and one time official photographer of the club, and Shaun Balfour for their photographs.

Thanks are also owed to men like "Derwent" "Fifer" "Don John" and "Onlooker" whose opinions of football matches, long ago in The *Fife Free Press*, *The Kirkcaldy Times* and *The Courier*, I have quoted frequently. Kirkcaldy is well covered for football coverage in newspapers.

But those who have helped me more than anyone else have been those supporters who have watched the games and endured the trials and tribulations of supporting a football team.

I refer to men like Bert Ross and Tom Murray of long ago, and George Proudfoot of today. There are others, many of them now long dead, (especially Bob Reid, goalkeeper in the 1960s) who have perhaps inadvertently given me the odd "titbit" about supporting Raith Rovers.

My source, for example, for the February 23 1924 scandal was impeccable, but I am bound by confidentiality (even posthumously!) from disclosing it.

To those whom I have omitted, my apologies, but I hope I can make it up to you by your enjoyment of the book.

David Potter
Kirkcaldy, July 2018

Contents

Acknowledgements	v
Illustrations	ix
Introduction	1
July	7
August	45
September	87
October	123
November	161
December	199
January	239
February	277
March	315
April	353
May	391
June	429
Index	467

Illustrations

In memory of the Raith Rovers players who died in the Great War	9
Sandy Archibald	11
James Logan, as a player	15
George Farm	22
Jimmy Nicholl takes his players on a pre-season run round the Beveridge Park	28
George Herdman	37
Team 1993-1994	46
Nottingham Forest 1967 Programme Cover	51
Team of 1985-86 all set to go. Unfortunately, performances did not live up to expectations!	56
The hard working but slightly disappointing team of 1932-33	58
All set for the Scottish League Second Division in 1902	66
Alec James	69
Hamilton Academical 1994 Programme Cover	71
Celtic 1995 Programme Cover	78
1910-11 — Raith's first season in the First Division of the Scottish League	80
Willie McNaught	85
Bobby Evans	89
Tommy McLean	99
Raith Rovers in 1953	102
Aston Villa 1960 Programme Cover	117
Raith Rovers in 2006	122
An agreeable and socially responsible moment in the club's history	130
Gordon Wallace, Player of the Year, 1968	139
Bayern Muchich 1995 Programme Cover	142
Scott Thomson	151
Andy Young	155
Pat Gardner	157
Raith Rovers in season 1977-78	166
James Logan as manager	171

Special trains for Edinburgh, 1921	175
Dr John Smith	179
Aberdeen 1995 Programme Cover	181
Murray McDermott	187
Andy Leigh	189
Gordon Dalziel turns away after scoring the equaliser in the League Cup final	194
Steve Crawford and Jimmy Nicholl with the Scottish League Cup	195
George McNicoll with Scottish Qualifying Cup	200
Ernie Till	205
Fur Week at Isaac Benzie's	206
John Urquhart against Rangers	210
John McGlynn	218
We all knew that Raith Rovers were an old club, but look at that date! Is that BC or AD?	220
St Johnstone 1993 Programme Cover	231
Raith Rovers 1905-06	234
Stark's Park in the 1920s. Pride of place is the new stand, opened on 30th December 1922	236
Raith Rovers Directors early 1950s	240
The punters on the old terracing	248
Willie Porter	259
Stark's Park in the early 1960s. Observe the old "cow shed" in front of the railway	264
Raith Rovers v Third Lanark 1950. Observe the rickety railway stand	269
Bobby Reid	272
Peter Hodge	280
A mock death card signifying the demise of Hearts in 1914.	286
Raith Rovers in 1921.	288
Raith Rovers 1937/38. Observe the club linesman with his flag	292
Director and retired goalkeeper Bobby Reid answers the call	296
Frank Connor, one of Raith's better managers.	299
Gordon Dalziel	301
Raith Rovers v Dumbarton 1988.	310
Raith Rovers v East Fife 1953.	318
St Mirren 1913 Programme Cover	324
Willie Penman, more commonly known as a goalscorer, proves his versatility	330

The Footballers' Batallion of World War I	334
Stephen McAnespie and Davie Sinclair with mascots	338
Raith Rovers v East Fife in the Scottish Cup replay	344
John Baird scored the goal that won the League Challenge Cup over Rangers.	359
Winners of the League Challenge Cup in 2014	360
A sign of the Premier League in 1993, a TV box!	364
Raith supporter Val McDermid who also writes crime stories	368
Raith Rovers 1922 in front of the old stand	378
The main entrance to Stark's Park until the 1990s	384
Raith Rovers 1949.	390
Moments of triumph were few and far between in the 2000s	392
Ian Porterfield	397
Frank Connor	402
Raith Rovers about to embark to Denmark for a summer tour	404
Jason Dair	409
Happy Directors in 2003 when promotion is achieved.	422
Can you spot the Prime Minister and the writer of detective fiction in the Directors' Box?	430
Malcolm McLure of Raith Rovers and Billy Steel of Dundee	434
Raith Rovers 1887, believed to be the earliest photograph ever taken of the club	438
Raith Rovers 1903/1904	442
Willie McNaught, Player of the Year awarded by the Supporters Club	452
Raith Rovers 2003/2004	458
A fine view of Stark's Park from the air	466

Introduction

Kirkcaldy is a very fine Scottish town. Once proudly industrial and built on two pillars — coal and linoleum, Kirkcaldy has probably felt the effect of de-industrialisation more than most places. Coal has now gone, a victim of the Thatcher v Scargill war of the 1980s which was bound to lead to the destruction of something, but linoleum still has a toehold and there are some days that the "queer like smell" is still there — almost like a ghost. Or a (w)raith in fact.

Why is Kirkcaldy's football team called Raith Rovers? No-one really knows, but there is an area of town, not all that far away from Stark's Park, called the Raith Estate. Why is that so called? Various scholars have worked hard to dig up meanings like "cattle enclosure" or "land near the sea" or whatever. But as likely an explanation as any could come from the medieval gentleman called Michael Scott of Balwearie. Read him up, if you will. There is a board about him at the top of the Beveridge Park. He was a wizard, a magician and one of his hobbies was necromancy, the summoning up of dead folk. It is not necessarily a hobby that brings any great success rate, one wouldn't imagine, but maybe some folk would imagine a few "wraiths" floating about the area of town where the Beveridge Park, Balwearie High School and Stark's Park are now. Knock off the silent "w" and we have "raith". Hey presto, as old Michael might have said!

Raith Rovers played their first game in 1883, apparently on the current site of Balwearie High School. They subsequently moved to Robbie's Park, inside the modern Beveridge Park. Robbie had apparently been a well-known local horse, it was said. In 1891, they moved to Stark's Park, Mr Stark having been a local landowner, and they have stayed there ever since. The ground is a funny one. The main stand, built in 1922, turns a corner and stops at the half way line. There was not much anyone could do about that because that is simply the way that Pratt Street runs. Opposite the main stand is the Railway Stand which does indeed look like a station platform. It was built in the 1980s to a great fanfare of trumpets, but it is sadly abandoned now, almost in the way that a child soon tires of its toys a few days after Christmas. It had replaced a quaint looking but distinctly decrepit and hazardous old structure which shook as a train passed and had advertisements for the *Edinburgh Evening News* and sundry coal companies all over it. It had character, but it also had dirt and dry rot and the spectators stood on cinders and railway sleepers, so it had to go.

At each end, there are two ugly looking structures built in the mid-1990s when the club was bullied into going for an all-seater stadium as prescribed by the gangsters of the now discredited SPL with its strong Rangers predominance. This body also had preposterous ideas like, for example, making Inverness Caledonian Thistle play their home games at Pittodrie in Aberdeen. (That is true, by the way, however unbelievable it seems now.) And now that a generation or two of footballing incompetence has condemned Raith Rovers to what looks like a fairly permanent exile from the Premier League, the two stands, particularly the away supporters' stand at the Beveridge Park end of the ground, are seldom full. The phrase "white elephant" barely covers them!

Raith Rovers supporters are usually very deprecating about their team. They are certainly not given to bouts of blind, irrational optimism nor unbridled enthusiasm. They will certainly not tell you that their team is the best in the world. They generally accept their place in life as something like the 15th best team in Scotland. Anything below that puts them down among Brechin, East Stirling, Albion Rovers and Forfar and that is a little infra dig. On the other hand, they cannot compete on any long term basis with the big city teams like Celtic, Rangers, Aberdeen, etc. They have their occasional success against the big boys — sometimes a spectacular one — and that is enjoyed all the more simply because it is so exceptional.

There have been several eras in history when Raith Rovers have been distinctly uppity. In 1898 they won five trophies, admittedly local ones. In the Edwardian days, they won the Scottish Qualifying Cup. The early 1920s under James Logan when Alec James and David Morris played, saw success, a more prolonged period in the 1950s when the "burglar proof" half back line of Young, McNaught and Leigh were around was better and lasted longer, and then came the mid 1990s when they yoyoed in and out of the Premier League, won the Scottish League Cup and dipped their toes in Europe.

Great, halcyon days, but they have to be balanced against the "down" eras — the 1930s, the 1980s and the early 2000s when things happened at the club which occasionally people outside the town simply would not believe and accused us of making it all up. But the club remains beloved of the town, and it is often said that the way the football club are referred to can tell whether someone is a Langtonian or not.

A native Langtonian will, for example, talk about "gress", and will invariably say to someone in April "market weather", whereas an incomer to the town like your author will say "grass" and admit that the weather in April can be changeable.

But it is "the Rovers" which gives it away, as if there are no others. Supporters of Albion, Doncaster, Bristol and a few others will disagree with this of course. But to a Langtonian, "the Rovers" are to football what "the Flyers" are to ice hockey. Axiomatic and defining. To the outsider, there is the attraction that they are no real threat to anyone. They have had their moments — they have won the Scottish League Cup and the Scottish Challenge Cup, but they have never been the Champions of Scotland, and with respect to those who run the club, probably never will. Yet a man who had never been to Kirkcaldy very often (if ever) in his life stepped off the train one day in 1972 to visit his son who was now living there and suddenly burst into Brown, Inglis and Moyes; Raeburn, Morris and Collier; T Duncan, J Duncan, Jennings, Bauld and Archibald. So clearly 1922 had had an effect on him!

The stewardship of the club has often been a source of much distress. In some ways they remind one of the song of Des O'Connor in the 1960s "I let my heart fall into careless hands". There can be little doubt that there have been times when those in charge of the club have done things that have defied belief. Yet in the same way that the Roman Empire could occasionally survive a crazy Emperor, the concept of Raith Rovers has survived some real dangerous idiots in its time, and we can all throw a name or two into the hat there.

It would be ambitious to say that Raith Rovers are the most eccentric team in Scotland. After all, there is strong competition, and Rovers are far from the only club in Scotland whose supporters have wondered why they keep on supporting them. They have also wondered from time to time whether one or other of the Directors of the club might benefit from a visit to a "shrink". Certainly, over the 135 years, there have been some weird goings on, and Raith Rovers have a strong claim to their particular place in the Hall of Madness, particularly when one considers the decade or so as the 20th century gave way to the 21st.

There has also been a certain amount of sheer wickedness. The great team of the 1950s simply grew old and died a natural, benign and genteel death, but the teams of the 1920s and 1990s were dismantled through sheer greed and transfer fees. Only to a point can we accept the "have to sell to survive" philosophy. That is the cant and humbug of rich Directors, put about by their loyal allies in the Press. It is not the view, necessarily, of the terracing punter. And the punter never did accept the "establishment" view of what happened in 1924 and 1981. Those of us with eyes to see can probably work out what it was all about, however.

But crime writers, Prime Ministers and millionaires can support the club too. More importantly, so do the men and women of Kirkcaldy, and they are very important. The days of the regular five figure crowds have long gone, but that reflects the way that society has changed as well. It used to be said of the Scottish working class, that a football match on a Saturday afternoon was "the 90 minute revenge on the rest of the week". The decline of heavy industry has changed all that, but it has not exempted a football team from its bounden duty to represent its community in an intimate and very personal way.

Every day of the year has seen something happening to Raith Rovers. Well, admittedly, late May to early July can see the club go into a kind of abeyance, a kind of summer hibernation, as it were, and it has not always proved easy for the author of this book to find a lot so say about the club on some days. He has nevertheless taken advantage of the very rich local history of the town of Kirkcaldy to fill a few gaps in the summer, when necessary.

This book is not a history of Raith Rovers and does not claim to be such. It is an eclectic choice of some of the fascinating things that have happened over the years to this fascinating club. The months of January and February may be said to have a predilection with the Scottish Cup. This is admitted, (it a fascinating and ancient tournament) but Raith Rovers seem to have a particular aversion to this competition, and their supporters hate to be reminded that both East Fife and Dunfermline Athletic have won it, but Raith Rovers haven't! One recalls the Ollerton Hotel, a now deceased hostelry in Victoria Road. In about 1972, a pound note was pinned to the wall above the bar with a small piece of paper saying "Raith Rovers to win the Scottish Cup by 1976. 20/1" I don't know if anyone took up this bet, but it would have been an easy £1.

Occasionally, the entries are, of necessity, mundane, but then again that author begs his readers to understand that games against Dumbarton and Airdrie in the 1930s may seem to be uninteresting now, but they were crucial then. Such is a supporter's love for his club. The reader may detect a certain preference in the writer for the 1920s. This bias is gladly admitted, for that was the time then they were good. It was also the time when they were bad. Raith Rovers are a perplexing club.

The best all-time team? In traditional 2-3-5 formation, may I suggest?

		McDermott		
	McAnespie		McNaught	
Young		Morris		Baxter
	Cameron		James	
Maule		Penman		Dair

But of course, supporters who have seen more games than I have, will disagree. That is not a problem. It would be a terrible Adolf Hitler kind of world if everyone agreed with each other.

The author is not necessarily a Raith Rovers supporter as such. He was born in Forfar in 1948 in a Celtic family. So he loves Forfar Athletic and Glasgow Celtic. On the other hand he has lived in Kirkcaldy since 1971, and has followed the fortunes of the local team with some interest, commentating for Hospital Radio for a spell in the 1990s and writing for a year or two for the programme.

Read and enjoy!

July

July 1 1923

This was the morning of the shipwreck, making Raith Rovers one of the few teams in footballing history to have survived such an occurrence.

Yet without wishing in any way to downplay what must have been a very scary moment for the Kirkcaldy men, it was hardly on the scale of maritime disasters like the *Titanic* or the *Lusitania*!

It happened off the coast of Galicia, in north-west Spain, as Raith Rovers on the *Highland Loch* were making their way to play a few games on the Canary Islands in a summer tour.

There had been a certain amount of fog and not enough lighthouses; suddenly the ship hit a rock.

A thoroughly dignified evacuation took place with some Rovers players earning plaudits for the help they gave to elderly passengers to get to the lifeboats, and everyone was saved, albeit in a rather deserted and remote part of the world.

The place is so remote in fact that the Romans called it "Finis Terrae" (Finisterre in Spanish) meaning "the end of the world".

After the damage was repaired and the ship duly refloated at the next high tide, some of the players were given the greatest honour that one can get on board a ship, namely being invited to dine at the captain's table!

When the news reached Kirkcaldy, the reaction was at first alarm, then relief before a certain degree of levity. It could have been a great deal worse.

July 1 2016

Raith Rovers Football Club

RemembeR The Somme 1916-2016

In memory of the Raith Rovers players who died in the Great War

July 2 1954

The end of the school term and the beginning on the summer holidays were marked by the Annual Prize ceremony of Kirkcaldy High School and Viewforth High School.

The Kirkcaldy High School one was held in the Adam Smith Hall, (just along the road from where the school was).

Mr R M Adam, the rector, used the occasion to stress just how cramped for space the old school was.

If they didn't move soon to their projected site at the north of the town, then the school would be "bursting at the seams". However, plans were well in hand, and he himself had seen the drawings, and it was hoped that they could move soon.

In fact it would be 1958 before it all happened). He congratulated and thanked everyone for their efforts and wished them all a happy holiday.

The main address was given by the Rev Flint of Kingskettle, convenor of the Education Committee in which he stressed the value of "character".

At Viewforth, in the absence of the rector, Mr Rollo, through illness, the ceremony was conducted by Mr Fraser, the Principal Teacher of Science, while Mrs Rollo presented the prizes and the assembly was addressed by Rev A Renshaw MacKay MBE of Bethelfield Church.

But no doubt the minds of quite a few of the pupils, boys in particular, drifted to the football fields, and the stories that Raith Rovers were soon to be starting training for the new season.

A few lucky folk would be able to see the World Cup final between Hungary and West Germany on their TV screens on Sunday night.

Sandy Archibald

July 3 1935

The economic depression of the 1930s may well have been receding, but Raith Rovers are still in a pretty poor shape according to the balance sheet issued today, ahead of the AGM on Monday July 8.

The club recorded a deficit for the last year of £1268 14 shillings. In the previous year there had been a balance thanks to the sale of a few players, but this had not been possible this year; no big team had been very interested in any Rovers players.

On the other hand, income generated from the turnstiles had shown a slight increase, and it was to be hoped that this could continue in future years.

Hopes were expressed that with the general improving economic picture throughout the country, and local unemployment steadily falling, there would be more money in the town and more chance of people attending football matches.

In addition there were one or two other positives. One had been the appointment of Sandy Archibald as manager. Archibald had been a good player for the club before he moved on to Rangers, and being a local Fife man, he had a certain affinity with the supporters. The other thing was that the Supporters Club was now a success. Relationships between the Supporters Club and the Board of Directors had not always been good in the past, but this year the Supporters Club had raised £11 from various fund raising activities, and Directors had gone out of their way to express their thanks. The club and the supporters were at least all in this together!

July 4 1927

Much regret was expressed, according to *The Fife Free Press* about the decision of Mr A G Adamson to stand down as Chairman of Raith Rovers.

The reason given was that he did not have enough time to devote to the job, as he had other business interests. Not everyone would express regret however.

Much as some people admired Mr Adamson's devotion to the club, like most Chairmen, he came in for a certain amount of criticism as well.

He had been involved in a fairly unsubtle and rather undignified — even venomous and spiteful — dispute with the Supporters Club, and would of course always be associated in the eyes of the support with the "asset stripping" of so many of the great players of the early '20s and the eventful departure of manager James Logan.

Mr Adamson had been with the club for over thirty years, and had seen the team rise from its humble Northern League days to eventual inclusion in the Scottish League Second and then First Divisions.

There had been some great days before the War including a Scottish Cup final appearance after a degree of success in the Scottish Qualifying Cup, and then the great days of the 1920s.

Raith's problem had been that the town of Kirkcaldy, although "fitba daft", could not, over a long period of time, really cope in terms of support with the big Scottish big cities, let alone the English ones. Mr Adamson would continue to be a Director and to serve with the SFA. His replacement as Chairman of Raith Rovers would be Mr James Bogie.

July 5 1945

The European War finished a couple of months ago, although the Japanese War was still going strong. Raith Rovers fans yearned for the return of a proper football season, but that would not happen until season 1946/47.

Today however it was a different kind of passion in Kirkcaldy and indeed the rest of Great Britain, for a General Election, the first since 1935, had been called throughout the United Kingdom.

This was to replace the Coalition Government, which had been in power since 1940 and had indeed served the country so well in wartime conditions.

It was not an entirely unfamiliar experience for Kirkcaldy folk for there had been a by-election in 1944, won for Labour by Tom Hubbard. It was the same Tom Hubbard who stood for Labour this time and he was opposed by the classical academic Douglas Young for the Scottish Nationalists, Major Guest for the Conservatives and John McArthur for the Communists.

Hubbard called for the implementation of the Beveridge Report on Health and Social Welfare, Young wanted an independent Scotland, Guest praised Winston Churchill and McArthur wanted an alliance with the Soviet Union.

The results would not be known for another three weeks (to allow for soldiers votes to be brought home from overseas) but it was generally expected that although Hubbard would win in Kirkcaldy, Churchill and the Conservatives would win in Great Britain.

July 6 1916

James Logan, as a player

July 6 1916

Lieutenant James Logan, who had played in the Raith Rovers side which had reached the final of the Scottish Cup in 1913, returned to his home in David Street today after a few traumatic days in France.

He had been with the Royal Scots in the first day of the Somme in 1916. Late in the day, he was found physically unimpaired but dazed, disorientated and unable to tell the stretcher bearers what had happened to him.

This was a clear case of shellshock, and he was also suffering from deafness. He was shipped home to Portsmouth and the decision was taken then that he might recover better in Kirkcaldy.

A horse-drawn taxi was awaiting at the station to take him home to his delighted and much relieved wife. He did recover quite well at home after a few weeks, but to his dying day he still retained a certain residual deafness and was never able to tell anyone what happened to him on that fateful day of July 1.

He did go back to the war, however, was promoted to the rank of Captain, and then, of course, when the war finished, became the manager of Raith Rovers in their great days of the early 1920s. He always said that the best therapy and cure for war trauma was football.

He was one of the players who might have gone further in the game but for the war. He was good enough, for example, to play for the Scottish Military v English Military in a game at Goodison Park in May 1916 a few weeks before the Somme.

July 7 1917

The weather was good for the Raith Sports held at Stark's Park this beautiful Saturday afternoon. The war had now almost reached its third birthday, and summer was the time when wives and mothers held their collective breath, for that was the time when the action was at its most intense. People had now learned to realise that newspaper propaganda was usually absurdly optimistic, and that things were not so rosy as they were presented.

Once again this summer Kirkcaldy had been badly hit by news of many casualties from France. There was however a determination to enjoy the Sports. Five-A-Side football was the highlight with teams from Cowdenbeath, Dunfermline, Raith Rovers, Denbeath Star, East Fife, Glencraig Celtic and the Royal Scots. East Fife won the tournament beating both Raith Rovers and a team called "Raith Rovers Munitions Workers" en route.

There were also athletic races, boxing and an impressive display of Swedish Drill by the soldiers and a Fancy Dress Parade put on by "female munitions workers". Private Flannigan of the Royal Scots won an event with the rather chilling name of "Bomb Throwing" (presumably with blank ammunition!). Musical entertainment came from the Pipe Band of the Royal Scots and the Dunnikier Colliery Prize Band.

Admission was sevenpence with "soldiers and sailors in uniform" fourpence and children free. Disabled soldiers were admitted free, and indeed given privileged status. Sadly, following last year's carnage on the Somme and elsewhere, there were an awful lot of them.

July 8 1923

Rovers opened their tour of the Canary Islands with a 3-1 win over Vigo, a team from Galicia, who were also on tour.

Ironically, they came from a town that was not all that far from the place where Rovers were shipwrecked. Some people had worried about how well they would recover from their shipwreck experience a few days ago, but that did not seem to be a great problem for the team now that they had arrived in the Canary Islands.

What was more of a problem was the hard ground, which did not have much turf, and the rough tactics of the Spanish team, who were not all that well versed in the rules of the game at this early stage of football's development — or at least they may have had different interpretations.

A local man who had been engaged to referee failed to appear, and Bill Inglis of Raith Rovers agreed to officiate. What particularly upset Inglis and the Rovers players was the "knee trick", which one presumes means a knee to the groin. However Tom Jennings scored twice (one from a penalty kick) and Alec James once.

The spectators were very partisan, and *The Fife Free Press* says that it was not all "milk and honey". Meanwhile back in Kirkcaldy, the cricketers could have done with some Canary Islands weather, for their game in the Beveridge Park against Edinburgh Institute was rained off after half an hour!

July 9 1921

Raith Rovers sent a strong Five-a-side team to the Royal Scots Annual Sports at Powderhall in Edinburgh this Saturday afternoon. Their team was Rattray, Inglis, Duncan, Neish and Collier.

The Sports began with tribute paid to the members of the Royal Scots who had fallen in the recent War, and in particular to the many men of their regiment who had perished in the Quintinshill Rail Disaster near Gretna Green of May 1915.

Rovers did well and actually beat a strong Rangers team by 1 corner to 0 in the semi-final before falling by 3 goals to 3 corners to the local side St Bernard's in the final, an outcome which went down well with the crowd.

Such tournaments, of course, meant very little, but it was a fine way of keeping fit in the summer heat. The season would begin on August 20, and a week after that would come the highlight of the calendar when the mighty Celtic came to town, eager to avenge their defeat that they sustained in April last season.

Meanwhile back at Stark's Park, Kirkcaldy High School were staging their Annual Sports and Mrs Oswald of Dunnikier presented the prizes which consisted of cameras, golf sticks and fountain pens. She might have done better to present someone with a stop watch, for the one that they had, malfunctioned and therefore, the exact times of the winners could not be recorded! On the cricket field, both Kirkcaldy and Dunnikier won, but at Three Trees Park (now known as the Ravenscraig Park) Nairn's lost to Auchterderran.

July 10 1923

While interesting things are going on in the Canary Islands and elsewhere, inciting the envy rather than the interest of football fans (for 1923 was a time when people found it hard to take foreign football in any way seriously) more mundane things were going on back home with the announcement of the fixture list for next season and the sale of season tickets for the new stand.

The impressive new structure had been opened in December 1922 and attracted a certain degree of interest and indeed curiosity, for stands did not often turn a corner as this one did! For season 1923/24, you could get a de luxe seat in "A" Stand which is described as having "Chairs" for £2 4 shillings and 6 pence, while Ladies' (sic — *The Fife Free Press* was not always good at apostrophes) and Boys could buy one for £1 5 shillings.

Even allowing for inflation and given the fact that admission to the ground for an average game was about 1 shilling, this seems to be an astonishingly good bargain, for Raith Rovers were a fine team in the 1920s and the season ticket allowed for 19 home League games, beginning with Dundee at Stark's Park on August 18. Rangers would be here on December 15 and Celtic on March 22. It was an exciting prospect, once the boys got back from their "holiday" in foreign parts and got down to the real football again.

Where are the Canary Islands, anyway? Oh, what it must be like to be a professional football player! Better than linoleum factories and mines!

July 11 1936

The Fife Free Press assured Raith supporters that manager Sandy Archibald was having no holiday this summer as he was too busy scouring the country looking to sign on new players. It was hardly surprising that he felt obliged to do this, because he had now been in post for a season and a half, and last season's performance was, frankly, awful.

Second bottom of the Second Division, well below teams like Montrose, Brechin, Forfar and worst of all, Cowdenbeath — towns of far smaller population than Kirkcaldy — was considered totally unacceptable for a team who had been fourth and third in the First Division only slightly more than a decade ago, and had this been an age in which managers were sacked as often as they are in the 21st century, Archibald would have been "released from his obligations" some time ago.

But Archibald, a Fife man from Crossgates who had played with distinction for Raith Rovers, Rangers and Scotland, was a hard worker and knew his football. He was aware that he had a difficult task, but he was also aware that finance was not in great supply either at the club or in the town itself.

Recently there had been more and more signs that the economic depression was over and that things were beginning to pick up. Hitler was a worry in Germany, but there was something comical about him as well.

In any case Great Britain had a new young King called Edward VIII. It was about time he was getting himself a Queen, though, was it not?

George Farm

July 12 1967

Rumours which had been spreading round the town were confirmed today when it was announced that Manager George Farm was leaving Raith Rovers to take charge of Dunfermline Athletic.

This was a major blow for the club, because Farm had just led Rovers to promotion to the First Division, and many supporters criticised the Directors for not making more of an effort to keep him.

It seemed to be sending out the signal that Dunfermline Athletic were a better option than Raith Rovers in terms of ambition, something that would never go down well in Kirkcaldy. It was a bad blow to the club just on the eve of their first season back in the First Division.

It would indeed turn out to be a smart career move for Farm who would lead the Pars to a Scottish Cup success the following year in 1968, followed by a good run in Europe the year after, although Farm himself would return to Raith for a less successful spell in the early 1970s.

Farm was famously outspoken and never took any prisoners. He had been a great goalkeeper in his time, playing for Queen of the South and earning caps for Scotland, but his most famous occasion was the "Stanley Matthews" English Cup final of 1953 when he kept the goal for Blackpool as they beat Bolton Wanderers 4-3. At one point in his life he also worked as a lighthouse keeper!

July 13 1935

With less than a month away from the start of the new football season at Station Park, Forfar against Forfar Athletic, *The Fife Free Press* assured its readers that Raith Rovers would be a far more difficult team to beat this year and would attract far greater crowds than they did last year under the managership of Bob Bennie.

Archibald was appointed in the middle of the season and impressed everyone with his "go ahead" methods of playing football, reflecting in many respects the way that he used to play, a decade previously, in the great Rangers forward line of Archibald, Cunningham, Henderson, Cairns and Morton.

One of the great things about Archibald was his natural, modest charm and ability and willingness to talk to fans, never forgetting that they were the lifeblood of the club, and in Raith Rovers' case, had had a rather thin time over the past few years. Already for this year, a few season tickets had been sold, with a slight reduction in price. There was, too, a little more money around and the hope was growing that the worst of the economic depression had past.

Today saw the first football match of the season being played at Stark's Park with Kirkcaldy Mutual Service Association taking on their Cupar counterparts in what promised to be an enthusiastic, if not particularly brilliant, football match. The game was to be kicked off symbolically by Sir Robert Lockhart, one time Provost of the town.

July 14 1956

Raith Rovers, currently doing well in the Scottish League First Division, proved their versatility today by beating Dunnikier at cricket at Dunnikier Park.

Dunnikier CC were originally the team of the Oswald family of Dunnikier House; they had started in 1856 when a group of young men (some of whom had played the game in the Army with English players when they served in the Crimean War) had approached Mr Oswald for a piece of ground to play on. Dunnikier were thus celebrating their Centenary Year. Later in the year, the famous Douglas Jardine of "Bodyline" fame or notoriety would speak at their Centenary Dinner.

Today they were beaten by Raith Rovers, containing Andy Leigh, Willie McNaught, Johnny Maule and supplemented by a few supporters like Dougie Diack who was more associated with Kirkcaldy CC.

Dunnikier batted first and scored 82, but it would have been a great deal less but for 31 not out from Nelson Ferguson, a man better known for his bowling than his batting. For Rovers, Andy Leigh and Bobby Buchan took the wickets. When Rovers went in, they too struggled but David Hutchison and Andy Leigh saw them home. It was a very pleasant day and a huge crowd attended.

Sometimes there was a certain disapproval of footballers playing cricket in the summer, lest they get injured, but there did not seem to be any problem here, for it was indeed good public relations, and as the new season was approaching, it was good training.

July 15 2016

It was a bizarre start to the season.

In the first place it was the earliest Rovers had ever started an official season.

In the second place, it was against Cove Rangers, opposition which Rovers had never faced before, in official competition at least.

Thirdly, the game was played at Station Park, Forfar before a crowd of not very many, 362 in fact.

It was a fine Friday night on what used to be regarded as the start of the Trades Fortnight summer holiday. The Scottish League had decided to revamp the League Cup and to re-introduce a sectional format on the grounds that in the past many teams only had one game and did not really make any money out of it.

This meant that the competition had to start earlier so as not to get in the way of League fixtures. Rovers were drawn in a section containing Cove, Alloa Athletic, Ross County and Montrose. Each team had four fixtures, two home and two away. The winners of each of the 8 sections qualified, as indeed did the 4 best seconds.

In addition to the early start, Cove's ground was out of commission so the game had to be played in Forfar.

Forfar's bakers missed a huge trick here by not having their pie stall open to sell Forfar Bridies — a cause of serious distress to Rovers supporters - but apart from that Rovers supporters departed happy with a 2-1 victory after Cove had gone ahead. However Kyle Benedictus and Lewis Vaughan scored for Rovers.

July 16 1904

Raith Rovers Sports were held today at Stark's Park before a large crowd in fine weather.

It was of course the start of the Kirkcaldy Holiday Week, and although very few people could afford hotels or boarding houses in 1904, there were nevertheless loads of day trips to Edinburgh and along the coast.

In spite of many people being away on day trips, Rovers raised £40, a large amount for 1904, but *The Fife Free Press* is highly critical of the arrangements. Proceedings were carried out at a very slow pace, and there was no method, neither by loudspeaker nor even by a board to tell spectators who had won the various events.

There were Athletics races and Cycling races, and The Trades' Band helped to enliven proceedings, but the main part of the time was taken up by whippet racing, a very popular pastime in mining communities at this time with dogs like "Daisy Bell" and "Little Molly" doing well.

There was then a five-a-side football tournament involving Kirkcaldy United, St Bernard's, Cowdenbeath and two teams from Raith Rovers. Raith Rovers eventually won by beating Kirkcaldy United by 1 corner, neither side having managed to register a goal in the now intense heat of the late afternoon. In the Junior and Juvenile section, Leslie Hearts beat Dunnikier Athletic.

The general feeling was that there should have been a programme issued, and more of an attempt made to tell the crowd what was going on, and it was no surprise to see some spectators slipping off in the direction of the Beveridge Park to see Kirkcaldy playing Cupar at cricket. A weakened Kirkcaldy side (many of their players were on holiday) chasing 138 were all out for 58.

July 1993

Jimmy Nicholl takes his players on a pre-season run round the Beveridge Park

July 17 1916

Today "a Director of Raith Rovers" received a letter from an officer in the Royal Scots telling him that Private James Scott of the "Footballers' Battalion" of Sir George McRae had been killed on the first day of the Battle of the Somme on July 1.

The delay was explained by the time that it took then to find the body and to identify it. Jimmy Scott, who had been born in Airdrie in 1895, had joined Raith Rovers from the Glasgow Junior side Petershill in summer 1913. He had originally joined the club as a left winger, but had shown some clear goal scoring potential and had been moved to the centre forward position, Not the least of his distinctions had been that he scored a goal against Celtic's Charlie Shaw on December 13 1913 at a time when Charlie and the rest of the Celtic defence had been considered impregnable. All in all, he scored 25 goals in 59 League games for the Rovers.

He had joined McRae's Battalion in the first season of the war, and had married a girl called Catherine Reekie in April 1915 in Airdrie. He has no known grave but his name is commemorated on a memorial at Thiepval. Reputedly, he was one of the first to fall on that fateful of July 1 1916. He was only 21, and his death was much mourned in Kirkcaldy, yet there were so many other deaths that in some ways the sheer horror of this one was simply merged in the general mass of all the other carnage.

July 18 2017

Rovers' chances of making any progress in the Scottish League Cup are now looking slim following their second defeat in a row to opposition from the City of Discovery. On Saturday they lost to Dundee United, and tonight at Stark's Park, it was Dundee who got the better of a hard working but somewhat uninspired Raith Rovers side.

The crowd was disappointing — something that speaks volumes about summer football — but they saw a good game won 2-1 by the men from Dens Park with all the goals coming in the final stages of the game. It was the 83rd minute before Dundee opened the scoring; Scott Allan' s free kick wasn't properly cleared and the ball spun to Moussa El Bakhtaoui, who stabbed the ball home — and was then booked for jumping on the wall to celebrate! But the determined Rovers equalised with what seemed to be the last kick of the game when Lewis Vaughan hit one from the edge of the box. That seemed to be a just reward for what Rovers had put into it, and the weaker brethren of the support who had gone home now rushed back to see the statutory penalty shoot-out.

But there was still a minute of two on injury time to be played and after Rovers had missed a good chance to win the game, it was Dundee who ran up the field; Jack Hendry rose high to head home a Paul McGowan cross.

This was extremely hard on Rovers, but the philosophers shrugged their shoulders and said "That's fitbaw for ye!"

July 19 1975

The football season was approaching and Raith Rovers had recommenced training with new manager local man Andy Matthew.

Everyone was keen to exorcise a few ghosts from Stark's Park after a few depressingly under-performing seasons, with Rovers still a million miles away from the new Premier League due to start in August. Quite a lot of supporters felt that to be the natural habitat for a team which had been in the old First Division for all the 1950s and about half of the 1960s.

Since 1970, the Second Division had been the order of the day. In the meantime, the summer had been very warm and pleasant but the town had been struck by a series of fires that look like all the world to be arson. Early this morning, at about 4.00 am, St John's Church in Elgin Street/Meldrum Road was burned down and this had followed another fire at Torbain School. The Church was completely ruined, and police were urging all public buildings to organise "Firewatch" rotas of volunteers or vigilantes. Other churches in the town did just that.

Jokes spread about the town whether it would be an idea to have a "Firewatch" at Stark's Park, or whether it might be a good idea anyway if the antiquated old stadium was burnt down!

Nevertheless, things were taken seriously until a somewhat disturbed young man was caught in the act trying to burn down another Church in town a few days later.

July 20 1907

Although cricket was still holding sway in the summer months, Raith Rovers were not entirely idle.

They sent a five-a-side team to compete in the Hearts Sports in Edinburgh but lost by 1 goal to 1 point to Hibs in the first round, meaning presumably that a point was given for a corner.

It was nevertheless an honour to be invited and encouraged the club to think that elevation to the Scottish League First Division was not far away.

They had applied earlier this summer but been knocked back. The club however was very ambitious, and were now a Limited Company, with a large take-up of shares.

They had made a profit last season and had now appointed one Peter Hodge as secretary from Dunfermline Athletic, and George Goodfellow, late of Hearts, was now the trainer.

Already the club had 15 players signed for the new season, including some new faces, although sadly John Manning had been transferred to Blackburn Rovers for the princely sum of £750.

Another good season in the Second Division would make it difficult for the Scottish League to resist their demands for First Division football.

Meanwhile the expansion of the town continued north of the railway. 1908 would see the opening of a primary school called the North, and the Old Kirk was able to build a "daughter" Church in Meldrum Road, now called Bennochy Church, but for a long part of its life known as St John's Church.

July 21 1992

Interesting times in Kirkcaldy, as the net tightened on Karen Carrick, leader of the ruling Labour group on the Council.

Basically, she had been caught telling "porky pies" about having degrees in both Law and Medicine and, instead of simply admitting that she had made a mistake, tried to brazen it out.

It was a matter of some interest to the 874 fans who came along this sunny night to see Raith Rovers take on Hibs in a pre-season friendly. It was a good idea to invite Hibs (Rovers had already played Hearts a few days previously) for Hibs, the holders of the Scottish League Cup were on a roll, having now finally managed to ward off the unwelcome attentions of Wallace Mercer, of Hearts, who had tried to amalgamate them with Hearts a couple of years ago.

They played well that night, beating a poorish Rovers team (who were trying out a few fringe players) 3-0 with Rovers giving very few indications of the great season that lay ahead of them.

This was the first season of the pass-back rule, whereby a defender was now not allowed to kick the ball back to his goalkeeper on pain of giving away an indirect free kick at the point where the goalkeeper touched the ball (invariably near the goal and in a dangerous position). Some experienced defenders found this rule difficult to handle, and there were a few examples of this tonight. Ms Carrick was sacked in disgrace the following day.

July 22 2003

It is not very often that Bradford City play Raith Rovers, but they appeared tonight for a pre-season friendly, with a reasonable crowd of 1100 turning out to see the rare, and possibly unprecedented appearance of the Bantams at Stark's Park.

Bradford City would always be recalled for the horrible fire in May 1985 where 56 lost their lives and countless more were injured and traumatised. Sadly only the real football geeks could tell you that they won the English Cup in 1911, beating the then great Newcastle United at the Crystal Palace.

The Bradford based *Telegraph and Argos* is proud that about 80 or so made the trip from Bradford, but it also says that they would have been better strolling along the "nearby prom in the pleasant sunshine", such was the standard of fare on offer.

Raith supporters were not quite so scathing, for the team actually played well and won 2-0. The first goal was a good one by John Sutton from a Martin Prest cross; it was Prest who scored the second goal, which can only be described as "bizarre".

It was the last minute of the game. Prest had ended up in the back of the net, and therefore could not be offside. He untangled himself and began to walk up the field when Bradford's Dean Windass passed the ball back to no-one in particular other than the bewildered Prest who, as the ball was a pass back, still could not be offside. He simply slipped the ball into the net, as the remnants of the small crowd collapsed in laughter! Not that it mattered, for it was only a pre-season friendly.

July 23 2016

It is a long trip to Dingwall from Kirkcaldy, but Raith's record in that very pleasant town with hospitable people is not too bad.

They beat Ross County there in 2012, and did the same today — in a sort of a way, that is, on a penalty shoot-out after a draw to earn an extra point in the Scottish League Cup.

The difference this time was that Ross County were actually the holders of this competition, having beaten Hibs in the final last March. Thus it was two former winners of the competition who entertained a smallish crowd of 1,173 at Victoria Park today.

Rovers were without their new signing Rudi Skacel but Declan McManus was playing. The game was a little turgid and someone with a sense of humour said "end of season stuff"!

It was probably too early to be playing football on this hot day, but it was Rovers who went ahead through an own goal. It had followed a good move involving Lewis Vaughan, but it was the luckless Cikos who knocked the ball into his own net. The holders now piled on the pressure but needed a penalty kick to equalise after Jason Thomson was adjudged to have brought down Brian Graham in the box, and Graham scored from the spot.

With both teams suffering from unusual conditions (for Scotland) there was no further scoring, and so both teams earned a point, and Rovers won the extra point after doing better in a rather incompetent display of penalty taking than the Staggies did. It was quite a pleasant trip down the A9 after that for the gallant band of Rovers supporters.

July 24 2001

It was as well for the 724 fans who came this Tuesday night to see the second pre-season friendly of the season (they had already played Livingston, a team which seemed to like buying Raith Rovers players!) that they did not know what was ahead of them — for season 2001/02 may well be the worst season of all — although, goodness knows, there are rivals and other contenders for that award!

However tonight we had rare visitors in York City, whose main distinction seems to be that they come from a fine city with Viking Museums, railway museums and a lovely cathedral.

They also are one of the few British clubs who begin and end with the same letter, and seem to have spent the 1950s in English Cup battles on muddy pitches and always losing gallantly.

They were also the last team in the alphabet usually, so you knew when listening to the results on the radio that the Scottish ones came next!

A recent connection was Peter Duffield, a man of many clubs but who had now found his way to Terry Dolan's Third Division side. Tonight's game was predictably low key, and strictly for the connoisseur (or even the football "geek") and the only goal of the game was scored by another soldier of fortune called George O'Boyle, now enjoying a brief dalliance with Raith Rovers. York were destined to finish 8th from the bottom of Division Three in England that year.

Rovers would do a lot worse than that!

Bert Herdman

July 25 1945

The first post-war season was approaching, although it would not be an official one and would still be considered "war-time football" with no Scottish Cup and no official Internationals.

This was because there were so many players still overseas, and indeed the war was still going on in the Far East. But Raith Rovers were prepared and today the managership of the club passed seamlessly from Willie Reekie to Bert Herdman.

It was not so much a palace revolution as a family agreement, for the men were brothers-in-law! Herdman would do the job on a part-time basis but this would later be upgraded to a full-time job, but it hardly made a lot of difference to Herdman, for his background was not a playing one, but a Supporters Club one.

Even in 1945 it was unusual to have a Manager who had never played the game at a professional level and everyone was interested to see how he would perform.

He would indeed last more than 16 years in the job. He was totally unpretentious, a little gruff on occasion and certainly with a propensity to lapse into bad language now and again. He also suffered from a bad stammer. But he had a welcome inability to suffer fools gladly, and this quality alone would serve Rovers well in the years to come.

Those who say that he was the greatest Rover of them all probably had a point. It probably helped that he was not a hired professional, but a manager with a genuine love of the club.

July 26 1945

Sheriff Principal John A Lillie KC made the announcement today at the Police Buildings in St Brycedale Avenue at about 3.30 pm that Raith Rovers supporter Tom Hubbard had been duly returned to represent Kirkcaldy at Westminster.

There was no real surprise about that, for Kirkcaldy had tended to vote Labour in the past in any case. Normally politics, even Westminster ones, played little part in the lives of those who worried only about the start of the football season (the fixtures were now out and Rovers would be at home to Arbroath on August 11 for their first match of the season) but this was different.

Those who had listened to the radio (the "wireless" as it was known in 1945) had heard of huge Labour gains in both Scotland and England, and that there was going to be a landslide victory for Labour.

It seemed odd that Winston Churchill, the hero of the hour, was being sacked, but there was more to it than that. Many of those who voted were still in the services, and had every reason to hate the officer class, but also the electorate had long memories of poverty, unemployment and misery in the 1920s and 1930s, which they associated, not without cause, with the Conservatives.

Things would now change from this day onwards with babies born in the late 1940s (the "baby boomers") not only surviving because of the National Health Service but becoming healthier, happier, better educated and destined to live longer. Wars often bring revolutions. 1945 did indeed bring a revolution, and fortunately in this case, a peaceful one.

July 27 1929

To-day's edition of *The Fife Free Press* is upbeat and optimistic about the start of the new season in a fortnight's time. Supporters will once again have "the indignity" of being called Second Leaguers, but it is better to be playing well in the Second Division than suffering repeated hammerings in the First, the reporter reckons.

A sign of the times however comes in the admission that Rovers have only eleven signed players on their books and there is as yet no recognised outside left. No great leeway for injuries there, then!

But training has resumed and the good people of Kirkcaldy have been treated to the sight of the players charging about the Beveridge Park of an evening, or a group of young men puffing and blowing their way along the Prom in their tracksuits. There has been the usual change of personnel with some departures and the influx of no less than five newcomers, the most exciting of whom was a man called Fred Panther, from Folkestone, who had last season scored a remarkable tally of 32 goals between Christmas and the summer. Clearly with a man like Panther, Rovers would come on by "leaps and bounds" this season, said someone, with a sense of humour that was not quite as good as he thought it was.

There was another chap, however, called George Drain, who had been a provisional signing last year. It was fervently to be hoped that Rovers would not go "down the drain". The opening of the new season was keenly anticipated.

July 28 1973

Raith Rovers today opened their season at Dens Park in sweltering heat in what was called the Dryburgh Cup. This was a short lived pre-season tournament in which the highest goal scoring teams in both Divisions were entitled to take part.

This tournament, like the League Cup this year, was played under an experimental law whereby you could only be offside inside your opponents penalty area and its lateral extension to the touchline, an extra line being drawn on the pitch to make this clear. It was a praiseworthy attempt to see more goals scored in the game, but unfortunately it did not work, and the experiment was soon abandoned.

A crowd of 4,000 were at Dens Park today but very few Rovers supporters seemed to have given up their holidays in order to attend. Those who did saw Rovers hold out well against a strong Dundee side who were parading their new signing Tommy Gemmell. Rovers took the game to extra time before Dundee managed to get the only goal of the game.

As the tournament was a knock-out one, this ended Rovers' participation in this competition. Indeed it was not really taken seriously at all, being just looked upon as a competitive pre-season friendly. Next week would see Dunfermline Athletic in the Fife Cup, and then the really serious stuff began the week after that with a trip to Stirling Albion in the League Cup. But manager Farm said he was quite pleased with the start of the season.

July 29 1920

The football season was fast approaching and Raith Rovers did a bit of unusual training this Thursday by playing cricket against Kirkcaldy Cricket Club at the Beveridge Park in front of a reasonable crowd on a fine summer evening.

Kirkcaldy CC, of course, in 1920 were quite good, and could attract crowds of over 1,000 to see them. Tonight the crowd would be about that, but it was sad to notice in the crowd so many young men, who used to play both football and cricket, now sadly disabled.

It was, of course, time to put the war behind us, the politicians said, but for some people that was not possible. Kirkcaldy batted first and reached 80, to which Raith Rovers replied with 63. Bill Inglis was Raith's best bowler with 5 for 43, although he could not beat the bowling of DC Gatherum who ripped through Rovers batting with 7 for 35.

A pleasant time was had by all and the officials of both sides wished each other all the best in their respective sports, and it was provisionally agreed to play a return game, football this time, at Stark's Park sometime on a suitable date.

The football season was scheduled to open two weeks on Monday with a League game against Scottish Cup finalists Albion Rovers, but there would be a few trial matches before then. Manager Logan seemed to be confident that this would be a good season.

July 30 1988

It is not often that tickets are sold for a pre-season friendly, but the visit of Graeme Souness' Rangers was considered important enough for such precautions to be taken.

In the event, there were loads of spaces and the crowd could pay at the gate. Rovers did well enough to hold Rangers to a 2-1 victory for the Ibrox side, and the game wasn't taken all that seriously. Not all Rangers stars were playing that day, but there was enough of them to persuade their fans to come from Glasgow to see the game.

There were some baddies among them as well, all with a chip on their shoulder for 1988 had been a bad year for Rangers, as Celtic had won a League and Cup double, and they were eager for revenge.

And yet there is no logic at all about some fans who stood and gave what looked like a Nazi salute as they sang "God Save The Queen"! Derek Johnstone was there, and visibly upset when very few supporters recognised him as he came out of the main entrance at full time!

Rovers had shown a steady improvement since the appointment of Frank Connor as Manager. Having won promotion in 1987, and stayed in Division One in 1988, it was now felt that an attempt should be made to gain further promotion to the Premier and with a starting XI of Arthur, McStay, Murray, Fraser, Dennis, Gibson, Ferguson, Coyle, Ferguson, Dalziel and Sweeney, things looked possible.

July 31 1983

It had been a long time coming, but today marked the end of the managership of Gordon Wallace, who had been in place since 1979.

A Dundonian, Gordon had played for Rovers between 1966 and 1969, and had also had a distinguished career as a player for Dundee.

The problem with his time in charge had been 1981, when promotion to the Premier League had almost been achieved, but for one reason or another had been thrown away.

After that, the team lacked credibility in the town as the depressingly low attendances would indicate, and Gordon left to become a Coach with Dundee United, then the Scottish Premier League champions, under the formidable Jim McLean. He would became manager of Dundee in time, but like everyone else, did not last long under the perpetually fluid set up at Dens Park and moved to Dunfermline for a similarly short-lived and unsuccessful time.

He has also been Coach at Raith Rovers, Arbroath and Forfar. There still remains in Kirkcaldy a great deal of affection for Gordon Wallace. His playing career saw him scoring many goals for Rovers in the promotion season in 1966/67.

In the first year of being in the First Division, when relegation looked inevitable until late in the season Gordon scored enough goals to become the Scottish Football Writers Player of the Year.

He scored a total of 264 League goals for various clubs. His managerial career was not without its moments either, for 1979 and 1980 saw Rovers respectable in the First Division and playing some good football.

August

RAITH ROVERS FOOTBALL CLUB
SEASON 1993 1994

August 1 1992

Eyebrows were raised today throughout Great Britain — and indeed the world — at the astonishing score line of Raith Rovers 7 St Mirren 0.

It was the first game of the season, and although pre-season form had been reasonably good, and manager Jimmy Nicholl had done a great deal of "talking up" his side, the extent of this victory over a team who had played in the Premier League last season was a remarkable one.

Naturally of course it was all put down to beginners' luck, but it had been a very impressive victory, with three goals from Gordon Dalziel, two from Craig Brewster and one each from Ronnie Coyle and Jason Dair.

It was not that St Mirren were a poor side. They were simply swept away by a team playing some of the best football ever seen at Stark's Park.

The crowd was a disappointing 2,254 with many of the St Mirren contingent departing the scene for a walk down to the prom early in the second half. This was the start of a really great season for Raith Rovers, and this day was also the establishment of a record.

Paul Lambert played for St Mirren that day. He would go on to win a European Cup medal with Borussia Dortmund. He is thus, without a shadow of a doubt, the only man in the history of football to win a European Cup medal and to lose 0-7 to Raith Rovers at Stark's Park!

Rovers fans, never given to excessive displays of enthusiasm, were happy but the pessimists were saying that it would not last.

August 2 1914

The weather had been absolutely beautiful this scorching summer, as worshippers made their way to the Parish Kirk to hear the preaching of Rev John Campbell. Today there is excitement and apprehension in the air as the international situation yesterday took a turn for the worse.

But *The Fife Free Press* appeared as normal yesterday. The football season is due to start in two weeks' time, the first fixture being against Motherwell, and the enthusiastic scribe is very happy to talk optimistically about Raith's chances. The players returned to training this week and great things are expected of Manager Richardson and his men like George McLay, James Logan and Fred Martin.

Raith have been a valuable addition to the Scottish League First Division since 1910, and although chances of winning it are extremely slim, nevertheless, they have held their own and it would be nice to have another go at the Scottish Cup in 1915, wouldn't it?

However, in August cricket is still king, and great tribute is paid to professional William Clements who will have his benefit match against Dunfermline next Saturday, August 8, and everyone should contribute generously, for he has been such a great servant this season as player coach and groundsman. Yesterday Linlithgow played at Beveridge Park and the weather was fine.

What could ruin such an idyllic summer? Only that Czar Nicholas II of Russia has involved himself in the dispute between Austria and Servia (as it is called), and so Germany might have to involve herself on the other side, then France, then Great Britain on the side of the Russians. If that happened, the Rev Campbell said, everyone must "do their duty". But defending the Russian Czar?

August 3 2013

Raith Rovers delighted their 1219 fans by beginning the new season with a 6-0 defeat of Queen's Park in the Scottish League Cup. The extent and scope of the victory was unexpected, even though it would have to be admitted that Queen's Park, that quaint old amateur anachronism still in existence a good 120 years after professionalism was legalised, were hardly top notch opposition. Yet they brought their supporters with them that fine if a little windy August day, and there must surely continue to be a place in Scottish football for Queen's Park.

Today however they were simply swept aside by a rampant Rovers side who were two up at half time through a header from Gordon Smith and then a fine drive from Joe Cardle. In the second half the floodgates simply opened and Calum Elliot scored twice before substitutes Greig Spence and Lewis Vaughan completed the rout.

To complete the misery for Queen's Park, Guiseppe Capuano was sent off by referee Stephen Finnie for two yellow cards. Neither of them looked all that bad, to be honest, and we even heard pleas for clemency to Mr Finnie coming from the main stand, for Rovers were 3-0 up at the time!

It was a good day for Rovers, however, and a certain spring in the step was evident as they bounced homewards. Was this the harbinger of a really good season? The fans had certainly waited long enough, and those who delighted in the fall of the once mighty had further reason for happiness that night when incredulous mobile phones told them that Rangers, penniless, bankrupt and friendless, had been beaten by Forfar at Station Park!

August 4 1998

The season kicked off eccentrically on a Tuesday night with the visit of Hamilton Academical for the first League game of the season.

Frankly, it was hard to be optimistic about Rovers' chances, for there was a fairly obvious financial problem. The building of the two stands at each end of the park had been expensive and Rovers' relegation in 1997 had not helped the cause in any way.

In addition, this year Hibs were in the First Division, and it was hard to envisage anyone other than them winning the League and getting the only available promotion spot.

Those who felt that way at the start of this game would have more cause for depression at the end, for it was a miserable 0-2 defeat from Hamilton. Hamilton were, quite simply, better. Rovers, although they did their best, were slower to the ball.

Yet as long as Jimmy Nicholl was about, there was some sort of hope for the club, it was felt, but this was an older Jimmy and he frankly lacked the quality of players that he had had earlier in the decade. Now only Jason Dair of his previous side was still at Stark's Park. Much interest centred on Dave Bowman, ex-Dundee United, a tough competitor but a man with a bad disciplinary record.

It was clear, however, that the coming year was going to be difficult. 2,316 people left Stark's Park rather apprehensive and depressed.

August 5 1967

Souvenir Programme
RAITH ROVERS

NOTTINGHAM FOREST
SATURDAY, 5th AUGUST, 1967

Kick-Off 3 p.m.

This is Your Lucky Number— N° 2440

FIRST PRIZE £2   SECOND PRIZE £1

Official Programme   **6d.**

August 5 1967

Rare visitors in Nottingham Forest came to Stark's Park, and therefore an eager 7,000 appeared on a sunny day to watch this pre-season clash.

"It was the best of times; it was the worst of times" says Charles Dickens in a "Tale of Two Cities", and this applied to Raith Rovers in 1967.

On the one hand, promotion had been achieved at the end of last year; on the other, manager George Farm had defected to Dunfermline. Serious doubts were expressed about Rovers' ability to stay in the First Division under new manager Tommy Walker, until recently a successful player and manager with Hearts.

Whether he could adapt to Raith Rovers, however, was another matter. It was the custom on this day (the Saturday before the season started properly) for Scottish teams to play English teams and Rovers had done well to persuade Johnny Carey's Nottingham Forest to appear in Kirkcaldy.

This was, of course, before Forest's great days under Brian Clough and they were often looked upon as the great under-performers of English football. They had won the English Cup in 1959, but had done little else to please their large support.

However, Joe Baker was playing for them and he scored twice as they beat Rovers fairly easily 5-1, Rovers consolation goal coming from a penalty converted by Ian Lister. The gulf however was there for all to see, and Rovers fans took a deep breath as they contemplated the task ahead. Forest, nevertheless, were a quality side.

August 6 1994

Raith Rovers today finished their pre-season tour of Ireland with a 2-0 win over Bangor, goals coming from Ronnie Coyle and Ally Graham.

Their other tour games had also been 2-0 wins, but of course pre-season friendlies mean very little, however much they are useful for the manager and the players.

Raith Rovers in 1994 were in a funny position. They had been relegated after one season in the Premier League, but they had not been in any way disgraced and had turned in some fine performances.

It was generally agreed that they had enough good youngsters to fight back in men like Steve Crawford, Colin Cameron and Jason Dair.

On the other hand, uncertainty surrounded the talented manager Jimmy Nicholl. It was no secret that Kilmarnock were interested in him to replace Tommy Burns who had gone to Celtic, and Nicholl, clearly an ambitious man, was tempted to move to a "bigger" club and that included Northern Ireland.

Normally relegation means "regime change" (rather like a defeat in war for a country) but it was to the credit of the Raith Board (who were themselves ambitious) that they were determined to hold on to the charming Ulsterman who was of course still young enough and fit enough to turn out as a player now and again.

It promised to be an interesting season ahead, and there would be many tough opponents, not least St Johnstone (another team with Premier League aspirations and also relegated last season) who would be calling at Stark's Park on Saturday.

August 7 1993

This was Raith Rovers first day at the top table — the Premier League. Everyone had been looking forward to the first game and 4,628 turned up to Stark's Park to watch it.

The opponents were St Johnstone, a club whom Rovers might reasonably have expected to defeat at home, but the game turned out to be a respectable 1-1 draw with Shaun Dennis scoring the equaliser for Raith Rovers; Colin Cameron and Gordon Dalziel both had hard luck at the end.

The crowd were quite happy with the performance, but reckoned that they were in for a tough run this season to make sure that they were not to be one of the three teams that were to be relegated. (This was so that the Premier League could be reduced from 12 to 10 in one of the confusing and recurrent debates about the optimum size).

Last year's talisman, Craig Brewster, had now gone as well to Dundee United. Brewster, himself a Dundee United supporter, had earned few friends in Kirkcaldy in the prolonged wrangling that took place over his possible departure. The Board had not handled things very well, either, by their failure both to grasp the realities of the situation and to move quickly for a goal scoring replacement.

But nevertheless, excitement prevailed in the town for this was a whole new situation for Raith Rovers, and there was also the added frisson of enhanced media coverage, for we were now among the elite!

August 8 1995

This Thursday night the following men made history for Raith Rovers — Thomson, McAnespie, Broddle, McInally, Dennis, Sinclair, Rougier, Cameron, Crawford, Taylor and Dair — as they stepped onto Stark's Park to play Rovers' first ever European game against Gotu Itrotterfelag, the champions of the Faroe islands.

The crowd on a lovely August evening was 5,082 and they saw Rovers take a confident 4-0 lead into the second leg with goals from Tony Rougier, Steve Crawford, Jason Dair and Colin Cameron.

It would be fair to say that they had played against more demanding opposition, but helped by new signings Alex Taylor from Partick Thistle and Jim McInally from Dundee United, they played confidently and finished the night well on top in the tie.

Some supporters had expressed a desire to go to the second leg ("Is the supporters club running a bus?" someone asked), and it was nice to see that some Faroese had made the trip to Kirkcaldy, with the Rovers supporters singing "You only sing when you're fishing" and other ditties like that.

It was of course very easy for folk to patronise the opposition — in truth they were not great — but it was sobering to find out that Motherwell had that night gone down to so called "easy" opposition from Finland.

In later years, the Faroe Islands international team would have their moments against Scotland — on one occasion winning 2-0 at half time before Scotland earned a humiliating draw — and of course, nowadays, Scottish teams regularly make fools of themselves against teams from smaller and poorer nations.

Team of 1985-86 all set to go. Unfortunately, performances did not live up to expectations!

August 9 1930

The season opened with a rather tough 3-3 draw against Albion Rovers.

There was a little history here for Raith Rovers had defeated Albion Rovers towards the end of last season in a game which effectively denied Albion promotion and promoted East Fife.

The Coatbridge men were not slow to suspect some kind of Fife conspiracy, and some of the tackles were rather coarse. *The Fife Free Press*, while praising the effort put into the game, does say that it "lacked finesse" but Rovers were due great praise for the way that they fought back from twice being two goals down to earn a draw, and with a bit of luck might have won the game at the end.

The crowd at the start was a disappointing 2,500 but increased steadily throughout the game. This seems to be saying something about the economic situation of the time in that spectators were usually allowed in free near the end of the game — many people were now suffering from the effects of the Wall Street Crash in America less than a year previously.

Albion were 2-0 up at half-time, but then player-manager Willie Birrell pulled one back. Albion then scored to make it 3-1 and for a while all seemed lost but Jackie McLaren and Fred Panther each scored to level matters, although Panther's equaliser was hotly disputed by Albion who claimed a hand ball.

The Fife Free Press was of the opinion that the Rovers team was basically sound, but envious eyes must have been cast at East Fife then making their First Division debut at Motherwell that day.

The hard working but slightly disappointing team of 1932-33

August 10 1963

The season opened not in the usual bright sunshine of opening day but in heavy rain as Rovers and a crowd of 4,460 welcomed neighbours East Fife for the opening League Cup match in a section also containing Arbroath and Dumbarton.

It was a new and much diminished Raith Rovers, for they had been relegated at the end of the previous season and now had to re-adjust to the smaller crowds and the more basic stadia of the Second Division.

1963 was a strange year. Not only were details emerging about a Tory Cabinet Minister having an affair with a girl from a working class background called Christine Keeler, but a highly organised gang of criminals had robbed the Royal Mail train in what became known as the Great Train robbery.

All this, and Rovers with a new Manager in Doug Cowie (who used to play for Dundee) and in a new strip, predominantly white with two narrow hoops, and with a few players that no-one recognised — yes, "the times they are a changin'" as the new song was about to say.

But credit to the new Rovers and East Fife — they served up a reasonable game of football in the rain. It finished 1-1, Rovers goal being scored by a fellow called Jackie Thoms, whom they signed a day or two ago from Bath City.

The usual banter, not all of it good natured, with the East Fife boys, news that the other game in the section had also ended 1-1, everyone headed home to dry out. It was as well that very few people knew what was coming, for this was not going to be a great season!

August 11 1984

1984 was the year for which George Orwell predicted terrible things for the world in the shape of dictatorships, spies and the original "Big Brother".

The truth of 1984 for Raith Rovers was a hundred times worse than that.

They were now in serious danger of losing any credibility they ever had in the town. Since 1981 when there had been a chance of promotion to the Premier League, the spiral had been continually downhill, and crowds were dipping alarmingly.

They were now in Division 2, the third and lowest tier of Scottish football, and today they opened their League season in England, in Berwick. Shielfield Park was still a Mecca for Celtic supporters on holiday. It was there that Berwick Rangers famously dumped the Glasgow Rangers out of the Scottish Cup.

If there was any advantage in playing Berwick it was that there was a direct railway line, and so a few, but only a few, Rovers supporters travelled to watch their team. They returned depressed having seen the team lose 1-2 with only a Keith Wright goal to cheer them up.

Not surprisingly, talk turned to other things — the miners' strike and discussion about who was the more loathsome, Arthur Scargill or Margaret Thatcher, England's latest thumping from the West Indies or the Los Angeles Olympics, (the American Mary Decker claimed that she had been tripped by Zola Budd, the South African who ran for Great Britain) and even, whisper it, could Kirkcaldy win the East of Scotland cricket League?

August 12 1950

Raith Rovers scored first and last against Third Lanark at Stark's Park in the opening day of the season to beat the Cathkin men 3-2.

It proved the truth of the old adage that a good beginning and a good end are all that matters with everything else less relevant!

Yet there were clear signs in the middle of the game that things were not all that well in certain departments of Raith's play. Willie Penman had the honour of scoring Scotland's first goal of the season after about one minute's play and then Johnny Maule put Rovers two up after 12 minutes, beating Third Lanark's young goalkeeper Ronnie Simpson.

But then Third Lanark gradually wore Raith Rovers down, came back through Henderson in the 67th minute and then equalised with Cuthbertson a few minutes later.

The 15,000 crowd were beginning to head homewards, reflecting that they had at least seen a good game of football in which a draw was a fair result, when George Brander scored a goal out of nothing with a fierce drive from well outside the box to give Raith Rovers a victory.

Third Lanark deserved at least something out of the game according to most newspaper accounts, but it meant that Rovers were off on the right foot. This was the first game of the Fife v Glasgow League Cup section, for in the other game that day Celtic beat East Fife. But Wednesday would see an important trip to Bayview for Raith Rovers.

August 13 1955

The season opened in splendid sunshine at Stark's Park with a crowd of almost 20,000 there to see the local derby between Raith Rovers and East Fife.

East Fife had done well in this trophy in the past, winning it three times; Rovers had reached the final in 1949.

Jim Cuthbert failed a fitness test and Ernie Copland was given the nod. The game could hardly have had a more explosive start, for there were two goals in the first 90 seconds before a lot of the crowd could get in, for there were still long queues all the way down Pratt Street at kick-off time.

Jimmy McEwan put Rovers ahead when an Andy Young shot was deflected to him, but then almost immediately fair haired Bobby Leishman of East Fife scored a brilliant goal from the edge of the penalty box.

15 minutes later Bernie Kelly put Rovers in the lead when his free kick was twice deflected on the way into the net. It was an odd goal but much hailed by the Rovers support. But sadly, that was about as good as it got for Rovers that day because Andy Matthew equalised before half time.

The Methil men, in the second half, simply took control of the game and the 4-2 score line was a fair reflection of the play. *The Courier* was quite scathing about the Raith inside trio of Young, Copland and Kelly whose passing was "unbelievably bad" as Rovers struggled to get back into the game.

A disappointment for the Rovers, but no time to lick wounds as a trip to Tynecastle beckoned on Wednesday night.

August 14 1943

Good news continued to flow from the front. The Afrika Korps was no more, defeated by the Desert Army finally at Tunis in May.

With Sicily now more or less secured, it was only a matter of time before the invasion of mainland Italy, with an invasion of France or Norway definite possibilities in the spring.

But in the meantime the football season started with Rovers once again in the North Eastern League, opening the season today with a good 3-2 win over East Fife at Bayview.

It is a mistake to dismiss war-time football as something of an irrelevance. There were indeed other major issues going on at the time, but people needed relief from it all, and football, cinema and theatre provided just that.

The crowd along the coast today was about 3,000 (for security reasons, the exact figure was not always given) and they saw a thrilling game with Willie Reekie's enthusiastic side scoring late in the game through Jackie Stewart to win 3-2.

It was a good start, but supporters who travelled back on the overcrowded train (in war time circumstances, East Fife was one of the few away fixtures that anyone could reasonably hope to attend) knew that, as always, team selection was often a hit or a miss with decisions having to be taken late in the day, depending on travel, leave or work considerations. Nothing is ever certain in life, but in war times this adage has even more validity.

August 15 1921

Raith Rovers' Scottish League season opened eccentrically on a Monday at Celtic Park, because the Celtic Sports were still going strong on the Saturday.

The crowd of 12,000 (there would have been more on a Saturday, one feels) saw a very good game which Rovers lost 0-4. The Press, both local and national, are adamant that although Celtic were good, Rovers nevertheless deserved something out of the game, for the half back line of Raeburn, Morris and Collier were outstanding for Rovers, and both Duncans in the forward line had a great deal of bad luck.

There had of course at the end of the 1920/21 season been indications that things were developing at a rate of knots at Stark's Park, and indications were good that this would be a fine season. (When Celtic came to Stark's Park on August 27 next week — another piece of eccentric fixturing — the result was a respectable 1-1 draw).

Today however, Celtic even without their "boy wonder" Tommy McInally, scored the goals at the right time with Archie Longmuir scoring early and then half way through the second half, before Andy McAtee and Joe Cassidy scored the other two as Rovers tired. It cannot be very often than a team loses 0-4 on the first day of the season, and yet comes home optimistic about the future but this is precisely what happened here. Celtic, a good side, won the League at the end of the season and Rovers were third.

August 16 1902

These were heady days in 1902!

The Boer War had now finished at the end of May after a few years of pitiless and pointless slaughter, King Edward VII and Queen Alexandra had been crowned at the Coronation last week (delayed for a couple of months because of the King's illness), Gilbert Jessop had hit a century in 77 minutes to help England beat Australia at the Oval — and Raith Rovers played their first ever game in the Scottish League Division Two.

This should have been a great day in the history of the club and an indication that the club now had truly great national pretensions, but in fact it was a huge anti-climax. The game was played at Bainsford, then the home of East Stirlingshire and it ended up a 4-1 defeat.

Alex Hynd scored from the penalty spot, but East Stirlingshire were clearly the better team, and *The Courier* was distressed that "the forwards have not yet settled down to their proper game", although it also states that the defence was good enough.

The weather was reasonably pleasant, and quite a few supporters made the trip to Bainsford on the outskirts of Falkirk to see Rovers in their new venture. Others however could stay at home and watch the Raith Band Contest or indeed the cricket at the Beveridge Park. Football had not yet really recovered from the blow delivered to it by the Ibrox Disaster earlier this year in which 26 people had died while watching the Scotland v England game.

All set for the Scottish League Second Division in 1902

August 17 1910

History was made this Wednesday night when Rovers travelled to Cappielow in Greenock to play Morton in their first ever Scottish League Division One match.

They had lost 4-1 to Hearts two nights ago in the Dunedin Cup, and they lost tonight again, although by a narrower margin, 0-1. "The weather was threatening, but the rain held off" says *The Fife Free Press* in a statement would have been appropriate to Greenock on many occasions since 1910, and there was an attendance of about 4,000.

Rovers team on this historic occasion was Ewing, Inglis and Cumming; Donagher, Aitken and Philip; Thorburn, McAuley, Gourlay, Simpson and Gibson, and *The Fife Free Press* is full of praise for their effort and "the better and prettier football was coming from the Rovers side". Unfortunately however, the Morton team, full of ex-Rangers players like Stark and May, got the only goal of the game when amidst "great enthusiasm" "Gracie headed the ball into the net".

Rovers forwards like Jimmy Gourlay and Fred Gibson were singled out for praise, but sadly they could not score. It was believed however by the journalist that Rovers were a good team and that they would "equalise matters" when Morton came to Kirkcaldy. They did in fact do this, and the start of the First Division campaign was quite a creditable one. One thing that Raith Rovers were already finding difficult was the travelling in the First Division. Greenock on the Wednesday night and now Aberdeen at Pittodrie on the Saturday!

August 18 1923

The season opened with a brilliant Raith Rovers display against Dundee at Stark's Park with the Rovers winning 3-0 with goals from Bill Inglis, George Miller and Tom Jennings.

Raith had of course only recently returned from their tour of the Canary Islands, and much play was made of the fact that goalkeeper Jimmy Brown was wearing a very bright "canary coloured" yellow jersey.

The Dundee based *Courier* is naturally upset and concentrates on the many shortcomings of Dundee, "the hundreds of Dundee excursionists will want to forget this one" and how they must have yearned for their talismanic Alec Troup, now transferred to Everton!

But "Dark Blue" also concedes that Raith Rovers were very good indeed and sings the praises of the half-back line of Raeburn, Morris and Collier who dominated the game, with Collier singled out for his "superior forcing qualities". No fewer than "four dandy shots" hit the Dundee uprights and one the crossbar, so the score might easily have been 8-0.

If there was any criticism it was the usual one directed at Alec James who tended to overdo the trickery and who missed out on a good goal scoring opportunity by his inability to resist beating the same man twice! The trouble was that the 18,000 crowd loved James and encouraged him in his ball play. There was a particular attraction in seeing a big brutal defender not even being able to get close enough to foul him! It was clear however even at this early stage that the future this season for Raith Rovers looked good.

Alec James

August 19 1959

The Raith Rovers fans who travelled to Airdrie this Wednesday night must have been pinching themselves in disbelief on the way home.

Raith Rovers had now started the season with four successive wins. It was not necessarily unprecedented, but it was certainly unusual. In addition it was the second successive Wednesday night that they had won at Broomfield, the home of Airdrie with the quaint, cricket-style pavilion in the corner of the park.

The first three games had been wins in the Scottish League Cup over Celtic, Airdrie and Partick Thistle, and this was the opening game of the Scottish League.

The win was totally deserved as acknowledged by *The Glasgow Herald* which also states that Airdrie contributed to their own downfall with their inaccurate close passing. Raith half backs Andy Young and Andy Leigh were singled out as being outstanding for Raith, keeping their forwards supplied with the ball.

Andy Young, in particular, a veteran now, often posed the question why he had not been chosen for Scotland. Tonight he hardly put a foot wrong as Rovers won far more convincingly than the 2-1 score line would have suggested. Rovers went ahead when John Urquhart scored from a Jim Kerray pass, and after Airdrie equalised with a header after a long throw-in, Tommy White, a lesser known Raith figure up to this point, scored the winner from an accurate Urquhart cross.

Raith finished the game well on top with their small knot of supporters jubilant and noisy.

Raith Rovers Football Club

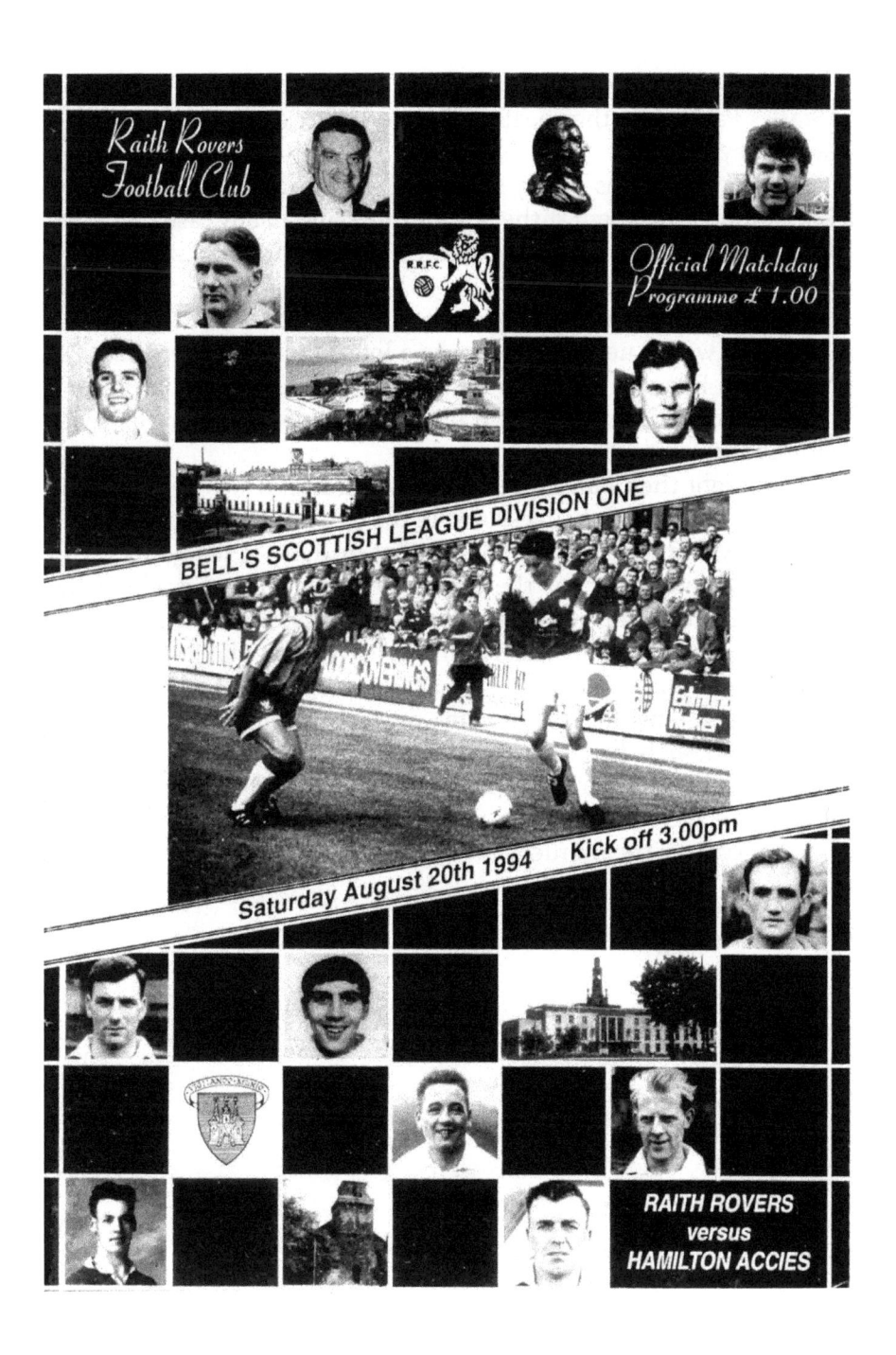

Official Matchday Programme £1.00

BELL'S SCOTTISH LEAGUE DIVISION ONE

Saturday August 20th 1994 — Kick off 3.00pm

RAITH ROVERS versus HAMILTON ACCIES

August 20 1969

At their fourth attempt, Rovers won their first game of the season at Stark's Park when they beat Airdrie 2-1 before a crowd of 2,907 this Wednesday night.

The low crowd was hardly surprising, for Airdrie don't really carry a big support with them at the best of times and in any case these two teams were more or less making up the numbers for Celtic and Rangers in this League Cup section.

Everyone accepted that Rovers had little chance of winning the section but would nevertheless make a lot of money! Rovers had lost narrowly to Rangers on the first day of the season, then had been a little short of luck at Broomfield before going down rather heavily to Celtic at Parkhead.

But tonight they won through against Airdrie. It was a remarkable game with all the goals being scored in the first half, Rovers goals being scored by Colin Sinclair and Alan Miller. It did not really matter in terms of qualification, for the chances of either team reaching the quarter final had long gone, but it was always a pointer for the rest of the season and made sure that Airdrie at least knew that Rovers would be no pushovers.

Times were tense for the Vietnam war was going on with unremitting ferocity, and such had been the violence and tension in Northern Ireland that the British Government had been compelled to commit troops. The idea at this stage was to protect the Roman Catholic community from the murderous Protestant gangs.

August 21 1926

Under new Manager, George Wilson, Raith Rovers recorded their first win of their new and much diminished existence in the Second Division as they beat East Fife 4-2 at Stark's Park in the second game of the season.

It was a great improvement from their narrow defeat by King's Park last week, and their supporters in the 5,000 departed happy. The crowd might have been a great deal more, but supporters of both sides were badly affected by the miners' strike which, unlike the General Strike which had been settled in a few days, was continuing relentlessly causing loads of problems with poverty and deprivation.

It was Rovers first win since the end of February, when they beat Clydebank and was much cheered by the support, who saw them go ahead when Owen Dorrans scored early on, then made another chance for Willie Allison. Allison then scored with a header before George Reay finished matters off with a penalty kick scored after a hand ball.

The Courier is rather scathing about East Fife's tactics which it says are "kick and rush" as distinct from the "close passing" game of Raith Rovers.

Both teams were on the verge of a remarkable season. Rovers would get promoted and win their way back to the First Division whereas East Fife would write themselves into the record books by becoming the first team to reach the Scottish Cup final from the Second Division.

August 22 1995

Rovers duly qualified for the next round in the UEFA Cup when they drew 2-2 with Gotu Itrotterfelag in Toftir, the capital of the Faroe Islands.

Rovers were 4-0 up from the first leg on August 8, so unless something dreadful was to happen, they were confident that they could get through and indeed they did with goals from Danny Lennon and Steve Crawford. When Danny Lennon scored in the first half, it was game over for the crowd of 350.

Those who went to the game had to keep reminding themselves that this was actually a European tie. About 40 travelled from Kirkcaldy to the game, and a lot more would have done similarly if they had not been deterred by the sheer inaccessibility of the place.

Some went by ferry, an experience — about 2 days each way —not likely to be repeated by some supporters who found the Atlantic a bit choppy even in August.

Others flew on a chartered plane from Aberdeen which was at least quicker but small and no more comfortable. Those who did go on the trip however and lived to tell the tale did at least have the consolation of being able to tell everyone that they saw the first ever away leg of Raith Rovers career in Europe. The next leg was even further away in Iceland and even further north, but accessibility was at least a lot better.

August 23 1969

38,040 were at Ibrox to see Raith Rovers play a great game against Rangers in the Scottish League Cup.

The final score was 3-3 and Rangers in fact were lucky to get off with a draw. Rovers could not win the section — it was always unlikely with both Rangers and Celtic being in the same section!

The significance of this game was that it gave Celtic the advantage, for each Old Firm team had beaten the other, and it would all depend on how they played against Raith Rovers and Airdrie.

Twice Rangers went one goal ahead through Alex MacDonald and Andy Penman, but on both occasions, Gordon Wallace equalised for Rovers. Then late in the game, Colin Sinclair put Rovers ahead to the sound of almost total silence apart from the cheers of the small Rovers support. Then as the boos and the catcalls began to intensify, Alex MacDonald equalised for Rangers. Pressure then rained down on Bobby Reid's goal, but Rovers held out for a deserved draw. Rovers' Manager at the time was old Ibrox favourite Jimmy Millar and he pronounced himself satisfied with the result.

So a draw meant advantage to Celtic — but the green and whites still had to come to Stark's Park on Wednesday night. The result meant that the noose was slowly beginning to tighten round the neck of Rangers' Manager, Davie White.

August 24 1997

Ex-Rovers player Willie Mathieson had a very narrow escape from death today.

The one time Rangers and Raith Rovers full back, now retired from football, was ringing the bell at the Old Kirk of Kirkcaldy for the Sunday service in his duty as an Elder. The bell was old, dating from the 15th century, and had been recast several times.

It was the tradition that the bell should be rung to summon the congregation to worship in the days when the congregation all lived in the High Street area, and the tradition was passed on.

Suddenly the tongue of the bell fell out and came hurtling down on Willie and other members of the congregation assembling for worship. It missed his head by a matter of inches and was so close that there was a rust mark on his shirt. Fortunately no-one was injured even though considerable damage was done to the wooden floor of the landing.

The Courier and *Fife Free Press* both reported this incident and Rev John Ferguson said how lucky Willie had been, and was not shy of using the word "miracle" in this context. The service went ahead as planned.

Willie, a Raith Rovers supporter from Cardenden played most of his career with Rangers, winning in 1972 a European Cup Winners' Cup medal in Barcelona and a Scottish Cup final medal in 1973, but played 13 games for Raith Rovers at the end of his career in 1976/77.

August 25 1984

Raith Rovers had a dreadful game today, losing 5-1 to the "Blue Brazil" of Cowdenbeath.

The game was played at Central Park, Cowdenbeath; the performance was every bit as bad as it sounded, but there was at least something to make Kirkcaldy sports fans happy today, for Kirkcaldy Cricket Club, for the first time ever, won the East of Scotland League Championship.

Some fans were even seen to leave early from Cowdenbeath, giving up on Raith Rovers, and dashing to Bennochy (where the doctor's surgery and a housing estate are now) to see the second half of the game against Leith Franklin.

If Kirkcaldy won that game, they would be champions. Unfortunately (and unusually for them this season) they were making a "pig's ear" of it (although it was put a great deal more crudely than that) for Leith Franklin, facing a demanding total of 243, were steadily chasing it down as catches were dropped, tempers were lost and the game was slipping away from Kirkcaldy with even professional Bob Carter unable to capture the wickets.

It looked bad. Then came news that the main rivals Stenhousemuir were losing to Heriots. The situation was confused, and there were of course no sophisticated mobile phones in 1984. It looked as if Kirkcaldy had captured enough bonus points to win the League — as long as Stenhousemuir lost! But Leith Franklin now beat Kirkcaldy. There was a long wait, until someone phoned the pay phone in the old clubhouse to say that Heriots had indeed beaten Stenhousemuir, and that therefore Kirkcaldy were the champions!

OFFICIAL PROGRAMME

Raith Rovers
FIRST DIVISION CHAMPIONS 1994 - 95

£1.00

BELL'S PREMIER LEAGUE
RAITH ROVERS F.C. v CELTIC
SATURDAY 26TH AUGUST 1995,
STARK'S PARK, KIRKCALDY.
KICK-OFF 3:00pm

August 26 2017

A very pleasant day was spent by all Raith Rovers fans along the coast at East Fife as their favourites beat the home side very comfortably by the score of 5-0.

The weather was nice and warm and the spectators got a good view of the sea and the surrounding countryside. (Normally the wind is howling and waves are threatening to sweep everybody out to sea!).

There is something rather exposed about New Bayview, and quite a lot of East Fife supporters preferred the old ground, which did have a great deal of character and history about it.

But good as the scenic amenities were, they were not as good as what was happening on the field of play, for Rovers put on the type of exhibition which, if seen oftener last season, would have staved off the horrors of relegation. Lewis Vaughan scored two, and Bobby Barr, Greig Spence and Liam Buchanan scored the others in what was essentially a rout.

The game was played on an artificial surface and one or two people might have been worried about that, but it wouldn't have mattered for Rovers could have beaten them today if they had been playing half-way up Largo Law.

It had been a good start to the season for Raith Rovers and Barry Smith pronounced himself happy. All that needed to be done now was to keep winning in this funny First Division which contained five teams beginning with the letter A.

1910-11 — Raith's first season in the First Division of the Scottish League

August 27 1910

This was a great day in Kirkcaldy (and Fife) football.

It was the first time that First Division football had been played in Fife. Raith had been accepted for the First Division (there was no automatic promotion or relegation in those days) and their first home game (they had already played and lost two away games at Morton and Aberdeen) was against the might of Rangers.

Rangers, a well-supported side, brought two "football special" trains from Glasgow, and publicans and restauranteurs did a good trade.

Rangers had won the Scottish League four years in a row around the turn of the century, but had since lost out to that other great Glasgow side called the Celtic.

A year ago their supporters and those of Celtic had rioted after being cheated out of extra time and destroyed Hampden. They were a wild bunch, but had one or two decent people among them as well.

Stark's Park had been specially extended for the crowd which looked to be upwards of 10,000. Rangers were 2-0 up before half time with goals from Alick Smith and Jimmy Gordon. Rovers fought back in the second half but without success although the crowd "round the ropes" enjoyed what the saw.

The general feeling was that Rangers were a very good side, but that Rovers would be good enough to do well and to earn a few points in this difficult League. Rangers' Manager Mr William Wilton was quite effusive in his praise of Rovers' efforts.

August 28 1915

The war had been going for over a year now, and already there had been significant casualties from Kirkcaldy and district.

Conscription was not yet in force, and the casualties were usually regular soldiers or volunteers who had joined in the first flush of excitement for the adventure.

Football had survived, but there were severe restrictions in that, for example, a player had to do war-related work as well as play football on a Saturday.

Raith Rovers were still in the Scottish League and today travelled with a squad of mainly youngsters to Shawfield to play Clyde, at that time a strong Glasgow team who had been beaten Scottish Cup finalists in 1910 and 1912.

Manager John Richardson was able to field the same eleven who had done well enough in the first game of the season against Airdrie.

This game was played in heavy rain throughout with the young Rovers performing well in front of a crowd of about 4,000, the crowd containing as always a smattering a men in uniform home on leave.

The Fife Free Press praises the enthusiasm of the youngsters and says that the only thing which let them down was their lack of composure in front of goal, whereas Clyde, with a slightly more experienced XI, particularly their veteran full back John Gilligan, took advantage of one of the few opportunities that they had when Scouller scored three minutes from time to consign Rovers to a rather unlucky 0-1 defeat.

August 29 1990

The affairs of Hibernian Football Club had been on the slide for many years, thanks to dreadful management and husbanding of resources with a particular desire to sell players to the extent that they now had very few players left to sell.

No strangers to the First Division, they were also a sitting duck, so Wallace Mercer thought, for an amalgamation with Hearts. The idea of one strong Edinburgh team was, in theory, a good one, but Wallace Mercer, an unashamed capitalist with unbounded ambition was emphatically not the man to do it.

He had raised such antagonism and hatred in Leith that Hibs, not too far from liquidation a short time ago, had now taken a new lease of life. Oh, the things that can be achieved by sheer hatred! But how would they do on the field?

Not too well, if tonight was anything to go by, for tonight a headed goal by George McGeachie of Raith Rovers at Stark's Park was enough to beat them in the 3rd round of the Scottish League Cup. 4,631 were there, as indeed was Mike Aitken of *The Scotsman*, who complained of the "idiosyncratic position of the Press Box" which made it difficult for him to see the game.

It was a good win for Raith Rovers and Jimmy Nicholl, and the reward was a trip to Ibrox next Tuesday night where Nicholl could meet up with his old friends again! The season was off to a good start for Rovers. Hibs supporters were just glad that there was still a Hibernian FC for them to support!

August 30 1939

Raith Rovers beat Burntisland Shipyard with a degree of ease 6-0 this Wednesday night at Stark's Park.

The weather was fine and sunny, but the mood of the spectators was far from bright.

There was the obvious footballing reason for this in that Rovers had not started the new season very well, but there was also the "International emergency", as it was called with rumours abounding that Hitler was about to invade Poland. If that happened, war would be inevitable.

As a general rule, young people were excited at this turn of events, but older people who recalled the war of just over 20 years ago looked upon the future with apprehension. There was however a quiet resignation that it was going to happen anyway, so it would be better to face it. In Kirkcaldy, the Air Raid Patrol was already in position telling everyone not to collect in the streets if there was an air raid and not to use a telephone if a raid was in progress! And everyone had been issued with a gas mask, which they were meant to carry with them at all times.

But on the field tonight, Raith Rovers gave their fans something to be happy about — the very impressive young Johnny Maule scored two good goals as did John Smith and Willie Dunn and Jimmy Kerr got one each. Stenhousemuir were due to come to Stark's Park on Saturday, but would it happen?

Willie McNaught

August 31 1957

Raith Rovers supporters did not know whether to laugh or cry today, as their team played magnificently to beat Rangers 4-3 at Stark's Park before a massive crowd of 25,000.

It was the last match of the League Cup section, but thanks to the system of goal average (i.e one divided the goals scored by the goals against), a 4-3 win was not enough. 5-3 would have done the trick, but it was not to be, hard through Rovers tried to get that final goal that would have made all the difference.

The game was a thriller with six goals scored (3-3) in the first half, but then Jimmy McEwan scored with about 10 minutes to go to set up a breath taking finale. It was also a very feisty encounter with Willie McNaught and Don Kichenbrand in particular conducting a private vendetta against each other all game.

John Urquhart scored one for Rovers and Jim Kerray two in the first half while Alex Scott and Johnny Hubbard did the necessary for Rangers.

Rangers supporters rejoiced noisily at the end, but it might have been better for them in the long run if they had not qualified for the later stages of the League Cup. This was the year in which they lost 7-1 to Celtic in the final!

Rovers' supporters could console themselves with the thought that, as this was the night on which Scottish Television started, the lucky few who had a TV which could take two channels had a choice of watching! It was a choice of the cowboys, in fact — Wells Fargo on BBC or Wyatt Earp on STV!

September

September 1 1965

Since they reached the final of the Scottish League Cup in 1949, that competition was one in which Raith Rovers had done surprisingly badly.

On only one other occasion had they even qualified from the sectional stages, but tonight's fine performance against Arbroath gave them a very good chance.

All they now had to do was draw with Queen's Park on Saturday. They had beaten Stirling Albion home and away, and drawn previously with Queen's Park at Hampden and Arbroath at Gayfield.

This Wednesday night's game was a cracker, but Rovers showed enough to tenacity to win through. Both teams scored in the first half, but then Rovers went ahead and looked comfortable at 2-1. But then it all happened in the last few minutes with Arbroath equalising and the Rovers scoring twice to lift the two points.

George Lyall scored a hat-trick and Pat Gardner notched the other goal. The 3234 crowd departed in fine fettle, convinced that they could now get a draw with Queen's Park and qualify (as it happened, they beat them convincingly 3-0) for the third time since the inception of the trophy.

There was little doubt that a fine young team was beginning to emerge under George Farm, with talented youngsters like Ian Porterfield and Pat Gardner developing well with the role model of Bobby Evans a fine one to follow. "Evans, as usual, was superb" was a cliché in newspaper reports in his Celtic days, and the same was true now. His red hair was slowly changing colour and he was maybe a little slower, but he was still always there when required, covering every blade of grass on the field. The future was looking brighter than it had for some considerable time.

Bobby Evans

September 2 1939

This was one of Raith Rovers more surreal games of football.

Hitler had invaded Poland yesterday, and as the game between Raith Rovers and Stenhousemuir began at 3.15 that afternoon, the House of Commons was in emergency session trying to persuade a reluctant Mr Chamberlain to do the needful and send an ultimatum to Germany. They did so, Germany refused to leave Poland and war was the result.

5,000 people were at Stark's Park. As at most games, the National Anthem was played and sung vigorously by the crowd, while all the time there were tears in everyone's eyes, not least those of the men in invalid chairs, not yet old men, but visible and obvious evidence of the horrors of war. Some of the crowd already had their boxes with a gas mask inside, as they tried to get excited about what was a dreadful game of football, won well 3-1 by Stenhousemuir, appropriately nicknamed "the Warriors".

No-one will know the name of the talented young man who scored a good hat-trick for Stenny, for his name is simple listed as "Junior". Three Raith men were exempted from the general panning of the team — goalkeeper John Moody, left winger Davie Duncan and right winger Johnny Maule, whose trickery with the ball would become legendary after the war.

The 5,000 crowd left depressed at the end, or should we say more depressed, for everyone knew that war was here and would be confirmed soon. In the meantime, the BBC radio assured everyone that the Polish Army was fighting bravely...

September 3 1910

Rovers had had a great tradition in the Scottish Qualifying Cup (winners and runners-up in recent years), so a defeat in the First Round hurt.

It hurt all the more when the defeat was to Dunfermline Athletic — bad enough at the best of times! — a club who were still in the Central League while Rovers were just starting their first season in the First Division of the Scottish League.

It was a serious blow, and *The Fife Free Press* does not spare the team, saying that they went out "almost without a fight" and refuses to make excuses about the strong sun and the wind being against them in the first half.

The truth was that Dunfermline (a club who had achieved little so far and clearly lagged behind Raith Rovers) had a point to prove and in modern terms were "up for it", having erected a temporary stand in front of their pavilion to accommodate more fans in their somewhat primitive East End Park.

Their fans were there in large numbers with "corncrakes" and a big drum, and when Croal scored what proved to be the only goal on the game in the 10th minute, they "waved their hats and sticks in the air" to celebrate.

They should have scored again when "for quite two minutes the ball danced about the goal line but no-one could send it home" in the rather improbable description of *The Fife Free Press*.

The second half, when Rovers had the advantage of the wind and the sun, should have seen them do better, but Dunfermline, with captain Jimmy Brown outstanding, remained on top, not disdaining the "lash the ball forward" style of play which at least tended to keep the ball in the other half! It was a sore blow for Raith Rovers.

September 4 1993

It was Raith's first season in the Premier League, and they had yet to record a win.

Supporters always knew that things were going to be a lot tougher in the Premier League than they had been in the First Division, which they had won by a considerable distance last season. It was the first season that Rovers had been in the top tier since 1970.

Today still did not bring that elusive first win but did at least bring a glorious finish against local rivals Dundee United, who had of course stolen Craig Brewster over the summer!

It was a beautiful sunny day before 5,304 spectators at Stark's Park, and Rovers were 0-1 down to a Billy McKinlay goal scored within the first five minutes of the first half. But Rovers fought hard, and gradually throughout the second half as they played towards the Beveridge Park end of the ground gained some sort of control over the situation with Colin Cameron and Jason Dair looking particularly impressive.

First Dair hit the bar and the ball bounced out, and then with literally seconds left, after a throw in on the Railway Stand side of the field, Cameron rolled the ball to player-manager Jimmy Nicholl who crashed home a great shot from well outside the penalty box. It is often said that grabbing a last minute goal for a draw is as good as a win, and the Raith faithful celebrated accordingly.

It certainly vindicated the manager's decision to keep on playing when so many had felt that he might give up that side of the game when the team reached the Premier League.

September 5 1931

Raith Rovers recorded a fine 4-1 win at Bayview in the derby game against East Fife.

Rovers were now back in the Second Division, and may have lost a little credibility in the eyes of some supporters as a result, but this was a local derby. On a hot, sultry kind of day with the threat of thunderstorms 4,500, including a lot of Rovers supporters on special trains, made their way along the coast to see the game. The 4-1 win, however, was a little flattering to Raith and Rovers were indebted to the three B's — Andy Bell, Tommy Batchelor and Jock Beath — for their solid defending.

For Rovers, Joe Cowan scored twice and the other goals were scored by Jacky Archibald and Jacky McLaren. It was a fine win for the Rovers whose form this season had been inconsistent so far. Supporters, naturally on a high, following a derby win, now felt that this might be the year for promotion again.

It was only when they got back to Kirkcaldy and the evening papers with the results came out that they learned that Fife's John Thomson ("Jock" as he was sometimes known in Kirkcaldy and Cardenden) had been carried off with a serious head injury in the Rangers v Celtic game at Ibrox. Worse news followed when the Sunday papers appeared the following morning after a night of speculation and anxiety.

John had been born at 74 Balfour Street, Kirkcaldy in January 1909.

September 6 1958

Today's Fife derby match between Dunfermline Athletic and Raith Rovers actually started with a thunderstorm going on overhead. It had to be abandoned after only 30 minutes play.

Only 5,000 were there, taking cover under what shelter there was (there wasn't much at East End Park until the early 1960s) and some of the crowd and players were, frankly and with cause, afraid for their lives.

The referee was the famous Tom Wharton, a man of huge bulk and therefore called "Tiny" by the fans. Not everyone was happy about it, but it was agreed to go ahead in view of the fact that the sparse crowd had paid their money.

After about six minutes, Rovers went ahead through a penalty sunk by Jimmy McEwan to the delight of the few Rovers fans behind the goal. The players were then taken off for a spell after a particularly heavy downpour, but came back after Mr Wharton had inspected the parts of the pitch which had suffered the worst flooding.

Dunfermline then equalized with a fine header from Charlie Dickson. But then after more heavy rain which flooded not only the field but also the bottom of the terracing, Mr Wharton decreed that enough was enough and there would be no further play.

This was a pity, for the game had been entertaining, and when the game was replayed on the Holiday Monday at the end of September, it was a good 3-3 draw on another very heavy pitch.

September 7 1957

Raith Rovers continued their good start to the season with a fine 4-2 win over Third Lanark today at Stark's Park.

Last week, they had beaten Rangers 4-3 at Ibrox (admittedly in a losing cause as they just failed to qualify from the League Cup section).

Today was the first game of the League season as they welcomed the men in red from Cathkin Park — the "warriors", the "Hi-Hi-Hi's" or the "sodgers" (because they were originally the 3rd Lanark Volunteers). In spite of the intermittent wind and rain, a crowd of 8224 appeared and most of them left encouraged by what they saw and full of optimism for the season ahead.

The half back line of Young, McNaught and Leigh was such that quite a few journalists suggested that Scotland could do worse than play the whole three of them in International matches, but the man of the moment was the charismatic, but occasionally indolent and lazy Bernie Kelly.

Bernie had had a nasty experience with his car last week involving a burst tyre, but then had been chosen at inside left to play for the Scottish League against the League of Ireland in Dublin in a fortnight's time.

Today, he showed why he was one of the most talked about men in Scottish football when he scored a hat-trick against Thirds. Veteran goalkeeper Jocky Robertson fumbled the first one, but the second two were real crackers. Thirds fought well and late in the second half had brought the score back to 3-2, but then Johnny Williamson scored the fourth to get Rovers off to a flying start in the Scottish League.

September 8 1971

For the third time in a year, Raith Rovers went up to Gayfield, Arbroath on a Wednesday night and returned on the wrong end of a 0-4 beating.

It had happened last year, and it had happened this year on the second game of the season in the League Cup, and here we were again.

Small wonder that the travelling support was a little more diminished than what one would have expected. It would have to be admitted, however, that Arbroath were a class outfit with clear and justified aspirations to reach the First Division again.

There did not seem to be any great problem at Stark's Park where 1-1 tended to be the score line, but 0-4 yet again reduced manager Bill Baxter to despair. Was there a problem with Gayfield, that curious little ground whose touchline was a matter of yards away from the North Sea?

Tonight it was Rovers who were all at sea with Murray McDermott in the Rovers goal, although far from error-free, keeping the score down to respectable levels.

The season had not really started well. Failure to qualify for the League Cup was, after all, the norm but after a bright start against East Fife on opening day, things had not prospered. It was not as if the players were poor — Jim Dempsey, Gordon Wallace, Ian Lister were respectable performers, but clearly an improvement was going to be required if Rovers were ever to challenge again for the First Division, considered to be their rightful place.

September 9 1922

Celtic Park had the flags at half-mast today in view of the death in a motor bike accident of their great player "Sunny Jim" Young.

Rovers found themselves struggling to field a team because of injuries.

Manager James Logan was compelled to give a Scottish League debut to a diminutive youngster called Alec James who had impressed in the reserves and in a Fife Cup game.

He was just 20 years old and came from Bellshill, and had just recently joined the club. He was however very small and thin, but that was by no means unusual in the 1920s when there was often a huge disparity in size between brawny defenders and scrawny forwards — one thinks of Patsy Gallacher, Hughie Gallacher and Alec Troup. The Welfare State, which would of course solve the problem of under-feeding, was still some 25 years away.

There did seem to be something special about this young man with his trickery, but even so, a debut against the League Champions on their own ground was a tall order. However, the 15,000 Celtic crowd were impressed by the way he made a fool of some of their defenders.

He did however dally when he might have scored, something that showed his inexperience and Celtic went on to win 3-0 over a fairly poor Rovers side, but as they headed for the train home that night, Rovers supporters reckoned that in young James, there might be someone for the future. He was retained next week for the game against Airdrie, a 0-0 draw.

September 10 1996

Raith Rovers, though no fault of their own, became the laughing stock of Scottish football when Manager Tommy McLean resigned after a week in charge!

He had been at the helm for one game — admittedly a very bad defeat at the hands of Aberdeen — but it was not unreasonably felt in Kirkcaldy that Raith Rovers were worth a little more than one week.

It reminded one of that Beatles record on the late 1960s called "Hello Goodbye". And yet a week previously there had been all the cant about "building a strong team" and "harnessing local support"!

But it was the summons of his, admittedly, fearsome elder brother Jim at Dundee United which caused Tommy's departure, for Jim had just sacked another Manager and wanted wee Tommy to do his bidding.

The whole thing smacked of nepotism and even corruption, but away Tommy went leaving behind a bewildered Rovers support wondering where one went from here. Yet, although Tommy had clearly disqualified himself from a long service medal, it was nothing like a record even in a job where "security of tenure" is an abstract concept.

Andy Young once had his jacket off to start working as Manager of Raith Rovers before changing his mind — but he hadn't signed anything.

Then we had Stevie Murray whose tenure at Forfar Athletic began on the Tuesday and stopped on the Friday, and he never saw them playing a game. The training session that he took must have been pretty awful, though!

Tommy McLean

September 11 2001

This day is, of course, well known for dark deeds. It was America's second "day of infamy", the first having been Pearl Harbour of December 7 1941.

This was the day that planes were hijacked and flown into the Twin Towers in New York. The ramifications of this day would go on for some considerable time.

The following night's European Champions League games were postponed, but it was too late (the Twin Towers had been attacked about 2.00 p.m. British Summer Time) to postpone tonight's domestic Scottish fixtures, in Raith Rovers' case a home game against Montrose in the Scottish League Cup.

Rovers had not started the season all that well — some good performances like beating Falkirk had to be balanced against a couple of shockers at the hands of Partick Thistle — and manager Peter Hetherston was beginning to lose the confidence of some fans.

Nevertheless, 1099 turned up to Stark's Park to see the game, and they were rewarded with a 1-0 win, the only goal coming from Darren Henderson, who headed home a Scott Crabbe free-kick in the 10th minute.

It was not an easy game for the Rovers fans to watch, for Third Division Montrose put up a good performance, easily the better team in the second half but unable to convert their chances.

The full time whistle brought some relief to the fans who thus could look forward to a run in the League Cup, but the main focus of attention in fans' minds was what was happening in the USA, and how the western world was going to react.

September 12 1995

TV Cameras, national Press, radio — the lot descended on Stark's Park to see Rovers take on Akranes of Iceland in the first leg of the UEFA Cup.

Football was big in Kirkcaldy at that time, and it was great to see such interest and support (from people who usually favoured other Scottish teams) as Rovers took on a team who contained quite a few men with experience in the English or European Leagues, and others with aspirations to do so.

Incredibly, Rovers were Scotland's only remaining representative in this competition, and it was nice to see Stark's Park looking so full with 5,824 spectators inside.

Raith opened the scoring in the 15th minute when Danny Lennon swept in, from the edge of the box, a good ball from the excellent Stephen McAnespie. Things were looking good for the Rovers but then just before half time, disaster struck and Akranes got their vital away goal as Thordursson picked up a lovely through ball and slipped it past Scott Thomson.

The second half was exciting, but it began to look as if Akranes were prepared to settle for a 1-1 draw with Rovers finding it difficult to get through an organised Icelandic defence. But then Danny Lennon tried a shot from outside the box and Rovers were back in the lead once again. With about ten minutes left Colin Cameron released Barry Wilson who scored the third goal.

The game finished with Stark's Park in raptures and Rovers fans delighted to have a 3-1 lead in a performance which was much praised in the national Press and TV.

Raith Rovers in 1953

September 13 1902

Having been defeated last week in the Scottish Qualifying Cup by Lochgelly United, Rovers turned their attention this week to the East of Scotland Qualifying Cup when the "soutars" of Selkirk came to Stark's Park.

It was probably true to say that football in Selkirk was in its infancy, and that they were better at rugby and cricket than the "association game".

Today they lost 11-0 to an efficient Rovers team, determined to make up for last week's disappointment.

The Courier says that Selkirk team contained some "well set up fellows" in terms of stature, but they were "sadly deficient" in the "science of the game".

Some were good runners but they had "little or no control of the ball". This makes one think that the Selkirk team were basically the guys not good enough to get a game for the rugby team!

Be that as it may, Rovers enjoyed themselves with Jimmy Smith going nap and scoring five, Tommy Cairns had two and Jock Eckford, Alex Hynd, Simpson Rankine and George Anderson scoring one each to entertain the crowd.

Latterly however, the crowd began to get bored with the proceedings and either went home or willed Selkirk score a goal. This score sadly set a precedent for Selkirk, for in December 1984, they travelled to Stirling Albion to lose 20-0 in a Scottish Cup tie.

Selkirk is a lovely Borders town with a very good rugby team, but it has been anything but a hotbed of Scottish football over the years!

September 14 1999

Having had a little bad luck in going out of the Scottish League Cup to Motherwell on penalties a month ago, a further blow was delivered to John McVeigh's mercurial side when they lost 1-3 at Livingston in the League Challenge Cup at Almondvale.

The Scottish League Challenge Cup (which would indeed be won in future years by Raith Rovers) was the competition for everyone except the Premier League clubs, and it was often felt that it was within Rovers' compass.

But tonight, Livingston were quite simply better as the potentially very talented Raith team of Didier Agathe, the two Toshes (Steve and Paul), Marvin Andrews, Jay Stein and Craig Dargo failed to function against a solid and determined Livingston outfit.

Rovers' fans were well represented in the 2223 crowd but as this game followed a 0-2 defeat by Morton on the Saturday in the League, things began to look bleak for Rovers.

Nevertheless, there remained a certain belief that under John McVeigh, an outspoken but determined character, things might yet improve after a year or two of disappointments. The historian must however tread carefully when describing the history of this club over the next few months and indeed years, for several things happened that frankly defy rational analysis.

John McVeigh, for example, would be suddenly sacked on 1 December for mysterious reasons, and the ramifications of that one went on for a few years after that. In the meantime the club continued to suffer. It was a disturbing time to follow Raith Rovers!

September 15 1965

Raith Rovers' run of eight games without defeat came to a spectacular end this Wednesday night when Celtic came to Stark's Park for a League Cup tie and won 8-1, before a massive crowd of 15,000.

Crowds had been slipping of late but this game was like old times again with huge queues at the turnstiles and the game having to be delayed by a few minutes to allow the crowd in.

It was generally agreed to have been the best display of attacking football seen in Kirkcaldy for many years as both McBride and Hughes scored three goals each and Lennox and Hughes one each, and even Raith supporters had to clap on occasion.

This was by no means a bad Raith Rovers team, and playing tonight but now at the end of his career was Bobby Evans who had of course made his name with Celtic playing for them between 1944 and 1960. Evans had made his name alongside Jock Stein (now Celtic's Manager) in the 1950s, and was still much beloved of the Celtic supporters.

Jock Stein was of course no relation to Bobby Stein who was playing for Raith Rovers at right half. Also playing for Rovers was Ian Porterfield who would score the famous goal that won the English Cup for Sunderland in 1973.

It was John "Jocky" Richardson who scored Raith's only goal that night. The team that night was Reid, McKeown and Gray; Stein, Evans and Porterfield; Hutchison, Gardner, Richardson, Lyall and McLean.

The really depressing news was that this was only the first leg. We still had to go to Parkhead in two weeks' time!

September 16 1959

Raith Rovers had bad luck this Wednesday night. They exited from the Scottish League Cup after a tough game against Arbroath at Gayfield which went to extra time.

They had done very well to qualify from a section which contained Celtic, Airdrie and Partick Thistle, winning all their games except for a narrow 1-0 defeat at Parkhead, and when they found themselves paired against the newly promoted Arbroath, they certainly fancied their chances.

The first leg was a 2-2 draw at Stark's Park which meant that everything depended on the second leg at Gayfield on the fringe of the great North Sea.

The game was even but goalless in the first half. Rovers were without Andy Young, probably their best player. Into Young's position at right half, they had brought Andy Leigh, who had recently lost his place to a talented youngster called Jim Baxter.

McNaught remained at centre half, and played brilliantly that night. But Arbroath, recently promoted to the First Division, just had the edge. Although Denis Mochan put Rovers ahead, Arbroath's inside right, Brown, equalised immediately. In the extra time period the same player managed to notch the winner. Rovers then hit the post in the very last minute, after what looked like a strong penalty was turned down when Mochan was pushed off the ball.

Two exhausted teams thoroughly deserved the plaudits of their fans at the end of the game, but Rovers fans were disappointed, feeling that they might have done better in the first leg at Stark's Park.

September 17 2005

A good but ultimately frustrating game was witnessed by a crowd of 1846 today at Stark's Park as Rovers drew 3-3 with Ayr United.

Ayr's equaliser came from a Raymond Logan free kick with virtually the last kick of the match when loads of Rovers supporters were heading home convinced that their early season League form was being maintained.

A great deal of attention centred today on Paul McManus who had been arrested on Wednesday night after a game at St Johnstone because his actual presence in Perth broke a condition of his bail order following a fracas in the Fair City a month ago!

The whole affair was treated with a certain amount of ridicule in the national press, for he was not likely to do any further offending in front of 2,000 witnesses!

Paul was allowed to play in this game however, and indeed it was he who scored Rovers' second goal with a fine header. This was after Ayr United had been 2-0 up.

Then soon after that Rovers seemed to have won the game with a good Neil Jablonski header. But prior to that, Paul Hilland had foolishly been sent off for two yellow cards, and the numerical advantage was significant in such a close game.

Although Rovers were now out of both the Scottish League Cup and the League Challenge Cup, their League form was played 6, won 3 and drawn 1, and the two defeats had come early in the season.

September 18 1915

Neither the war nor the football season were going well for Kirkcaldy at the moment.

The Fife Free Press contained many death notices of soldiers who had been killed, or what was perhaps worse for the family, those posted "missing".

Death could at least bring some sort of closure, but for those missing, there was the agony of their mothers and wives simply not knowing. In a week or two's time, the Battle of Loos would begin with its horrendous casualties and things would get worse.

Raith Rovers had not yet recorded a victory this season and travelled to Hamilton to play at Douglas Park in a game which *The Fife Free Press* struggles to say anything good about, possibly the best word about Raith Rovers being "moderate".

But this is hardly surprising in war time circumstances with the struggles of player availability and transport. Yet the crowd was a reasonably good one of 5,000 on a dull but dry day in Hamilton and their supporters saw a good 2-0 victory for their side with goals coming from Kelly.

Rovers were well served by Bill Inglis but the half backs and forwards were an uncoordinated bunch, and questions were already being asked about the advisability of players travelling to the west of Scotland after their compulsory Saturday morning in the munitions industries.

Maybe a regional set up would be better? Kirkcaldy United, for example, supplemented by a few "guests", played a great game today to draw with Dundee Hibs.

September 19 1921

This was the local Monday holiday in this part of Lanarkshire, so Raith Rovers travelled to Broomfield Park to take on Airdrieonians.

Two weeks ago they had gone to Albion Rovers and lost, but today they turned on a great display of football and won 2-0, impressing the 3,000 crowd to such an extent that some of them didn't so much turn on their own team as begin to support Raith Rovers with applause for some really good play in the half back and forward lines.

The home team started well but Jimmy Brown in goal was in fine fettle and having survived the first difficult five or ten minutes, Rovers launched a sustained counter attack which lasted more or less until the end of the game when Airdrie were awarded a soft penalty when the ball ran down the arm of Dave Morris. Neil "drove hard but missed the goal" says *The Courier* laconically.

Raith's two goals were good ones. The first was a classic "three card trick" from a corner taken by Bobby Archibald which found the head of Tom Duncan who nodded on to Bobby Bauld to finish the job. Then after a fine piece of work involving the Duncan brothers on the right wing, Tom Duncan sent over a lovely ball right on to the brow of Tom Jennings who "headed through with the opposition looking on".

It is interesting that this win by Raith Rovers was as much praised by the Glasgow-based newspapers as it was by those in the east. *The Glasgow Herald,* for example talks about a "capital performance by the bustling Fifers".

September 20 1941

Funny things happen in war-time, but this one was, by any standards, excessive.

Rovers beat Leith Athletic 9-5, a score line that one does not get very often in any class of football.

Rovers had already been beaten 8-1 by Rangers and next week they would go to Pittodrie to lose 7-1, so high scoring seems to have been a feature of war-time football — presumably because defences didn't have a chance to train together.

Raith Rovers had played in season 1939/40, but had been in abeyance the following season of 1940/41. They were now however in the North Eastern League.

The immediate threat of invasion seemed to have passed, but the war was in deadlock with neither side able to deal a knock-out blow to the other. Germany had however turned its attentions eastwards and Britain now had an unlikely ally in the Soviet Union.

1,200 saw this astonishing game of football in which Rovers were 7-2 up at half time. *The Fife Free Press* gives Leith Athletic a pat on the back for keeping trying in the second half and for not giving up, but it also adds wryly that the goal nets had to work overtime today for they stopped 14 goals, and there were one or two close things as well.

For the record it seems that George Whalley scored 4, Francis Joyner 2, Willie Masson, John Gould and the impressive young Willie McNaught (with a penalty) 1 each, although the crowd left dazed at the sheer amount of goals scored which made it look like a basketball match.

September 21 1912

Not all Raith Rovers supporters were sanguine about their prospects for this season in the First Division after a bad start.

Following a good win over Hibs last week, they travelled today to Fir Park, Motherwell for a clash labelled "steel v linoleum" and earned an honourable 1-1 draw.

It was all the more praiseworthy because of the loss of full back Davie Philp with a dislocated arm just before half-time. The weather was warm this equinoctial day ("too warm for the players" opines the *Fife Free Press*) in the heavily industrial Lanarkshire town.

Motherwell in 1912 wore blue but were getting fed up with having to change for their home games (as was the normal practice in these days) for too many other Scottish teams wore blue. Today they changed to red, and the following year they would make a permanent change to claret and amber in conscious imitation of Bradford City who had won the English Cup in 1911.

They were a fine side, their only problem being the one that would haunt them all their life — namely, that they were just geographically too close to Glasgow. 0-0 at half-time, Motherwell took advantage of their numerical superiority after the loss of Philp, and scored through Jimmy Bellamy, the Englishman who had won a Scottish Cup medal with Dundee in 1910.

But Rovers, inspired by James Logan at centre half, fought back and equalised through Harry Anderson four minutes from time. Outstanding for "the linoleum" was reserve goalkeeper Jimmy Mackie, a man who had been with the club for many years but had never really impressed.

September 22 1925

One of Rovers' saddest moments took place today when Alec James was transferred to Preston North End for a fee reputed to be £3,250.

The signing took place in what is now Station Court, but was then the Station Hotel, the representatives of "proud Preston" (as they were still called after their glory days of the late 1880s and early 1890s) having arrived off the train half an hour previously.

This brought an end to the Kirkcaldy career of the man who may well have been considered to be Raith's best ever player. He was small, tricky, could score goals and in some ways was typical of the age, the small man with the baggy pants reminding so many people of Charlie Chaplin.

But his heart had not been in the team for some time. On the Saturday before his transfer, for example, the team had gone down 0-3 to Falkirk, and it had been clear to everyone that he was not happy. It had also been clear that some of his team mates with less ability but more commitment were less than happy with him.

His father-in-law, trainer Dave Willis, had gone to England in the summer and the departure of James was merely one episode in the haemorrhaging of talent from the club at this depressing point of the club's history.

"Wee Aleckie" or "Jimmy" however left very happy memories in the town, and his subsequent success with Preston and more especially Arsenal made everyone proud to say that he had played with Raith Rovers first. And he himself was proud of that as well!

September 23 1922

Raith Rovers maintained their fine early season form with a 2-1 win over Kilmarnock at Rugby Park before 9,000 fans.

Kilmarnock were a good side who had won the Scottish Cup in 1920 and were always hard to beat at their own ground.

This time however, "Onlooker" of *The Fife Free Press* was very impressed by the Rovers who played a "fine sprightly game" and were without a "weakling" in their side.

This was in spite of Kilmarnock scoring early on. But the diminutive Alec James continued to impress with loads of "trickiness" and it was he who scored the equalising goal with a fine shot from the edge of the penalty area which gave the goalkeeper no chance.

But it was the winning goal from Johnny Borland which not only delighted the small band of travelling Rovers fans but also brought out a reluctant round of applause from the Ayrshire crowd.

He broke through all on his own and scored one of the best goals ever seen at Rugby Park — certainly on a par with the famous one that Jimmy Quinn of Celtic had scored on the same ground on Christmas Day 1909. Borland almost scored another immediately afterwards but the ball went narrowly past the post.

It was the opinion, however, both of "Onlooker" and of most of the scribes of the national press that the man of the match was centre half David Morris. "Davie" was superb on the ground and in the air, going back and going forward (as centre halves did a lot of in the 1920s) and although Kilmarnock pressed hard for an equaliser, Rovers held out for a deserved victory which made up for some of the poorer performances seen earlier this season.

September 24 1960

The evening newspapers made for pleasant reading tonight on the way home in the train.

They showed Raith Rovers in fourth position following a very creditable 1-0 win over Hibs at a sun drenched Easter Road.

Rovers had now won three games out of four in the League — the defeat, admittedly, being a painful one at the hands of Dunfermline — but today's game contained a lot for the travelling support to be happy about.

The goal was scored by Andy Matthew, a fine goal high into the net from a narrow angle following a quickly taken throw-in from John Urquhart. This had followed several near things at either end with Willie Wallace looking particularly sharp for Rovers.

On the other hand, Hibs felt that they might have had a penalty kick when Joe Baker was brought down, but referee Willie Brittle (sometimes called "brutal Brittle" because of his hard approach to the game) said no. In the second half, Hibs, playing down the slope, had more of the pressure piled on by men like the veteran Willie Ormond and the talented Joe Baker, but goalkeeper Jim Thorburn had a good game and Rovers held out for a narrow win.

The game was not to the liking of the Hibs faithful in the 14,000 crowd, for they resented their rock bottom position at the foot of Division One and they turned on their players in a way that surprised the Raith Rovers fans. But then again, Hibs supporters had seen better days — and not all that long ago either — and took badly to a defeat from provincial Raith Rovers.

September 25 1973

Raith Rovers' miserable start to the season continued with a depressing 0-3 defeat at home to Hamilton Academical.

This game was moved to the Tuesday night from the scheduled Wednesday.

Scotland, who were playing Czechoslovakia in a World Cup qualifier on the Wednesday, were going to be on television (a rare treat for 1973 and the boost that it gave the country when they won was quite something!).

But if fans could look forward to the International, there seemed to be little to look forward to from Raith Rovers this season, for this was a dire performance. As is often the case, at the time when you need a break, you don't get one. Rovers were unfortunate in that they came up against a slick Hamilton outfit who had started the season well.

One or two refereeing decisions didn't go Rovers way, but that was no excuse. Rovers were simply outclassed, and the booing and catcalling showed what the 2117 fans thought of it all, as did the steady homeward trickle throughout the second half.

Inevitably in such circumstances, there were the "Ah'm no coming back" cries of those who had said the very same thing at the last game, and there were also the usual knowing remarks about the players refusing to do what the manager told them, training ground rebellions etc. It was clear that George Farm's tactics were not working as well in his second time with the club as they had in his first time.

September 26 1995

Raith Rovers qualified for the next round of the UEFA Cup after a bare-knuckle ride in Akranes, Iceland.

They actually lost 0-1, but having won 3-1 at Stark's Park, this was enough to see them through, although those who were good at Maths and also understood the away goals rule, knew that another goal conceded was curtains for Rovers.

200 supporters were there to share the agony and many more listened to the BBC radio commentary in the early evening of this fine autumn night.

Rovers did very well, with goalkeeper Scott Thomson outstanding, to withhold the Icelandic pressure in the first half. Early in the second half Arnar Gunnlaugsson managed to poke the ball over the line in the aftermath of a corner kick. From them on in, it was permanent pressure on the Rovers goal, with even out-and-out forwards like Jason Dair and Steve Crawford sometimes appearing to clear the ball out of defence.

Shaun Dennis had a great game in central defence, as did the sometimes accident-prone Ronnie Coyle, and the Dutch's referee's final whistle, much beseeched for by the Rovers contingent, was a wonderful relief.

My own memory of this game was walking round the Ravenscraig Park, transistor radio cocked to my ear, watching a beautiful sunset and then hearing, above the commentary, a few voices singing "No, no, no, Geordie Munro!".

The singing was not great, but the sense of triumph for Jimmy Nicholl and his men was almost tangible over the airwaves.

September 27 1960

OPENING FLOODLIGHT FIXTURE

Aston Villa v. Raith Rovers
TUESDAY, 27th SEPTEMBER, 1960

Kick-off 7.30 p.m.

JIMMY McEWAN

Needs no introduction to the Stark's Park supporters, we wish him well.

Its amazing how he played so consistently in Senior football and was only recognised last season in a Scottish jersey for the League v. Wales; it has happened before.

SOUVENIR PROGRAMME - - THREEPENCE

Thos. McGilvray & Son, 64 Hill Street, Kirkcaldy

September 27 1960

The Stark's Park floodlights were officially inaugurated tonight in a friendly match against Aston Villa which Rovers won 2-1 goals scored by Bernie Kelly and Willie Wallace.

Aston Villa, for whom Jimmy McEwan now played, sent a fairly strong team, and it was a good game well enjoyed by the 10,000 or so fans who were there.

Floodlights had proliferated throughout Scotland during the last few years, Rovers having played a competitive match under them as early as 1956. They certainly provided enough light, and it was interesting to see the four shadows that followed each player from each pylon.

The advantages were the obvious ones that one could play night football, and that Saturday games even in darkest December could start now at 3.00 pm and the club could be sure that they game would finish with everyone able to see what was going on.

Part-time players who worked at another job during the day could now train under them at night with a ball instead of the aimless running round and round the streets in the dark as they used to do.

But the main advantage was that the light provided was first class, often better than daylight! There had been some objections (as there always are when some social progress is being made!) but now that people saw their advantages, the voices of the Luddite few were stilled.

Some grounds would be slower than others to have floodlights — Hampden, for example, conservative as always, would not have them until the following year.

September 28 2013

Contests between Raith Rovers and Falkirk tend to be keenly fought and close affairs, something that perhaps explains the rivalry between the fans.

When the rivalry extends to throwing things at one another, however, the explanation has to be one of limited intelligence. There was a little of this in the environs of the ground today, but it duly fizzled out.

The day was a pleasant one and the crowd numbered 1715 to see if Falkirk could avenge their exit from the League Challenge Cup a few weeks ago.

It did not look like it when Rovers scored in the first five minutes when Grant Anderson hammered home a Joe Cardle corner kick along the ground before quite a lot of the crowd had been able to take their seats.

Thereafter the crowd were treated to non-stop action with both teams going all out, and Raith had several chances to finish the game, notably by young Lewis Vaughan, who failed to pick up a good through pass from Calum Elliot.

The pessimists were telling everyone that we might pay for that, but the optimists were heading towards the exits, happy with their team who had now won 4 League games out of 7, as they thought.

In the third minute of added on time a misplaced goal kick came to Kris Faulds who realised that, at this stage of the game, he was as well having a go. He did just that, charging through a static and clearly exhausted Rovers defence before hammering home a great goal to stun the home crowd and to excite what was left of the away support at the far end.

It was a disappointment, but more fair-minded supporters agreed that Falkirk were worth their draw.

September 29 2004

Today ended the most astonishing few weeks in the chequered, varied and occasionally eccentric history of Raith Rovers.

Claude Anelka resigned as Manager.

He stayed on as Director of Football for a few more days before quitting from that job as well.

It is often said by fans that "the Manager knows nothing about football". It is not often, however, that this statement is literally true, as it seems to be here.

Trading on the name of his brother Nicholas Anelka who was indeed a great player with Real Madrid and various top English teams, Claude basically bought his way into the club in the summer, and when Antonio Calderon (himself no great shakes as a Manager) left at the end of the 2003/04 season, Claude insisted on taking over.

Such was the weakness of Raith Rovers' financial position that they could not resist his pecuniary blandishments, and the footballing world watched in amazement as Claude indulged himself in his hobby.

Players were brought in from abroad, and it was stated that the intention was to make Raith Rovers the third force in Scotland.

The results were appalling, the football was worse and when you talked to people outside Kirkcaldy, you experienced great difficulty in persuading them that this was actually happening and that you were not having them on.

Eventually after eight defeats out of nine, a "palace revolution" took place. It was beyond astonishing and difficult to parallel in any other club at any point on history. But it did happen!

September 30 2006

Rovers were struggling in autumn 2006.

Indeed the whole decade of the "naughties" as they came to be called were not exactly a land flowing with milk and honey at Stark's Park.

A particular problem seeming to be the inability to find a manager who could stick around for long enough to build a team.

The departure of Gordon Dalziel as manager had been deplorable but perhaps inevitable after the poor early season form of the team, and his replacement Craig Levein had no look of permanence about him.

He was only at Stark's Park in the shop window as it were, until such time as a better offer came along.

It duly did in the shape of Dundee United and then eventually Scotland, and he was only really at Stark's Park for about seven weeks during which time he could hardly have expected to do all that much.

Today was a profoundly disappointing 0-1 defeat at Ayr United, a team with which Rovers tend to have a lot in common except for the obvious fact that they are at different sides of the country!

The previous day Rovers had signed from Hearts an Icelander called Hjalmar Thorarinsson on an emergency transfer loan until January and he appeared today as a substitute, but to no avail.

Craig Pettigrew of Ayr United scored the only goal of the game in the 81st minute, and the Rovers supporters in the poor crowd of 1330 had little to cheer them on the long journey home.

But then again, no-one ever said that it was easy to support Raith Rovers!

Raith Rovers in 2006

October

October 1 1949

Rovers' free scoring centre forward Willie Penman had a "near death" experience at Celtic Park today!

After an accidental clash of heads with Celtic's Alec Boden, Willie was dazed, and in those days smelling salts containing ammonia were used to revive a player.

The trainer was administering them under Willie's nose when he revived suddenly and accidentally knocked the smelling salts into his mouth and swallowed some!

This was a very serious matter, and Willie had to be carried off, where he was attended to by Dr Fitzimmons, Celtic's doctor.

Incredibly the cure was to scrape some plaster off the dressing room ceiling, put it in some water and put some cotton wool in the water which Willie was then instructed to suck. He was then given an emetic and vomited profusely to empty his stomach!

Amazingly, this rather primitive method of treatment worked, and Willie was able to return to the field to finish the game which ended in a creditable 2-2 draw.

Willie was lucky to be alive, but he might even have won the game if it had not been for a great save by Celtic's goalkeeper Willie Miller. His mouth and throat felt like they had been on fire for a long time after that, but the important thing was that he survived.

Some Raith Rovers supporters may have been heard to say now and again "Celtic make me sick", but Willie was grateful to their doctor for doing just that!

October 2 1926

As Robert Burns might have said, "Alas! Alas! A devilish change indeed!"

The wonder was that Raith Rovers still managed to attract a crowd of over 3,000 to see Arthurlie.

A few years ago it was Rangers and Celtic who came calling, but Rovers were now relegated and it was Arthurlie from Barrhead who were the visitors.

They had once put Celtic out of the Scottish Cup but they were now struggling against the economic circumstances of the time, the same as everyone else.

The General Strike had been a fiasco in 1926, but the Miners' Strike was still continuing to its tragic conclusion with clear signs of deprivation now obvious in the mining villages and even Kirkcaldy itself, as the Miners Union, now in desperation, threatened to call out the safety men, and risk flooding the pits for ever.

In these circumstances, football might have provided some sort of relief, but Rovers, after a reasonable start to their Second Division campaign, had lost last week to Bo'ness and now failed to impress against this team, of determined players but limited ability.

Rovers only goal was scored by full back Jimmy Porter from a twice-taken penalty, but Arthurlie's goals were good ones, and Rovers fans were left to contemplate a future that was far from bright, something that was made all the worse by the thought of the recent departure of all the great players of a few years ago.

That had been a glorious interlude in Kirkcaldy's misery, but a short one.

October 3 1936

This 6-1 thumping from Forfar Athletic at Stark's Park may not technically and mathematically have been the biggest hammering in the history of the club, but it was the most humiliating in the eyes of the supporters since well before the Great War.

It was unexpected as well, for although Rovers had lost their previous game 4-1 to Cowdenbeath (slightly tarnishing a more than reasonable start to the season) that game had been put down to poor refereeing.

That excuse would simply not do today for Mr Welsh of Wishaw had a good game, and in any case Rovers scored first from a penalty.

But Forfar had the wily old George McLean back playing for them after a long career in English football and he immediately spotted a weakness in Rovers' goalkeeper with the unlikely name of Tom Crosskey.

Forfar twigged that he maybe had a weakness with balls from a distance, and the instructions were to pepper him with shots. After McLean equalised, Willie Black scored another four and George Preston another one as the Rovers defence, disjointed and arguing with each other, were pulled apart and made error after error.

The incredulous Forfar men took full advantage. By about half way through the second half, many of the Rovers supporters in the 5,000 crowd were on their way home shaking their heads in disbelief at such ineptitude.

The Courier reporter may even have had his tongue in cheek when he wrote "That is not Championship form. Things have to be tightened up if the promotion bid is to last!" It was what might be reasonably be considered stating the obvious.

October 4 1909

This Holiday Monday Raith Rovers had attractive visitors in Newcastle United, arguably the best team in Britain — and currently English League champions.

They had not as yet won the English Cup, though, having lost three finals at the Crystal Palace, commonly known on Tyneside as the "Palace of Doom".

Raith Rovers management are rightly praised by *The Fife Free Press* for their imaginative ability to bring the very best of opposition for prestige friendlies.

They were rewarded when a crowd of 5,000 turned up (including a few with "thick Geordie accents" who arrived off the train with the team) to see the game, even though it was far from a full Newcastle United team.

Frank Watt, the manager of Newcastle United and himself Scottish, from Edinburgh, did however include some of their Scottish players, like Tommy Sinclair, Sandy Howie, Wilfred Low and George Wilson (from Lochgelly, who would one day be manager of Raith Rovers). The best of them all, Peter McWilliam, captain of Scotland and commonly known as "Peter The Great", had just recovered from injury and was not risked.

The game was a very one-sided 5-0 win for Newcastle, and Rovers supporters enjoyed the footballing treat from their chivalrous opponents who declined in the second half to add to the 5-0 score line at half time.

All this was while a major political and constitutional battle was going on in the background. This was the ongoing battle between the Liberal Government and the House of Lords who had refused to pass Lloyd George's Budget. A crisis was in the offing, but the sympathies of both Kirkcaldy and Newcastle were with the charismatic Lloyd George.

October 5 1946

This was the first season of the Scottish League Cup, a trophy that was played for in war-time and was called the Southern League Cup for teams in the Southern League.

But now in the first official season, it had been introduced to add another competition to the season.

In future years it would be played at the start of the season in a sectional format on Wednesdays and Saturdays, but for the moment it was on Saturdays, as midweek football was not encouraged after August and September lest it encourage absenteeism and disrupt post-war recovery.

Rovers found themselves in a three-team section of Dundee and Stenhousemuir. They had lost their first game to Dundee but today travelled to Ochilview to play the Warriors of Stenhousemuir.

A crowd of 1,600 turned up (crowds were high in 1946 with all the soldiers now home, everyone having a job and optimism in the air) to see a thrilling game in which *The Falkirk Herald* is highly critical of the many chances missed by the home team who had a pre-war Celtic star called Charlie Napier in their ranks, and also a promising youngster by the name of Willie Ormond.

But Andy Young with a "30 yard pile driver" opened the scoring for Raith in the second half; about ten minutes later Jackie Stewart scored a second.

Stenhousemuir, who had hit the woodwork in several occasions, then made the result a little fairer when Morrison scored with a "well taken" goal near the end.

It was quite an entertaining and closely fought game, but the best team of the section would appear to be Dundee.

October 6 1923

Sometimes even the best to teams simply have a bad day, and this was one of them.

Raith Rovers totally collapsed before Hibs, at Easter Road, and lost 0-4, to the immense disappointment of the large contingent from Kirkcaldy who had travelled across on the train.

Hibs were a good enough side — they were last season's Scottish Cup finalists — although they often lacked consistency.

Rovers had had a good season so far, winning all their games in September except for one. On the October Holiday Monday they had defeated Leicester City 5-1 in a friendly.

But today, too many players had an off day — centre forward Tom Jennings was sadly anonymous, Dave Morris had no success in dealing with Jimmy "Sniper" McColl, and no-one divided opinion on the train back home more than Alec James.

Everyone admitted that today was not one of his better ones, but the majority of the supporters still thought the world of "Jimmy" or "Jamesie" or "Baby". "Derwent" however of *The Kirkcaldy Times* has a real go at him, describing him as the "spoiler of many a good chance" because of his "love of the spectacular".

The problem with Alec, it was agreed, that he could never resist the temptation to show off, and entertaining the public often took precedence over delivering a good quality ball to a well-placed colleague. Team work was something, it was generally agreed, which James had to work on, although there was little doubt that he was a crowd pleaser when he was on song.

An agreeable and socially responsible moment in the club's history.

October 7 1901

It was Holiday Monday in Kirkcaldy. Hearts were the attractive visitors bringing quite a few "capitalists" (i.e those who lived in the capital, rather than those whom Karl Marx and Ramsay MacDonald did not like!) to see the game.

They were the holders of the Scottish Cup, which they had now won three times, and were looked upon as one of the leading lights of the Scottish game.

Today however was the opening fixture of the East of Scotland League contested by Hearts, Hibs, Leith Athletic, St Bernard's, Raith Rovers and Dundee.

Although two of their players had "lost the train" as *The Courier* puts it, Hearts were well on top in the first half. They left the field three goals up "to the chagrin of the Langtonian faithful". Laing, who was "playing vice Oswald" (meaning that Jimmy Oswald was injured and John Laing took over) had a particularly unfortunate game.

But you could never tell with Raith Rovers, and in a quick spell early in the second half Alex Mackie, then Geordie Anderson, then Charlie Moodie (with a long range shot) equalised things for Raith while the Hearts defenders began to bicker with each other.

Then just at the end, Mackie scored again for Raith to record a famous and much celebrated victory, the political point about it being that it strengthened Rovers case for admission to the Scottish League.

Meanwhile the South African war showed only partial success, and the odd thing was that the casualty lists showed that more men were dying of disease and infection rather than in military action. Little wonder young Lloyd George and others were wanting an end to it all!

October 8 1892

Local bragging rights were definitely won by Raith Rovers today when they beat Kirkcaldy 6-0 in what *The Fife Free Press* calls the Edinburgh Shield, although it is more commonly known as the East of Scotland Shield.

Great local interest was reported in this game, although Raith had the more consistent form, and had whipped a team called Lassodie 14-0 in a previous round of this competition.

In addition Kirkcaldy's star man, Cameron "was badly and could not do duty".

Raith took the field in a new dress of blue with a "collar and cuff" attachment, and looked quite smart with every man in the "pink of condition and ready for the fray".

In the equally contested first half, Eck Suttie scored twice, but one was disallowed for offside, but then in the second half, Raith simply took command, Willie Dall scored a hat-trick, Davie Walker scored "a brace" and Suttie scored again to make the score a comprehensive 6-0.

But clearly the reporter wants to cheer up the Kirkcaldy supporters by saying "there is not six goals between the sides" and that "Grieve, the Rovers custodian, kept out some grand shots and once or twice saved miraculously", but the triumphant Rovers supporters standing round the ropes would not agree as they cheered and applauded their team off the park.

"The game could not be characterised as a brilliant game of football" said the *Fife Free Press*. Rovers supporters would beg to differ, and no doubt the point was discussed with animation as the fans went home past the recently opened Beveridge Park, which everyone agreed was an asset to the town.

October 9 2001

The time was when the arrival of Hibs for a League Cup tie would have attracted over 20,000 to Stark's Park, but tonight a crowd of 4,601 was considered satisfactory.

Raith's form had been mixed so far, but the arrival of Alex McLeish's Premier League Hibs side would be a serious challenge to Manager Peter Hetherston.

Hetherston had the misfortune to be in charge of the club at a time when some supporters questioned the wisdom and even the sanity of some in the Board Room in the context of the transfer comings and goings. They were, to put it mildly, bewildering.

Hetherston was a solid football man though, and was doing his best for the club. Hibs were a team who baffled their supporters as well. They had reached the final of the Scottish Cup last year, but were occasionally capable of dire performances.

Tonight Rovers held them well for the first half, and if anything had the better chances, but then early in the second half, old Rovers' favourite Craig Brewster and now very much a soldier of fortune playing for Hibs, scored early in the second half with a tremendous drive; from then on, Hibs slowly took command.

Then just at the end Brewster killed Rovers' fast fading hopes with another splendid goal from a distance. This defeat had a disastrous long term effect on Raith Rovers, for they now went into freefall after this result, and by December Peter Hetherston had moved on.

October 10 1973

A large crowd of over 7,000 were at Stark's Park to see the second leg of the League Cup quarter final against Hibs.

The first leg at Easter Road a few weeks earlier had seen Rovers fight hard to lose very narrowly 2-3, one of Rovers goals being scored by Joe Baker — who was given a round of applause for doing so by those of the Easter Road faithful who remembered him.

Rovers were not doing all that well in the League Division Two, but hopes were expressed that they might even pull off a shock tonight. It was not to be, however, for Hibs scored through Eric Schaedler in the first half and then Alan Gordon late in the game.

Apart from the occasional foray from Joe Baker who still looked as if he could win the day for Rovers, Rovers were never really in the game, and Hibs, a good side under Eddie Turnbull and indeed the current holders of the trophy, won comfortably.

It was one of those times when footballing fans were needing something to cheer them up, for war was raging in the Middle East, and the miners and the Conservative Government of Edward Heath were squaring up for a confrontation.

On that very day came the news that the US Vice President Spiro Agnew had resigned for tax evasion, thereby increasing the stress on the President Richard Nixon who was already himself under pressure as the world saw the net tightening on him for his part in the Watergate affair. The world, it would have to be said, was in a crisis.

October 11 1919

The Sunday Post pulled off a real coup here when it persuaded Steve Bloomer, the great England centre forward of the 1890s to come to Kirkcaldy to do a report on the game against Rangers.

It was Kirkcaldy's first really big game since the War with 16,000 present, many of them from Glasgow, a few of them, incongruously, wearing captured German helmets with "Come On, Rangers" painted on them!

Bloomer himself attracted a few to see him sit in the stand. Interned in Germany during the war and called "the ghost" because of his pale complexion, Steve was no "ghost writer" for he was seen to take notes as he watched the game.

The game itself was a little disappointing. Rangers were the better team and deservedly won 2-1, but a lot hinged on the referee Mr Hamilton who gave Rangers an early penalty for handball and then denied Rovers one for an equally obvious offence.

Jimmy Gordon scored the penalty for Rangers and then before half-time Sandy Archibald (ex-Raith Rovers) scored to put the Rangers 2-0 up. To their credit, Rovers kept battling throughout the second half, scored one through a man with the unlikely name of Fletcher Welsh and might have had yet another penalty, according to Mr Bloomer.

It was however no disgrace to lose to this Rangers team for whom Andy Cunningham and Tommy Cairns (rightly called "Tireless Tommy" for his efforts) were outstanding, but Rovers' big fault was hesitating in front of goal and not shooting often enough. (And that was the opinion of the best centre forward of them all!)

October 12 1912

After a series of drab and distressing draws, Raith Rovers suddenly hit form. Before 3,500 fans at Stark's Park, they defeated Queen's Park 5-0, to the great enthusiasm of their supporters and the Press, whose coverage of Rovers up to now had tended to concentrate on their finances and the strange things that went on behind the scenes. (Nothing changes!)

The Fife Free Press was a little more restrained than the writer in *The Courier* who gets carried away using imagery like Queen's Park being "swamped" and Rovers playing with "renewed vigour".

The defeat of Queen's Park was always a great thing, for Queens, the pioneers of the Scottish game 50 years ago, were still looked upon as "snobby", for when professionalism was legalised in 1893, the Hampden men had remained staunchly amateur.

Rovers' half back line of McLay, Logan and Anderson were singled out for praise, although Anderson was inclined to hold on to the ball rather too much. "McLay and Logan were at the top of their form, their fine height being a conspicuous advantage. It was his "inches" that enabled Logan "to score from a corner, the fine goal that he had".

This was the game, probably in which Logan won his spurs. He was a centre half which in 1912 was a role not so restricted to defence as it is now for centre halves were expected to join the attack. The other goals were scored by Tom Cranston and Fred Gibson, one of Gibson's coming from a penalty.

October 13 1917

The war was continuing with its unabated ferocity, although rumours, justified as events proved, persisted that Russia was on the point of collapse.

There was no resolution on the Western Front, though, as the dismal catalogues of war casualties in *The Fife Free Press* continued to show in spite of absurd propaganda headlines like "Successes of the British Army".

Raith Rovers were no longer in the Scottish League because of travel problems, mainly, and now played in the Eastern League, today travelling for the first time ever on competitive business to play a team called Dundee Hibernian at Tannadice Park.

This team had been founded by Dundee Irishmen in 1909, and after the War would change their name to Dundee United in 1923.

3,500 were in attendance, quite a few of them being soldiers in uniform, either on leave, or some of them wounded and home for recuperation purposes.

Agreeably, the Rovers brought a reasonable amount of supporters with them on the train, one of the benefits of war being that, as everyone had a job, there was a fair amount of money in the economy and people were more able to afford train fares and entrance fees for football matches than previously.

They saw a good game which ended 1-1. Rovers opened the scoring with a header from John Wightman, but the Hibs equalised near half time with a goal scored by the famous Jimmy Bellamy who had played in the team which won the Scottish Cup for Dundee in 1910. Also playing for the Hibs that day was James "Napper" Thomson who would make his name for Dundee after the War.

October 14 1950

15,000 were at Stark's Park to see Raith Rovers play St Mirren.

The team were on a high, having defeated Celtic last week at Parkhead (a rare achievement).

Today saw a 2-0 win over St Mirren in a game that was drab at times but Rovers had goals from Les Murray in the first half and Andy Young in the second half just at the time that it began to look as if the Paisley Buddies were coming back into the game.

Ironically in view of what happened later in the weekend, left back Willie McNaught "did not have a happy time" according to *The Courier.*

Perhaps he was unhappy at having been passed over yet again for selection for the Scotland team to play Wales in Cardiff next Saturday. But his fortunes were about to change, for he was sitting in his house in Rosabelle Street the following day when a knock came to the door.

This was "Fifer", the reporter of *The Kirkcaldy Times,* breathless and excited, having come straight from his office in Kirk Wynd where a "wire" had come in to the effect that Sammy Cox of Rangers, Scotland's left back had injured his leg yesterday playing against Third Lanark.

This meant that McNaught was to play for Scotland, Raith's first International cap since Davie Morris of 25 years ago. It was a "grand Sunday" said McNaught, and he played well enough in the 1-1 draw next Saturday.

Gordon Wallace, Player of the Year, 1968

October 15 1966

Station Park, Forfar before 1106 fans was the venue for the debut of Gordon Wallace.

Knowing that Rovers had made a profit last year, and irked by a defeat by Morton recently, Manager George Farm paid £3,500 to bring Wallace from Montrose. He was a proven goal scorer, and it was a clear sign that Rovers did not intend to stay in the Second Division for very long.

Forfar were a respectable team this season after one or two awful years, but today they were swept aside by a Rovers team that, with veteran Bobby Evans still superb at the back, simply meant business.

Wallace scored one and had a hand in two of the other goals as Rovers romped to a 5-1 victory. Bobby Gardner scored early, and then Wallace showed his quality when he fired over a cross to allow Jocky Richardson to score with a lovely diving header. Pat Gardner then scored before half time to make it 3-0 and more or less game over with Rovers supporters in full cry with their cry of "Jocky, Oi, Jocky, Oi, Jocky, Jocky, Jocky, Oi ,Oi ,Oi" in honour of Jocky Richardson.

Gordon Wallace then scored with a header before he sent over another lovely cross to find the head of Bobby Stein.

Forfar scored a consolation goal with a penalty kick, but it was a fine victory for Raith Rovers, and their supporters travelled home over the new Tay Road Bridge (opened a month or two previously) believing that good things were on the way.

October 16 1954

Raith and their supporters came back in the train from this game at Easter Road, Edinburgh with a grievance, feeling that Hibs' late winner by Ward was a foul on goalkeeper Charlie Drummond, unspotted by referee Mr Yacamini of Perth.

It had been a good game attended by a crowd of 18,000 and although the strong Hibs team, even without the injured Laurie Reilly, had more territorial possession in the second half, Rovers felt that they had done enough to earn a draw.

Rovers had started brightly and had taken the lead with a snap shot from Davie Duncan after a good pass from Bernie Kelly. Hibs had equalised soon after, however, with a fine surprise shot from Buchanan. Rovers twice had the ball cleared off the line with one of them looking like a penalty for hand ball when Higgins blocked an Andy Young shot.

But it was Hibs who were awarded a penalty in the second half when Eddie Turnbull was brought down. Willie Ormond caused tremendous distress to his supporters when he blasted wide, missing the goal by several yards. "He nearly hit the corner flag wi' it" said an unhappy Hibs supporter.

But then Hibs got their controversial winner and Rovers had no time to fight back. An unlucky day, alleviated to a certain extent by the news from Cardiff that Scotland had beaten Wales 1-0 through a goal scored by Paddy Buckley of Aberdeen.

October 17 1995

Raith Rovers F.C.
versus
F.C. BAYERN MUNCHEN EV

UEFA CUP
SECOND ROUND
FIRST LEG

EASTER ROAD STADIUM,
EDINBURGH

TUESDAY 17TH OCT. 1995
KICK OFF 6.00 PM

OFFICIAL SOUVENIR PROGRAMME £2.00

October 17 1995

In a decision not 100% agreed with by their fans, Raith Rovers moved their game v Bayern Munich in the UEFA Cup to Easter Road, mainly because UEFA insisted that all the fans had to be seated.

They attracted a crowd of 12,818 to Edinburgh, helped by the staging of a boys' game before the big game, and proceedings started at 6.00 pm. It was also the school holiday week and that too helped to boost the attendance.

The selling of Stephen McAnespie a few weeks earlier was a big blow to the playing side of the club, even though it did a great deal for the financial situation and it helped them build the two monstrosities behind each goal which hardly enhance the beauty of the ground.

Bayern Munich won this game 2-0 with a goal from Jurgen Klinsmann in each half. It certainly wasn't a total humiliation as some had predicted, and it was generally agreed that Davie Sinclair had been outstanding at the back.

It wasn't even that Rovers played badly; it was simply that Bayern Munich were a superb team who really should have been in the Champions League rather than the UEFA Cup.

Rovers had a few good moves as well, forcing Oliver Kahn to save once or twice. Not many supporters or pundits gave Rovers much of a hope in the Second Leg in a fortnight's time, but some 1,000 or so fans were determined to go to Germany to find out!

October 18 1924

Raith Rovers today beat Cowdenbeath 3-1 at Stark's Park in what *The Fife Free Press* described as a "decent, clean game".

It was well refereed by the man now generally regarded as the best up-and-coming referee of them all, Peter Craigmyle of Aberdeen. (He would indeed be Scotland's No 1 for the next twenty years).

Rovers' star man was a young left winger by the name of Tommy Turner, recently signed from St Roch's in Glasgow. He partnered Alec James on the left, and the pair of them lacked "height and avoirdupois". Today Turner, who scored a goal, was a better player than James, who played an "aimless, selfish sort of game".

Rovers' other goals were scored by Tom Jennings and George Miller, but the writer "Derwent" also pays tribute to the men from Cowdenbeath. Star of the game was once again Dave Morris, who proved to be an "impassable barrier" for the Cowdenbeath forwards.

It was to be hoped that the report of this game was a little more objective than the accounts of the General Election campaign where *The Fife Free Press* found it difficult to even pretend to hide its somewhat blatant Liberal sympathies and its clear desire to see Mr Murray beat Tom Kennedy, the sitting Labour MP.

The minority Labour administration of Ramsay MacDonald was seeking a new mandate. In this it would be unsuccessful, but so too was the *Fife Free Press*. The popular Tom Kennedy kept his seat when the election came on October 29.

October 19 1961

Today Bert Herdman stood down as manager of Raith Rovers to be replaced by Hugh Shaw.

Bert had been manager since 1945, and his 16 years of service included four Scottish Cup semi-finals, one League Cup final and consistently good form in the First Division since their promotion in 1949.

He was unusual in many respects, not least because he had never played professional football himself and had gained the manager's job via the Supporters Club.

Similarly when he was removed from the job as manager, there was a distinct lack of taking the huff, throwing a tantrum or selling a story to the newspapers, for he stayed on to work for the club as a fundraiser.

He was a very unpretentious man, well known in the town and not afraid to stand and talk to fans. Nor did he make the mistake of trying to court popularity. He had a stammer and it was often very embarrassing to listen to him, although there was a veritable plethora of stories about him.

He once summed up a player as "having nae richt fit, nae left fit, cannae heid a ba' but he's no a bad player"! On another occasion when told that the opposition were a good football team with passing a feature of their game, he told his men "weil, keep the ba' up in the air. They cannae play fitba' if the ba's up there".

He looked stern and frightening to youngsters, and indeed he was not a man to suffer fools gladly, but he was genuine and loved his football club with a passion. He still attended games right up to his death in 1968.

October 20 1962

It was almost in a spirit of defiance that 2837 fans appeared at Stark's Park to see bottom of the First Division table Raith Rovers take on second bottom Clyde.

Form had been disappointing, to say the least, with hammerings from Dunfermline Athletic, Airdrie and last week a scarcely believable 10-0 doing at Pittodrie from an incredulous Aberdeen who weren't doing all that well themselves.

In these circumstances, it was hardly surprising that manager Hugh Shaw rang the changes including three debutants in Jimmy Smith, David Boner and Morris Aitken.

In a sign of the new age, quite a few supporters appeared with a "trannie", a pocket size transistor radio, to listen to news and commentary from Cardiff where Scotland were playing Wales.

They would also deliver more important news if necessary, for the Soviet Union and the USA were picking a fight with each other about Cuba!

Clyde had one-time Scotland Internationalist Harry Haddock in their ranks, but he had clearly slowed down a little and it was Rovers who did the early running scoring through Bobby Adamson close to half time with a shot from just outside the penalty box which the goalkeeper really should have saved.

It was a long time since Rovers had left the field to a round of applause and 1-0 up, but in the second half Clyde struck back with a goal from Jim McLean (yes, that Jim McLean of Dundee United in later years!). McLean then had hard luck with a shot that squeezed past the post, and Clyde finished the stronger team. But a 1-1 draw it was, Scotland beat Wales 3-2 and the world was still in one piece.

October 21 2017

This turned out to be one of the less happy days of supporting Raith Rovers!

It takes the best part of four hours to get to Stranraer from Kirkcaldy. Quite a few brave Raith supporters decided to take the risk of going there, in spite of the dire prognostications on the BBC about Hurricane Brian, which was meant to do some dreadful things to that part of the country.

And yet it was fine in Kirkcaldy at about 10.00 when they set out. It was fine in Glasgow — the Scottish League Cup semi-final between Celtic and Hibs was played with no bother at all — and even as far as Ayr there was no real problem until the road, which had been dual carriageway up to that point, began to get narrow, hilly and very wet and windy.

Never mind, they made it to Stair Park, a ground which even its best friends would have to describe as primitive, and there they found a pitch that was more or less totally unplayable.

The referee, Mr Ross, aware perhaps that people had come a long way, decide to give it a go. It lasted 37 minutes during which time Lewis Vaughan scored for Rovers and Scott Agnew for Stranraer, but by then Mr Ross decided that enough was enough and time to go home.

Home! The Green Green Grass of Home of Tom Jones or the Ithaca of Odysseus were both as elusive as Kirkcaldy was that night.

Roads blocked, cars in ditches, people lost and not getting home until about 1.00 am on the Sunday! And then the hurtful thing was that it had been fine in Kirkcaldy and elsewhere! People said, innocently, "What kept you?"

October 22 2016

It is always a rewarding experience to beat Falkirk, particularly at their own ground.

Today was no exception as 4,334 spectators saw a fine 4-2 victory for the Rovers at the Falkirk Stadium which looks nice, but was as yet sadly incomplete.

There was a weird incident today when referee Barry Cook sent Falkirk Manager Peter Houston to the stand in disgrace when he was actually warning Raith manager Gary Locke! Houston seemed merely to try to intervene and to say something of the "All managers get excited in the heat of the moment" sort of stuff, but Mr Cook did not see it that way.

Raith's hero was two-goal Mark Stewart, a man with a mission — for he was ex-Falkirk (quite a few players had had times with the other team today) and also a man who had had some frustrating spells with injuries — and his goals came at vital times to put Rovers ahead in the first half, and to confirm the victory near the end, the other goals coming from Ian Davidson and Declan McManus.

Falkirk might have had cause to rue a few missed chances, but there could be little doubt that Rovers deserved their fifth win of the season and their second away from home. It caused the incurable optimists to talk about promotion and a return to the Premiership next season.

Sadly it did not quite work out that way, but the events of early 2017 must not disguise the fact that autumn 2016 saw some fine performances.

October 23 1937

King's Park are a team that is no longer with us.

They played in Stirling, but failed to resume after World War II during which their ground at Forthbank was badly damaged by a bomb, and they were replaced by Stirling Albion who now play at Forthbank but on a different site.

They were never one of the leading lights in Scottish football and today they were well beaten to the tune of 5-1 by a Raith Rovers team who were beginning to impress everyone in the Second Division by their goal scoring prowess.

Today Tommy Gilmour scored a hat-trick while Norman Haywood and Johnnie Whitelaw scored the others in what was a fine victory for Sandy Archibald's talented side.

5,000 were there to see this game but one of them, "Fifer" in *The Fife Free Press* was none too impressed with the performance, saying it was not "really convincing" against a poor team. Yet the team had only lost one game this season, and looked comfortable at the top of the League.

Some of the football played reminded supporters of the great days of 15 years ago, and Sandy Archibald, who had of course played for Rovers before his dazzling career with Rangers, was clearly an ambitious and motivating Manager, perpetually cheerful and affable and always happy to talk to supporters and to give quotes to the local press.

He had had some poor times with Rovers in the last few seasons, but had painstakingly built up a side that looked as if it could be good enough to gain promotion.

October 24 1942

The newspapers this morning were buzzing about a possible "push" that had started yesterday in the African desert some 65 miles west of Alexandria.

People however, after their heartbreaks in the Great War, were a little cynical of "good" news which fell flat a few days later. However a battle was raging at a place called El Alamein and the news was so far encouraging.

Raith Rovers travelled to Tynecastle to play Hearts Reserves in the North Eastern Premier League. In the horrendous circumstances of war time football training sessions were virtually impossible. Manager Willie Reekie would often wake up on a Saturday morning without a clue what his team was going to look like.

It was hard to criticise the team, who were near the bottom of the League. They did try hard to give fans some entertainment in those difficult days.

Today, however, there was a momentary break in the all-encompassing gloom, when they won their first away victory of the season. They certainly left it late to get the winner, for Davie Duncan scored it with virtually the last kick of the game. All this was after Rovers had gone down 0-2, and had pulled the lead back through two goals from Brand and Mackie.

It was some sort of relief, but better news would become apparent in the coming week or so, that the breakthrough in the desert was indeed a success.

Rovers' team that day (and some are just names, in that we do not even know their Christian names) was Robinson, Hickman and Cairns; Phypers, Low and Conway; Hurrell, Brand, Mackie, Smith and Duncan.

Scott Thomson

October 25 1994

Raith Rovers, tonight at McDiarmid Park, Perth, pulled off one of their biggest triumphs of their history when they beat Airdrie in a penalty shoot out to reach the final of the Scottish League Cup for the first time since 1949.

The game was a remarkable and dramatic one with Rovers scoring in the first half. In a goalmouth scramble Gordon Dalziel who appeared to have been fouled, fell on the ground but was able to tap the ball to Ally Graham who scored.

Rovers then seemed to be quite comfortable until well into the second half. Then came the controversial moment of the night: goalkeeper Scott Thomson was given the red card for handling the ball outside his penalty box.

The actions of Mr Crombie, the referee, and the stand side linesman in sending him off were technically correct but almost absurdly draconian.

It meant that young trainee goalkeeper Brian Potter had to come on and that a Raith player, Davie Kirkwood, had to come off. Yet Rovers held on for a while until Steve Cooper scored with a long range drive from well outside the penalty box.

About 15 minutes remained at that point and things looked to favour Airdrie, but 10 man Raith survived and took the game through extra time to a penalty shoot-out.

Then in an ending that no-one could have possibly imagined, young Brian Potter earned his niche in Raith Rovers history when, with the score at 5-4 for Rovers, he dived to save Alan Lawrence's penalty. It was Boys' Own stuff, and the bonus was that it was all true!

October 26 1935

It is not often, mercifully, in the sometimes lamentable history of Raith Rovers that the chronicler has to detail a hammering so comprehensive as today's 0-6 victory at the hands of St Mirren at Love Street, Paisley.

The saving grace was that the game was not watched by many Rovers supporters, for October 1935 was a month of thrashings (East Fife, Alloa Athletic and Leith Athletic had already beaten Rovers convincingly) and it was being openly discussed on the streets whether Raith Rovers should "pack in".

Indeed *The Fife Free Press* devotes equal coverage to the creditable exploits of Dunnikier Juniors who beat St Andrews 5-1 at Beatty Crescent.

Phrases like "worse and worse" and "completely outclassed" were used about Raith Rovers but fortunately, the doomsday scenario of closing down didn't come about. It was, nevertheless, a dreadful time for the Rovers.

Today, Bob Allan, a talented full back, was played out of position at centre half and St Mirren (a good side who had reached the Scottish Cup final eighteen months previously) simply ran through the panic-stricken defence at will. The score might have been double figures, had it not been for an inspired performance by "Junior" in the goal, a youngster good enough to be given another try.

Manager Sandy Archibald had now been in harness for about a year, and although he still retained some sort of credibility because of his brilliant playing career for Raith Rovers and Rangers, there would have to be some sort of improvement soon.

October 27 1956

Third placed Raith Rovers today travelled to Love Street, Paisley to take on St Mirren.

After the customary disappointing exit from the League Cup, early season form had been good apart from a bizarre 4-6 beating from Airdrie, and even the west of Scotland journalists were admiring their form.

8,000, including a fair amount of Rovers supporters, were at Love Street today to see a creditable 3-3 draw, although St Mirren deserved credit for having played a large part of the second half with 10 men after an injury to Neilson.

Against that, St Mirren's first goal was rather fortuitous, being an own goal scored by Willie McNaught. For Rovers, Ernie Copland scored twice and Bernie Kelly once, Copland's second goal being the culmination of a brilliant piece of team work involving several men.

Indeed this goal looked like being the winner until Devine equalised for St Mirren late in the game. A draw was a fair result, however, and it maintained Rovers position of third in the First Division.

Bert Herdman had a few moans to the local paper, but was generally happy with the result.

Elsewhere, it was generally agreed that injury-hit Partick Thistle were unlucky not to beat Celtic in an uninspiring League Cup final at Hampden.

More seriously, Hungary was now in open civil war against the rule of the Soviet Union with uncertain rumours flying about concerning the whereabouts of the great football player Ferenc Puskas, and there was still a great deal of tension in Egypt concerning the Suez Canal.

Andy Young

October 28 1950

It was a shame that the Scottish League Cup final (in which Motherwell beat Hibs) overshadowed this fine performance by Raith Rovers in the national press.

It might otherwise have grabbed national attention, for it was a game which seemed to encompass all that was good about Scottish football in this golden age.

The Courier is of the view that this was one of the best Raith Rovers performances since they gained promotion some eighteen months ago. They were 0-2 down to a good Falkirk side at Brockville, but a good crowd of 10,000 (at least 2,000 from Kirkcaldy according to some estimates) saw them fight back to win 3-2.

The Courier does however make one error when it says that Andy Young at centre-forward "has found his true position". Andy was indeed a good centre forward, but most Rovers fans of the time were of the opinion that he was far better at right half in later years.

However today he scored the first goal by simply being in the right place at the right time, then played a large part in the equaliser when he "sent in a whizz-bang" which the goalkeeper could only parry as far as Willie Penman.

The winner came when Young beat a man and slipped a fine ball to Johnny Maule who finished the job. This result put the hitherto somewhat inconsistent Rovers fifth in the League, and set the town talking for the local derby (well, it's 30 miles but still fairly local) against the strong-going Dundee on Saturday coming.

Pat Gardner

October 29 1966

Raith Rovers' title charge was temporarily derailed today at the primitive Cliftonhill Stadium of Albion Rovers.

The game was played on a dull, but dry and slightly cold day before a poorish crowd of less than 1,000 with not as many Rovers fans there as one might have hoped.

They saw a hard-fought but less than totally inspiring performance by their team who went ahead towards the end of the first half when Pat Gardner swept in an Ian Lister cross.

The second half saw Raith well on top but unable to score again and finish the game, and as often happens in these circumstances, the opposition came back and Jenkins equalised for Albion Rovers well into the last quarter of the game.

Then the home side went for it with Rovers indebted to Bobby Reid in the goal for a few good saves. One man stood out for Albion Rovers, and that was inside right Tony Green, a man who would play six times for Scotland after he went to Blackpool and eventually Newcastle United — where his career would be cruelly cut short in 1972 by a bad injury.

It was the opinion of many that he was one of the most talented players of that era, and he certainly was very impressive that day. George Farm, the manager of Raith at the time, was not totally happy with the team's performance but a point away from home is not always a bad result.

This was the day of the Scottish League Cup final at Hampden where Celtic beat Rangers 1-0.

October 30 1948

"In the Stark's Park Board room, in the dressing room, in Kirkcaldy streets, in packed buses and trains leaving the ground there was only one opinion — we have just seen Raith Rovers play the greatest game of all their history". That was the view of *The Courier*.

It was a justified one as Rovers had just beaten East Fife in the quarter final of the Scottish League Cup. East Fife were, of course, the holders of the trophy and some 26,000 tickets were sold for this match. In the event, inclement weather reduced the attendance to a little over 24,000.

Those who were there saw a truly memorable Rovers performance in which they were 3-0 up at half time with a penalty from Johnny Maule and two others from Tommy Brady and Francis Joyner.

But East Fife had Henry Morris, and he duly scored a hat-trick which would have levelled the scores if Willie Penman had not scored for Rovers in the middle of it all.

Time running out, 4-3 for Rovers and East Fife, with a huge support behind them, pressing hard, until Francis Joyner scored a lovely individual goal tearing through the East Fife defence to make the final score 5-3.

It was breath taking stuff, and the writer of *The Courier* singles out Johnny Maule as the man of the match but also pays credit to men like Willie McNaught and captain Tommy Brady (whom it calls "Tim" Brady!) who was influential even when injured and playing on the wing!

It is a game that is still recalled with pleasure by those old enough to have been privileged to watch it.

October 31 1995

The Hallowe'en Ghost Walk at the Old Kirk and the High Street was in full swing.

It consisted of characters from Kirkcaldy's past like Adam Smith, Robert Adam and Thomas Carlyle who would suddenly appear and talk to groups of people about their past lives.

Suddenly a man appeared and told the ghost of James Gillespie (a 17th century cleric) that Raith Rovers were beating Bayern Munich 1-0 at half time.

The ghost simply laughed and shook his head. Even a 17th century Presbyterian knew that was simply not possible! After all Bayern Munich were several times winners of the European Cup!

In fact it was true, for, Raith Rovers having held their own in the first half, Danny Lennon then with a free kick had scored for Raith Rovers just before half time, and the result was that everyone who was there was able to take a picture which showed the scoreboard at the Olympic Stadium saying Bayern Munchen 0 Raith Rovers 1.

It was a score-line which raised a few eyebrows all over Europe, and it even raised the possibility of another goal and one of the great European shocks of all time.

It was not to be, though, and Bayern scored twice in the second half to win the leg 2-1 and the tie 4-1.

Rovers had done something for Scottish football though and Jimmy Nicholl was always tickled at the idea of Bayern Munich getting shouted at by their manager for getting beat at half-time by Raith Rovers!

November

November 1 1969

A brave and spirited fight back from Jimmy Miller's side was not quite enough to earn a point against Hearts at Tynecastle today for Raith Rovers.

Rovers' form had not been great of late, but they had had a series of respectable draws to add to their solitary win over Airdrie on the first day of their League season.

Here they had bad luck in front of a disappointing crowd of 6,231 at Tynecastle. Rene Moller had put Hearts 1-0 up before half time. After a goalkeeping error early in the second half, Alan McDonald put them two ahead.

When the same player headed a third a minute later, it looked all over for Rovers, but scarcely had their celebrations died down when the sometimes undervalued Mike Judge pulled one back for Raith.

It was an opportunistic score, but it proved the old adage that a team is never more vulnerable than when they have just scored a goal. And it was Judge again who "judged" a Benny McGuire cross to bring Rovers right back into the game in the 75th minute. This set up a fine finish, with Hearts indebted to veteran goalkeeper Jim Cruickshank for a few good saves and his general calming influence to keep Rovers out; another veteran, Ralph Brand, one time of Rangers, had hard luck for Rovers.

As significant as anything was the loud cheer from the Hearts fans at the final whistle, for they had not won since September 13, and Rovers were left to rue their early defensive lapses.

November 2 1912

Strange, unfathomable goings on at Stark's Park earned their due reward when Rovers went down 3-5 to Hamilton at home on a rainy day.

The score-line actually flattered Rovers, for it was 1-5 until the last few minutes when Hamilton relaxed.

Half back James Logan had to withdraw before the game, and Jimmy Gourlay, the centre forward, was injured shortly after the start.

In addition to this, Hamilton Accies were a good side (they had been in the Scottish Cup final just eighteen months ago). Their centre forward, Rippon, scored a classy hat trick, but there were other reasons as well for this strange Rovers performance.

They had just sacked their "Secretary" (as Managers were sometimes called in 1912) Peter Hodge. Just why they felt they had to do this a matter of two weeks after they had beaten Celtic and three weeks after they had beaten Queen's Park, no-one seemed to know, but there had been a fairly public argument between Hodge and this trainer Jimmy Aitken about training methods, and now the pair of them had left the club.

Yet the results had been good. Today however Raith Rovers were poor and *The Courier* uses the word "disjointed" to describe both the defence and the attack.

The removal of the successful Peter Hodge from his post was not, of course, the last crazy decision to be made by the Raith Rovers Board over the years. Hodge was still at Stark's Park, serving his notice. History does not record whether he had a smile on his face at the end of this game or not.

November 3 1923

Raith, whose home form had been very impressive of late but who were struggling away from home, earned a draw in the wind and rain of Love Street, Paisley against St Mirren.

The talking point, however, was not the 1-1 draw, hard fought for and creditable though it was, but the sending off of Alec James.

"Derwent" of *The Fife Free Press* is clearly of the opinion that James was hard done by, and that the referee Mr Stevenson of Motherwell was looking for a "scapegoat".

There was quite a lot of "rough stuff" in what seems to have been a classic example of Scottish football played in bad weather with maybe not an awful lot of skilful play on view, but loads of effort and will to win.

James was "was not the worst offender" according to "Derwent", but one does not have to an expert in reading between the lines to twig that this means that James was guilty of something.

7,000 were at Love Street that day including a "commendable few" from Kirkcaldy, and they saw St Mirren go ahead with a strange goal — one which owed everything to the strong wind. A goal kick travelled more or less the length of the park and found Merrie who swept the ball home from the edge of the box.

In the second half with the elements in their favour, Rovers pressed, and then with the wind and rain making things almost impossible, James scored with a shot high into the roof of the net. Rovers then might have won, but when James upset the referee once too often and got "the long walk", they settled for a draw.

November 4 1961

Stark's Park looked good under the floodlights this crisp slightly frosty day, but there was little good football played by Raith Rovers today as they went down to Falkirk in what could yet prove to be a vital relegation match.

The management of the team was a matter of some concern. Bert Herdman was not having his appointment renewed, but was still in charge until they got someone else, apparently Hugh Shaw, recently sacked by Hibs.

The crowd of 2935 was shocked within the first ten minutes when Willie Ormond, one time of Hibs' Famous Five and in future years to become the manager of Scotland, put over a harmless looking lob, presumably meant to be a cross, which everyone left alone and it ended up in the back of the net.

The Evening Times remarks acidly that goalkeeper Willie Cunningham "played the role of a spectator". The play was then described variously as "aimless" "undistinguished" and "lacking in punch" until after half time when Rovers brought John Urquhart inside, swapping places with John McNamee.

This produced a little spark, but it was Falkirk and Willie Ormond who scored again, this time from a corner kick in the 78th minute.

Ten minutes later with many of the Rovers fans already heading up Pratt Street for their tea, Willie Benvie scored a consolation goal for Rovers, but it was noticeable that that there was no mad rush back in by the fans to see what might have been an exciting finale.

Raith Rovers in season 1977-78

November 5 1977

Rovers today entertained Stenhousemuir in this Division Two fixture.

Clearly Rovers' priority this year had to be promotion, for there were an awful lot of people who felt, with a touch of snobbishness perhaps, that Rovers were far too big a club to be in Division Two, the lowest tier of Scottish football.

Possibly, they were not naturally a Premier League team, but surely for a town the size of Kirkcaldy, Division One was the natural habitat. As if to prove this point, only 1,267 turned up at Stark's Park to see the men from Ochilview.

They saw a good, but not inspiring Rovers performance with goals from John Hislop, Ronnie Duncan and Andy Harrow in a 3-0 win, but the goals did not come until after the 72nd minute. The barrackers were beginning to make themselves heard, but even more noticeable was the slow drift towards the exits with the odd piece of abuse hurled at manager Andy Matthew before the first goal was scored.

But, as is the way with football fans, a goal changes everything and by the end of the game, fans were singing the praises of their team once again.

A more sober reflection however by the time that everyone went out to their Guy Fawkes celebrations was brought about by a glance at *The Sporting Post* which indicated that Rovers were only fifth in Division Two, a position that was not really good enough for those who recalled the great days of 20 years ago.

November 6 1948

Raith Rovers stayed joint top of Division "B" with a 4-1 win over Dundee United at Tannadice Park.

The Dundee-based newspapers, *The Courier* and *The Sunday Post* both insisted that Dundee United were the better team but it was simply that Raith Rovers got the goals.

The crowd was a healthy 12,000 for a "B" Division game and consisted of quite a few supporters who had travelled up on the train this morning.

Very few people owned cars in 1948 and even if they did have one, the Tay Road Bridge was still 18 years in the future, so it would have been necessary to travel across the river on the "Fifie" ferry or go round by Perth.

Tannadice Park was also a rather primitive place, as befitted the poor team of the city, who had never really lasted very long in the First Division even in the years that they earned promotion.

The stand was small and clearly now beginning to show its age even though it would be around for another 10 years or so, but Dundee United always did have enthusiastic fans.

Today however was Rovers' day and Francis Joyner scored three good goals while Jimmy Ellis scored the other. Willie Penman who had had a good season so far, scoring goals in other games, failed to find the net today, but that was probably because he was so well marked.

There may have been an element of truth in what was said about Dundee United playing the better football, but it is goals that count, and Raith departed from Tay Bridge Station on the 5.40 train delighted with what they had achieved.

November 7 1942

The news was good!

As the crowd of about 1,000 made their way to Stark's Park to see Hibs that fairly dull but stereotypical November day, they had already heard the BBC News on the radio.

It confirmed what they had read in the morning's papers — that the British Eighth Army's triumphant march was continuing; they were now approaching Mersa Matruh with the aerodrome already in the hands of the RAF Regiment.

There was therefore a spring in everyone's step, for at long last there was something for everyone to be happy about. "Advance, Britannia!" was the cry.

There was less to be cheerful at Stark's Park for this North Eastern League game between the Rovers and Hibs Reserves, which Rovers really should have won with a degree of ease, was a 1-1 draw.

As it was, they struggled to get a draw and only a shot ten minutes from time by Willie Mackie, a recent recruit from the juvenile side Raith Athletic, earned the Rovers a point.

While every game was hard-fought and keen, and defeat and victory were taken very seriously by the crowd, it was difficult in war-time circumstances to talk about "form" for the team chosen to play for Rovers was often vastly different from the one which actually took the field.

However recent news from Africa encouraged everyone to believe that things would soon be changing for the better. But in the words of the King and Elliott song of the previous war "There's a long, long trail a-winding into the land of my dreams".

November 8 1919

The conflict had now been over for almost a year, but the fairly large contingent who travelled across the Forth by train to see Rovers play at Easter Road were appalled to see the sheer amount of war veterans begging for money at Waverley Station.

Most of those who had served were now home, but getting a job was not always easy in the changed circumstances of the post-war world.

There were also still an astonishing amount of men still in uniform, for wars were still going on in Ireland, the Middle East and Russia.

But the most distressing sight was that of so many young men with one leg, one arm or serious facial scars.

At Easter Road, there was the usual sight of the blind, admitted free, and getting a "commentary" on the game from a volunteer. Those of the Rovers persuasion who watched the game might have wished that they couldn't see what they were seeing for this was a very poor Rovers side who went down 0-2 to Hibs, both goals being scored by John Wood. Rovers fought well once the two goals went in, but to no avail.

Rovers' form was unpredictable this season, but this was perhaps excusable in the difficult situation still prevailing in a society which had not really as yet come to terms with the effects of the Great War. Captain James Logan had recently been appointed manager, and big things were expected from him.

James Logan as manager

November 9 1957

Continuing their bright run of form, Raith Rovers went to Fir Park, Motherwell and won 2-0.

It was a crisp autumn day in Lanarkshire, but Motherwell, a fine side with good players like Archie Shaw, Willie McSeveney and a promising youngster called Ian St John, were no real match for a vibrant Raith Rovers side. Their half-back line of Young, McNaught and Leigh was now generally regarded as the best in the country, with the added advantage that they were a unit who understood each other and worked together.

It was generally felt by the gentlemen of the Press that the game deserved a larger crowd than the 11,000 who were there. After Bernie Kelly had missed a chance, it was Jimmy McEwan who put Rovers ahead on the 15 minute mark with a somewhat half-hit shot which went in off a post.

Then a few minutes later Bernie Kelly put Rovers two ahead. Although Motherwell fought well and piled on the pressure, Rovers defending was quite superb with Willie McNaught outstanding in nullifying the threat of St John.

Rovers too had their opportunities, but there was no further scoring in the second half. This was Rovers' sixth League win of the season, they had drawn three times, and their only defeat had been to East Fife. They were now second in the League, but Hearts were still undefeated and they looked formidable.

Rangers, still struggling with the psychological trauma of losing 1-7 to Celtic in the League Cup final three weeks ago, lost today to Kilmarnock at Ibrox and were struggling near the bottom of the League.

November 10 1923

Alec James, who had been sent off last week at St Mirren, was sent off today again in a home game against Falkirk!

It was an odd sort of decision by Mr Rennie of Dalmuir, and the journalist of *The Courier* is rather at a loss to explain it.

The game had been hard fought but nothing really untoward had occurred, although one or two players on each side, James included, had had a "talking to" by the referee.

Then in a rather "simple sort of affair", James and Tom Scott of Falkirk clashed, but no real violence was seen. The referee then talked to James and was seen to point in the general direction of the tunnel.

James, presumably not realising that he had been sent off stayed on. The game re-started, then the referee noticed that James was still on, so he stopped the game and again pointed in the direction of the dressing room. (This was long before the use of red cards).

This time James went, but the other Raith players protested and compelled Mr Rennie to consult his linesman. This he did, and to the mystification of all concerned, Scott was called over and invited to depart as well.

It was a mystery, but *The Fife Free Press* uses the rather odd phrase "in grips" to describe the incident and implies that Scott had to go as well to prevent a riot! All this should not be allowed to hide the fact that this was a very good 3-0 win for Raith with a penalty scored by Bill Inglis and two fine goals from George Miller and Tom Jennings.

November 11 1922

Four years had now passed since the end of the Great War, as it was now being called.

Due reverence was paid to the fallen before the start of the game against Third Lanark at Stark's Park today. In 1922, this involved everyone and everything coming to a standstill at 11.00 am for two minutes silence. In later years, it would be moved to the nearest Sunday but for the moment it was whatever day November 11th fell on.

In addition there was a certain amount of excitement in the air for there was to be a General Election in the country on Wednesday and the 6,000 crowd on its way to Stark's Park were canvassed and lobbied by supporters of both Tom Kennedy, the Labour candidate, and Robert Hutchison, the Liberal, who was also attracting the Conservative votes — so much in fact that the Conservatives didn't even bother to stand against him.

The game against the side from Cathkin wasn't "of the most interesting nature", but it was decided 1-0 in Rovers favour by a marvellous goal from 20 yards scored by the diminutive Alec James of whom some were predicting a great future.

Third Lanark, although they had famous players in Willie Hillhouse and Tommy McInally, did not really gel together as a team, and Rovers, once they got their noses in front, were able to break up the Cathkin side's attacks with ease.

The full time whistle was greeted with a certain amount of relief by the Rovers fans for they had lost their previous three fixtures.

November 12 1921

"Rover" of *The Fife Free Press* tells a bizarre tale of how he and several other member of the Press were interrogated as they entered the ground at Stark's Park today.

All this seems to have been because he "Rover" had the audacity to criticise the performance of the team a few weeks ago! But the issue of the "freedom of the press" disappeared fairly quickly.

Rovers today turned on a brilliant performance to beat Ayr United 5-0 to the delight of the 7,000 crowd. "Rover" is delighted with the change of tactics which no longer involved "running into a brick wall" with craft and guile being deployed instead.

And it was a splendid Rovers side — arguably their best ever of Brown, Inglis and Moyes; Raeburn, Morris and Collier; T Duncan, J Duncan, Jennings, Bauld and Archibald. Even though three of the goals were scored after Ayr United's centre forward, Quinn, was injured with a broken collar bone, Rovers would have won well anyway. The two wing halves in particular, Jimmy Raeburn and Will Collier, were outstanding. Tom Jennings scored two and the others were scored by Tommy Duncan, Bobby Bauld and Will Collier.

It was a splendid performance by the Rovers, so much so that the North British Railway Company decided to lay on three Football Specials to take supporters to Edinburgh to see them play at Hearts next week, a ground where Rovers have never won.

These were heady days for Raith Rovers!

Heart of Midlothian v. Raith Rovers.

SPECIAL TRAINS FOR EDINBURGH.

The North British Railway Company, with their customary enterprise, have arranged for special trains to convey the supporters of Raith Rovers to Edinburgh to-day. A train will leave Thornton at 12.40 p.m., calling at Dysart at 12.48, Sinclairtown 12.52, Kirkcaldy 12.58, Kinghorn 1.5, Burntisland 1.12, Aberdour 1.19, and Inverkeithing 1.35. Another train will leave Kirkcaldy at 1.8, calling and Kinghorn at 1.15, and Burntisland 1.22, while a third train right through will leave Kirkcaldy at 1.15. The return fare third-class from Thornton is 3s, and from the other stations 2s 6d. Return trains leave Edinburgh (Waverley) at 7.20, 7.27, and 7.35, calling at Haymarket five minutes later.

November 13 1993

Raith Rovers today pulled off a great result at Ibrox when they drew 2-2 with Rangers.

It was Rovers' first season in the Premier League, and they had had a few creditable results, doing better than some people had expected, but it was widely believed that to-day would see a rather large hammering from Rangers.

Rangers themselves had had a few inconsistent results but had nevertheless already won the League Cup, and were doing well at the top where they were chasing their 6th title in a row.

42,611 saw a good game with Rovers leading quite a few Rangers supporters to agree that they would not be relegated at the end of the season.

They did however (unusually at Ibrox) get the better of a refereeing decision when Gordon Dalziel scored what looked like a softish penalty awarded by referee Hugh Dallas, thus dispelling the rumours that Dallas came to referee games with a sash and a flute in his bag!

But after Mark Hateley had equalised with a good header, Mr Dallas proved his impartiality by awarding a softish penalty for Rangers, converted by Hateley as well.

With the game now looking over and done with, Rovers then delighted their small band of supporters by scoring a late equalizer. Ally Graham, who had joined the club this season from Motherwell, headed in a Jason Rowbotham cross. Rangers felt a little aggrieved and really should have won on the run of play, but it was a good draw for Raith Rovers.

November 14 1992

Although October had brought more draws than it did victories, Raith Rovers were still nevertheless undefeated in the Scottish League when the local derby with Dunfermline appeared on the horizon this dull, typically November day.

Rovers had defeated the Pars in the game at the start of the season at East End Park, and were undefeated in all competitions since their exit from the League Cup at the hands of Hibs in mid-August.

There were encouraging signs that the crowds were beginning to come back to Stark's Park as well, encouraged by the good reports they had heard and also impressed by the good public relations of the earnest and ambitious young player-manager Jimmy Nicholl.

Today's game attracted 5,794 — one might have expected a few more — and they saw a good hard-fought Fife derby in which Rovers emerged victorious, thanks to a Steve Crawford goal early in the second half.

Dunfermline had retaliated, and Rovers were more than once indebted to Tom Carson for several saves, but there was also a solidity about the centre of the field with Nicholl and Dalziel taking charge of proceedings, and Peter Hetherston also showing up well.

The dangerous Craig Brewster did not score today, but did enough to compel the Pars defence to mark him well. Although the final whistle was greeted with a cheer of relief rather than triumph, Rovers supporters departed with enhanced confidence in their team for the rest of the season.

November 15 1958

A statistically rather remarkable day — six games out of nine in the old Scottish First Division ended in draws.

This encounter between Aberdeen and Raith Rovers at Pittodrie was one of them, ending 2-2 in what was generally agreed to be a good game.

It did not however stop elements of the traditionally hard-to-please Pittodrie support from turning on their team with a slow handclap!

Aberdeen, League Champions in 1955 and winners of the League Cup in 1955/56 had not done so well since then; their fans obviously expected better than a 2-2 draw with Raith Rovers.

Raith more than held their own in the first half until Jackie Hather, a few minutes before half-time, scored with a lovely left foot drive which gave Charlie Drummond no chance.

Then it all happened in the first five minutes of the second half. First Billy Little scored a second for Aberdeen, and that looked like game over. Johnny Urquhart with a fairly simple tap-in pulled one back and then George Dobbie picked up an Andy Leigh pass and with a lovely run scored the equaliser.

This did not please the home support, who seemed to detect an element of complacency in their own defence, with even a few mutterings about bribes and bookmakers, a surprisingly common motif in the 1950s — in an 18 team First Division, there were quite a lot of games with not very much at stake.

In the latter stages Hugh Baird of Aberdeen clashed with Jimmy McEwan of Raith Rovers and both were booked. Dickie Ewen of Aberdeen was carried off with a leg injury, but Rovers could not cash in on their numerical superiority.

November 16 1934

One of Raith Rovers' greatest supporters died today at the age of 79.

This was Dr John Smith who died of "pulmonary congestion". He practised medicine at Brycehall, the house in Kirk Wynd where Wood's Lawyers Office is now.

Born in 1855 in Mauchline in Ayrshire (where Robert Burns lived for a spell), Smith was one of the pioneers of Scottish football, becoming in due course one of the legends of the game.

He played in the early days for Queen's Park and Scotland, scoring a hat-trick in the Scotland v England game in 1881. Of the five games in a row when Scotland beat England, "Dr John" played in four of them. He also won the Scottish Cup with Queen's Park in 1881 and 1884.

He also refereed the Scotland v England game in 1892 and played a few unofficial Internationals at rugby as well. By the time he came to live and practise medicine in Kirkcaldy, he was too old to play for Raith Rovers, but he was a keen attender almost to the end of this life, taking great joy and pride in the great side of the 1920s.

He was also very keen on Bowls, Cricket and Golf. A huge man, about 6 foot 2, he was well known and instantly recognised with his horse and Brougham carriage long after other doctors had moved over to motor cars.

He was well loved and respected throughout the town, and Raith Rovers were well represented at his funeral in the Old Kirk and Bennochy Graveyard.

November 17 1894

Raith Rovers' last five games had all been against Cowdenbeath.

It was almost a relief to get to play anyone else, even though Cowdenbeath's replacements were their near neighbours Lochgelly United.

Rovers had eventually beaten Cowdenbeath in both the Scottish Qualifying Cup and the East of Scotland Shield, and it was in the latter competition that Lochgelly came to Stark's Park.

The crowd was a good one, but the weather was not of the best description with rain and "a strong westerly breeze blowing towards the pavilion goal" (a description that raises an interesting question about where the pavilion was!)

Lochgelly were very impressive and half-time was reached with the "colliers" (as they were called) 3-1 ahead, Rovers goal having come through Jimmy Richardson. Eventually after an exciting second half with the wind now favouring Rovers, they scored towards the end through full back "Eck" Oag, but it was too dark for the reporter of *The Fife Free Press* to follow the play with any confidence!

They seemed to have got an equaliser but Mr Waugh, the referee, gave a corner kick instead although Rovers claimed that the ball had gone between the posts. (Goal nets had not yet, apparently, arrived at Stark's Park).

The final whistle came with the ground almost completely dark and the crowd relying on the very few gas lampposts in Pratt Street to see their way home, or in the case of the triumphant Lochgelly men, to the Railway Station.

Rovers' fans were not too despondent for next week they had to look forward to exotic visitors, called the King's Rifle Volunteers, from Dumfries, in the first round of the Scottish Cup proper.

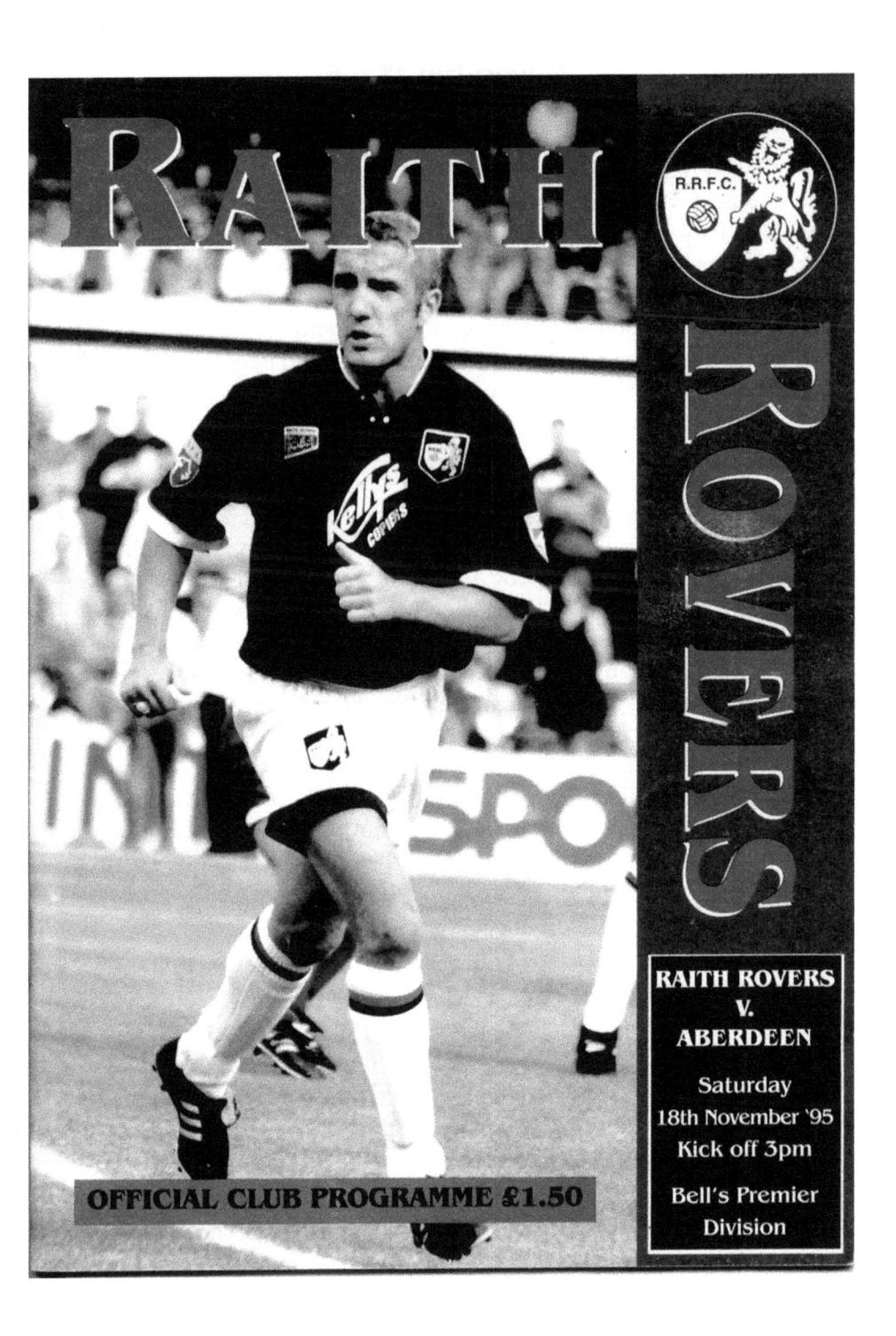

RAITH ROVERS

OFFICIAL CLUB PROGRAMME £1.50

RAITH ROVERS V. ABERDEEN

Saturday
18th November '95
Kick off 3pm

Bell's Premier Division

November 18 1961

Raith Rovers were in clear relegation trouble in November 1961, and Dundee were surprising everyone by their League title aspirations.

In recent weeks they had beaten both Celtic and Rangers, but today at Dens Park they had to dig very deep indeed. In a game which left Rovers fans bewildered that they did not get at least something out of it, Dundee beat Raith 5-4.

A crowd of 14,000 on a rather misty day attended; they were amazed to see Rovers take the lead with a goal from, of all people, Andy Leigh — a magnificent shot it was from well outside the penalty area.

Dundee pressed hard but both Ibrox and Parkhead resounded to the cheers of the crowd as the half time scoreboard showed Dundee 0 Raith Rovers 1.

But then the game became like a basketball match. First Dundee scored twice through Alan Gilzean. Rovers scored three through Mike Clinton, Ian Laurie and Bobby Adamson. 4-2.

It looked like a major shock, even when Dundee pulled one back to make it 4-3.

But then, sickeningly at the very end, Dundee scored twice, the winner coming from veteran Gordon Smith, now pursuing a Scottish League medal with three separate teams.

It was real tough luck for Rovers, although the game did not say much for the quality of the defending of both teams. Newly appointed Manager Hugh Shaw however had nothing but praise for the commitment of his men, and it certainly looked as if, on this form at least, they would be good enough to avoid relegation.

November 19 1966

A dull, rainy day (once again the word "dreich" was used for football in Scotland in November) was enlivened by a fine Raith Rovers performance.

They came from behind to defeat Berwick Rangers 4-2 at Stark's Park.

Pat Gardner — who had needed a late fitness test to determine whether he could play — scored a hat-trick, but the man who made the forward line tick was Gordon Wallace, the man who had only arrived about six weeks ago from Montrose.

He scored the other goal but his main contribution was in the way that he held up the ball and distributed it. The defence had not looked any too clever at the loss of the Berwick goals.

Bobby Evans was not at his usual best, but he rallied and made no further mistakes as Raith powered forward for their third win a row, something that was clearly promotion form.

Ian Porterfield had a good game as well today and was already attracting some attention from English clubs. Any stranger sitting in the Stark's Park stand with a soft hat and a warm raincoat was immediately suspected of being a "scout".

Rovers were now second in the League behind Morton, and the visitor to Stark's Park would be aware of two things. One was the enthusiasm of the players who obviously enjoyed working for Mr Farm, The other was the related one of the upbeat atmosphere of the supporters, whose pessimism and negativity had now gone, to be replaced by a genuine belief that the club was wanting to be promoted back to the First Division.

November 20 1920

It had been a topsy-turvy season so far in a topsy-turvy world, as the war had now been over for two years but without as yet any sign of "the land fit for heroes to live in".

At Stark's Park, results had been inconsistent, and home form had not been all that great, leading to quite a large amount of criticism in the letter columns of *The Fife Free Press* about performances.

Last week's 0-1 defeat by Clyde at Stark's Park had been particularly painful. Today, however, injuries compelled Mr Logan to field a fairly makeshift side to take the field against Morton, a side who had played several good games this season.

The weather was dull, as November days tend to be, but Rovers delighted the crowd of 7,000 with a 2-0 victory, the goals scored by lesser known players George Waite and John Dunn.

"Townsend" in *The Kirkcaldy Times* stressed however that today's well deserved win over one of the better teams of the League was all down to team spirit, with not a weakness in the team.

"So excellently did each player perform his work that to comment individually on the team would mean simply a recital of pleasant platitudes". He would not hesitate to choose the same team for the next game, he said.

In the event Mr Logan did exactly that — but the next game was at Celtic Park and a 0-5 beating was the outcome! Nevertheless, Mr Logan was slowly building up a good team. A few players had yet to arrive, but the nucleus was there.

November 21 1959

This was one of Raith Rovers best ever performances in their history as they beat Rangers 3-2 at Ibrox, having been 0-2 down in the first quarter of an hour.

They do not win very often at Ibrox; in fact 35 years had passed since they last did it. Today's result was even more commendable, for Rangers were currently League Champions of Scotland, and were just back from travels in Europe, where they had beaten Red Star Bratislava in the European Cup by drawing away after a win at home.

This put them in the quarter finals of the European Cup. But Rovers too were on a high, because they had just beaten Hibs last week, and they had unearthed a young left half called Jim Baxter.

Almost 40,000 were there to cheer Rangers after their European success, with Alec Scott on the right wing looking virtually unplayable.

Rangers, in all white, went two ahead with a goal scored by Davie Wilson made by Scott, and then Scott himself scored.

But hardly had the songs of triumph got started from the Copland Road end, when Rovers equalised with two fine shots from the edge of the penalty box, one by centre forward Jim Kerray and another from Jim Baxter.

That was the score at half time.

Rangers then pressed and might have scored but for some fine goalkeeping from Charlie Drummond.

It was to be Rovers day; Jim Kerray scored the winner.

The Evening Times headline is of an "Ibrox Kerray-on" but the Rangers management looked at the other Jim, Baxter by name, and wondered.

November 22 1980

Rovers consolidated their position at the top of Division One.

Referee Mr Knowles of Inverurie had his work cut out in a hard fought 1-0 win in a sometimes feisty encounter against Hamilton Academical.

News from Kilbowie Park in Clydebank that the "Bankies" had drawn with Hibs meant that Rovers were now on their own at the top of the League.

That was a great feeling for the 2342 crowd as they made their way home this dreich November (all November days seem to be "dreich" in football reports, don't they?) after having seen Gordon Wallace's side win by a solitary Colin Harris header.

It should however have been 2-0, but Ian Ballantyne missed a late penalty. This might have cost Rovers dear, had Murray McDermott in the goal not been on top form. Rovers had not lost a game since October 1, and there was now noticeably in town a far greater desire to talk about football.

Give or take the occasional good result, there had not been very much to get excited about for the last decade or so, and now this was a pleasant change with Donald Urquhart looking as good a player as anyone in Scotland.

Symbolically too, now that the old coal shed (as it was unkindly called sometimes) had been demolished with plans to build a new seated enclosure in its place, there was a feeling that Raith Rovers were now in a new era. Could supporters even contemplate a place in the Premier League?

Murray McDermott

November 23 1963

It was a terrible late November day as Rovers set out on the team bus to Stranraer.

One of the problems of Raith's relegation to the Second Division was that they now had to visit grounds like Stair Park, Stranraer which was a very long way away for a game that would inevitably be very poorly attended.

One topic would have dominated the conversation on the long journey down and that was last night's news from Texas of the assassination of President John F Kennedy, for whom a minute's silence was held at several grounds, something that was rare for a man with no obvious connection with Scottish football.

When the game did start, Raith "were seldom in the picture" according to *The Evening Times* but nevertheless managed to go in at half time winning 2-1 with goals from Ian Laurie and Felix McGrogan.

Laurie scored again in the second half but so too did Stranraer, and the home team were perhaps a little unlucky not to gain a draw.

Rovers, who had not had the best of starts to the season, were now sixth from the bottom of the Second Division and looking to climb a little higher!

This was actually not a bad performance, and those very few supporters who went with them would have enjoyed what was a rare victory up to now.

Car radios (still a fairly new phenomenon in 1963) would be listened to avidly on the way home to see if there was any more news from America.

Andy Leigh

November 24 1956

A bizarre occurrence took place at Rugby Park, Kilmarnock in the teeming rain; Rovers lost Andy Leigh at half time.

As is often the case in wet weather, a good game was being served up by two of Scotland's form teams of the moment. Some of the tackles were a bit robust, but possibly looked worse on the wet surface than what they really were.

Killie had scored through Frank Beattie and then just on the stroke of half-time, Eddie Mays headed another.

Referee Mr P Fitzpatrick from Glasgow had already had a word with Bernie Kelly about a minor piece of what is now called "handbags" with Kilmarnock's MacKay.

Now he was seen to be booking Andy Leigh, after he had blown for half time. No-one seemed to know what it was all about, and of course, there were no yellow or red cards in 1956.

It was only when the teams re-appeared and it was noticed that Raith Rovers were a man short, that it became apparent that Leigh had in fact been sent off.

It was apparently for something that Mr Fitzpatrick had overheard, something that a more experienced referee might have chosen not to listen to.

As it was, it was a fatal blow for Rovers who would now have the wind and the rain in their faces in the second half — and with only ten men!

Kilmarnock scored again after five minutes of the second half, once more through Frank Beattie, and Rovers then simply folded against a very strong and compact Killie team. The 0-3 score line was a hard blow to Rovers.

November 25 1967

It is not often that the European Champions appear at Stark's Park, but this is exactly what happened today when Celtic came calling.

It was like the halcyon days of 10 or 20 years ago. Long queues meant the kick-off had to be delayed to allow the 16,536 crowd into the ground.

Rovers, in their first season back after promotion were struggling to hold their own. So too were Celtic, a great deal less impressive this season than they had been last season. In addition, they were not long back from a traumatic and disgraceful trip to South America in an unsuccessful quest for the World Club Cup.

Today Rovers surprised everyone by appearing in blue jerseys without numbers (not illegal, but certainly unusual).

This was possibly a point being made by manager Tommy Walker about Celtic not wearing numbered jerseys either (they had their numbers on their pants), but it certainly seemed to disorientate the Celtic players, for Rovers put up a good display and at half time there was nothing between the two teams.

In the 57th minute, after John Hughes was brought down by Bobby Reid, Tommy Gemmell scored the resultant penalty, the ball hitting the bar before going in.

10 minutes later old Rovers favourite Willie Wallace added a second with a fine shot. Rovers kept fighting, though, and with a bit of luck might have pulled at least one goal back.

Jock Stein, Celtic's manager paid tribute to Rovers after the game for putting up such a good show.

November 26 1955

Rovers today had attractive visitors in Aberdeen.

Aberdeen had won the Scottish League (deservedly) for the first time in their history in April; a month ago they had won the Scottish League Cup by beating St Mirren.

Football had never been so big in Aberdeen, and as a result there were loads of red and white tammies, scarves and rosettes mingling in the crowd today, which looked to be a great deal more than the 10,000 estimated by the Press.

Because of their involvement in the League Cup, the Dons were behind in their games played, but like Rovers, they were comfortably placed in the middle of the League.

The crowd saw a good well fought game in which Aberdeen went ahead early after a pass back from Willie McNaught did not have enough weight on it, and Aberdeen's Paddy Buckley was in like a flash to guide ball home.

But this Rovers team knew how to fight, and the rest of the game saw them pressing hard with several chances. Scotland goalkeeper Fred Martin was playing well in the Aberdeen goal until in the 73rd minute Jimmy McEwan was on hand to equalise for the home side.

The last 15 minutes were played at a frantic pace on a heavy late-November pitch, but no further goals resulted and both teams were given a loud round of applause at full time.

Rovers had had a mixed November, losing to Hibs and Falkirk, but beating Kilmarnock.

November 27 1994

This was the day when it all came good for Raith Rovers, and they won the Scottish League Cup.

They did so at Ibrox this Sunday afternoon when they beat Celtic on a penalty shoot-out.

It was the first national trophy that they had ever won, and was much celebrated at the ground itself and in the town for the next few days.

Their opponents were by no means one of the better Celtic teams, but it was generally agreed that Raith deserved their win.

The crowd was 45,384 and Raith Rovers were given the Govan Stand (across from the Main Stand).

Steve Crawford scored first for Raith, but then Andy Walker equalised before half time. When Charlie Nicholas scored for Celtic in the 84th minute, it looked all over but Gordon Dalziel equalised after Celtic goalkeeper Gordon Marshall failed to hold on to a Jason Dair shot.

Extra time proved goalless, and so it was on to penalties.

Each team's allocated five penalty takers took their penalties and scored, then it was down to sudden death.

Welshman Jason Rowbottom scored for Rovers, but then Scott Thomson saved Paul McStay's penalty.

It was a tragedy for Paul McStay but ecstasy for Rovers and their Manager Jimmy Nicholl, and all the supporters who were there that day would remember it for the rest of their lives.

The men who won the trophy for Raith Rovers were Scott Thomson, Stephen McAnespie, Julian Broddle (substituted by Jason Rowbotham), David Narey, Shaun Dennis, David Sinclair, Stephen Crawford, Gordon Dalziel (substituted by Ian Redford), Ally Graham, Colin Cameron and Jason Dair.

Gordon Dalziel turns away after scoring the equaliser in the League Cup final

Steve Crawford and Jimmy Nicholl with the Scottish League Cup

November 28 1914

Today's game, a 1-1 draw against Dundee at Stark's Park played in icy and wet conditions would have ramifications.

Some of the Rovers players, notably Logan, Todd and McLay had decided that they were going to join up in McCrae's Batallion for professional football players, but they would not be taken to France for some time, and indeed would be available for selection for most of the rest of the season.

That was not the issue, however.

The game was a good one; even the Dundee-based *Courier* was of the opinion that Raith Rovers were the better side who deserved more than a draw. Indeed their report of the game contains no account of any untoward incident.

Yet, apparently, the referee Mr Kelso of Hamilton and the two linesmen had stones thrown at them by irate supporters.

The incident was duly reported and on Tuesday December 8, the Emergency Committee of the SFA met in Glasgow and decided that Stark's Park would be closed from December 14 until December 28. This was of course a major embarrassment for the club, who duly promised that they would "root out" such troublemakers.

It also meant that the game against Third Lanark on December 19 would have to be played at East End Park, Dunfermline. Many people of course felt that a solution to the problem would be conscription to the army — on the grounds that if anyone wanted to be aggressive, there were loads of Germans there.

It was beginning to be apparent by now that the war would certainly not be "over by Christmas", as everyone had said in August.

November 29 1924

Raith Rovers travelled to Dens Park, Dundee and played a disappointing game to lose 0-2 to the hitherto underperforming Dundee.

Dundee were always a well-supported side in the 1920s and today attracted a crowd of 10,000 including a fair amount who had travelled up on the train from Kirkcaldy.

The Courier is naturally full of praise for the Dundee side but says that Raith Rovers were disappointing; in the absence of Tom Jennings the forward line lacked "punch".

Tellingly, Rovers best player was goalkeeper Jimmy Mathieson, something that says a certain amount about the run of play. Halliday scored the first for Dundee. When the ball rebounded off the bar from another Halliday drive, McDonald had no problem in "putting the leather among the strings" as *The Courier* quaintly put it.

There was no doubt that this was a great disappointment for the Rovers fans who had already seen some of their best players transferred, and were reconciled to the loss of some more.

At the moment however, they still had David Morris at centre half and the tricky Alec James up front. There was no problem with James's ability to beat a man. Sometimes however he was not quite direct enough, and he sometimes found it difficult to resist showing off.

But the problem in 1924 for Raith Rovers was, quite simply, lack of cash. Or was it? Would a little more determination to hang on to star players not work wonders?

November 30 1946

It was perhaps fitting that on St Andrews Day it should be Andy Young who won this game for Raith Rovers.

They recovered from an indifferent first half on the back of a few previous results which one could not even dignify with the word "indifferent". They were simply awful.

Ayr United were duly beaten 4-1 on a sodden pitch after several hours of grim November rain. Amazingly, 3,000 (most of them standing in the rain) turned up to watch this game at Stark's Park, but these were the days when people flocked to football matches.

The great thing about Andy Young was his versatility (it was his versatility that would prevent him from winning a cap for Scotland in that the selectors never really knew what position he would be played in) and today he was at inside left and scored a hat-trick even though two of them were from the penalty spot.

Harry Muir scored the other goal, and Jacky Stewart had hard luck with several others. *The Sunday Post* is convinced that positional changes (with basically the same personnel) were all that was required for the Rovers, although the writer is also impressed with centre half Angus McGillivray who had recently joined the club from Arbroath.

The weather remained awful but Rovers fans remained happy as they went to the pubs or took their wives/girlfriends to one of the many cinemas in Kirkcaldy at that time, after perhaps listening on the radio to a programme of Scottish music to commemorate Scotland's patron saint.

December

George McNicoll with the Scottish Qualifying Cup

December 1 1906

Raith Rovers enjoyed arguably their biggest success to date when they won the Scottish Qualifying Cup. Today 13,000 were at Easter Road to see them beat St Bernard's 3-1.

This followed a 2-2 draw, but this victory was a great triumph for the Rovers side who had been in the Second Division of the Scottish League since 1902 and were now beginning to attract attention.

There was not yet any system of promotion and relegation to the First Division, but this achievement did a lot to help their cause.

George McNicoll, a man who had already won this competition twice with other clubs, opened the scoring for Rovers, then they went further ahead through a rather fortuitous own goal before John MacDonald made it 3-0 before half time.

Rovers then held what they had for most of the second half but in the last few minutes the light began to fade.

St Bernard's pulled one back through Finlay in a goalmouth scramble, and then were were awarded a penalty, but fortunately goalkeeper Bill Dowie saved.

The final whistle saw joyous scenes from the Raith support, and even more happy scenes when the Cup came home that night. The huge trophy had been presented at the meal at the Imperial Hotel in Princes Street by James Liddell, the vice-president of the SFA.

The Scotsman, although clearly sorry that an Edinburgh team did not win, admits that Raith were the better side.

The players were then presented with their medals at a special ceremony at the Adam Smith Halls a fortnight later. The team was Dowie, Inglis and Cumming; Moodie, Manning and Grierson; Mitchell, Wilkie, McNicoll, Dalrymple and MacDonald.

December 2 1905

Supporters made their way this dull December day to Stark's Park to see Rovers take on Abercorn of Paisley in the Second Division of the Scottish League.

The country was seething with rumours of the impending resignation of Conservative Prime Minister Arthur Balfour. In fact, he would not resign until Monday, precipitating a General Election in the New Year which would be a Liberal landslide.

Abercorn were one of the founder members of the Scottish League in 1890 but had fallen recently on bad times and would go defunct soon after the First World War.

Today turned out to be one of the best performances of the hitherto topsy-turvy season with Rovers winning 5-1 over a very disappointing "Abbie" side.

Admittedly two of the goals were softish penalties duly converted by McDonald, but the other three were good goals scored by Mitchell, Wallace and Gray.

This result put Rovers into fourth position in the League, and although the 1,000 or so spectators went home happy, they were nevertheless realistic enough to work out that more consistent form was needed if they were to top the League and eventually — their aim — to bring First Division football to Kirkcaldy.

This was Rovers fourth season in the Scottish League Division Two but there was as yet no automatic promotion or relegation, so Rovers would have to play well and show that they had sufficiently good facilities for playing at a higher level.

Today's was the sort of performance that impressed everyone in the West of Scotland, however.

December 3 1955

It was a sign of just how far that Rovers had come in recent years that a defeat at Ibrox was considered to be a misfortune, rather than one of those shrugging of shoulders and "What can you do about it?" philosophical sighs.

Mind you, this defeat was a fairly comprehensive one to the tune of 0-4 and Rovers' only possible excuse was the absence through illness (flu) of left half stalwart Andy Leigh, a vital cog in the half-back line of Young, McNaught and Leigh.

As a result, young Hamish McMillan had to be drafted into what was not really his best position and the side generally did very badly.

Rangers had not themselves been having the best of times — some two and a half years had passed since they had won any trophy — but today they really turned it on and started to show signs of the form that would win them the League in season 1955/56.

Their best players were the South Africans, Johnny Hubbard and Don Kichenbrand and it was Kichenbrand who opened the scoring with a lovely goal as he hooked a rebound off the bar into the back of the net.

Raith fought hard, but Rangers went further ahead when Ulsterman Billy Simpson scored. The second half was pretty much all one-way traffic with Rovers sorely indebted to goalkeeper Charlie Drummond for keeping the score down.

However, Rangers scored another twice before the end through Alec Scott and Billy Simpson again. It was a sobering day for Rovers, but they were still respectably placed in the Scottish First Division.

December 4 1948

Rovers travelled to Recreation Park, Alloa with a large travelling support (something that rather gives the lie to the perceived historical belief that the 1940s were a time of depression and poverty) and beat the local side 5-1.

Other than a blind spot against Dunfermline, Rovers' form in 1948 had been every good indeed and as the year drew to a close, supporters looked forward to 1949 with the prospect of promotion from Scottish Division "B".

There was also Scottish League Cup final against Rangers to be contemplated.

Today, the half time score of Alloa 0 Raith 1 was an absolute travesty, for Rovers had been all over them with Ernie Till, Tommy Brady and Johnny Maule outstanding.

The second half saw Rovers get their rewards in terms of goals - Willie Penman had two and George Carson, Jimmy Ellis and Francis Joyner one each.

The season had been all about the goal scoring exploits of Willie Penman so far — he had scored six against Stirling Albion and on another two occasions he had had four, and seldom did a game pass without him scoring at least once and that was with him being man marked, and sometimes with two defenders on him!

His long legs, his athletic frame and his turn of speed were great for Rovers supporters to come and see, but there were many other great players as well. It was a happy bunch of Rovers fans who came back to the Lang Toun tonight.

Ernie Till

December 5 1953

In the middle of a terrible run of form (they had not won since October 24) Raith Rovers travelled to Pittodrie to play Aberdeen, generally regarded as one of the form teams of the year.

It was a day on which Glasgow in particular was blanketed with fog, and quite a few west of Scotland games did not go ahead. There was no such problem in Aberdeen — at least it wasn't quite so bad — but the day was cold and unpleasant.

Such was the local enthusiasm for the Dons at the moment that 14,000 turned up with a few brave Rovers supporters as well.

Some had arrived on the train with their wives who had decided to go to the famous department store Isaac Benzie's in George Street for their Christmas shopping.

The wives probably made the better decision, for although the score was only 2-0 and Rovers never really gave up, they were well beaten by a fine Aberdeen side for whom Graham Leggatt was outstanding.

It was Leggatt who scored the first goal with a header, then the prolific centre forward Paddy Buckley scored the second near the end.

Rovers' goalkeeper George Johnstone had played for Aberdeen, won a Scottish Cup winner's medal with them in 1947 and was still a hero at Pittodrie. In spite of a generous reception from the Aberdeen fans, Johnstone had a poor game today and even injured his hand at one point.

Although everyone agreed that the Dons were a class outfit and that not many teams could live with them on this form, it was also clear that Rovers faced a real fight against relegation.

December 6 1958

Frost and fog — a frequent phenomenon in the west of Scotland in the 1950s before the various Clean Air Acts took effect, threatened to put this game off, but it went ahead as planned.

This was unfortunate for Raith Rovers, because they lost 0-4 to the very strong Airdrieonians at Broomfield.

As Rovers had lost to Clyde the previous week at Shawfield, Rovers trips to the West of Scotland in those days were not really very successful.

Today there was no real excuse, and they were simply beaten by a better side. Maybe they believed that the game should not have been played in the first place, but certainly they approached the game in an over-cautious fashion and paid the penalty losing two goals in each half.

McGill scored two and Sharkey and Rankin one each, and Rovers — with a questionable team selection of a half back line of Leigh, McNaught and Baxter, with Andy Young at inside right, had no answer to the onslaught.

The fog began to thicken in the second half — it caused a premature end to the games at Celtic Park and Cathkin — and Rovers may have entertained hopes of an abandonment, but Mr McTaggart kept the game going, and Rovers had no real complaint.

Rovers were at the start of a really bad run and would not win another game until early February. Airdrie on the other hand were having a good season, and were now third in the Scottish League First Division behind Hearts and Rangers.

December 7 1968

It was like old times again today at Stark's Park this cold, dull but dry December day as Rangers came to town.

There were long queues at the turnstiles and the kick-off had to be delayed by 10 minutes to allow the crowd in to see the new Rangers.

They had recently been on a spending spree, paying £100,000 to Hibs for Colin Stein. Recently Alec MacDonald had been added to the squad in an attempt to catch and overhaul Celtic, who, nevertheless, showed few signs of weakening.

The new arrivals had not yet, however, managed to unseat Cardenden's Willie Johnston from the Rangers team. Rovers' manager Jimmy Millar, once of Rangers, did not have such resources at his disposal but he did at least have a settled team of honest triers including his one-time Ibrox colleague Ralph Brand.

The ground was well filled, with even a hint of a crowd disturbance when a missile landed on the track behind the goal at the sea end of Stark's Park.

Rovers held Rangers quite well until half time with the game well poised. It was just as if someone had pressed a button in the second half as Rovers were simply swept aside by the Rangers tide.

First MacDonald scored with a header when the ball came off the woodwork, then John Greig missed a dreadful penalty which he ballooned way into the crowd.

Then, to the delight of his fans, Colin Stein headed a second goal before Bobby Watson scored near the end to make it a comprehensive win for the Ibrox side. For Rovers, the only crumb of comfort was that the bottom two teams, Falkirk and Arbroath both lost, which meant no change at the bottom.

December 8 1956

Today saw Rovers best ever performance against Rangers as they beat the Ibrox side 5-1 at a packed Stark's Park.

Rovers had been going well, and there was even talk of a challenge for the Scottish League this year. This was generally ridiculed by the cynics, but after this day, the cynics were a little quieter.

It would have to be said that Rovers got their fair share of luck to win 5-1 with the last two goals possibly exaggerating the difference between the sides.

The weather was cold but there was no problem with conditions for the early start in these pre-floodlight days, and there was, as always, a sizeable Rangers presence there.

It was Rangers who scored first when Sammy Baird finished off a cross from Johnny Hubbard. But then the man who would be the man of the match, Bernie Kelly, a talented but occasionally lazy player took over. Bernie was a self-confessed Celtic supporter and enjoyed himself today! He scored the equaliser before half time, heading home a cross from Johnny Williamson and then dominated things in the second half.

But it was John Urquhart who scored two goals, prodding home a simple one, and then scoring one with a lob which deceived George Niven, as Urquhart himself slipped and fell, and had no idea that he had scored. 3-1 to Rovers, and that was it, thought one Burntisland-based supporter, and he headed down to the prom to get his bus to avoid the crowd.

But then he heard a roar and another roar, and was somehow convinced that Rangers had equalised to make it 3-3. Wrong! It was Ernie Copland who had scored, and Rovers had stunned all of Scotland by winning 5-1. Only once in a very dark blue moon does this sort of thing happen to Rangers.

John Urquhart against Rangers

December 9 1916

After results like today's the question is seriously being asked how long can Raith Rovers continue?

Some of their men had joined up, others were likely to be conscripted, and yet others had to do shifts on Saturday mornings in the munitions industry.

But today Rovers eventually managed to scrape together a team to travel to Dens Park to play Dundee, only to lose very comprehensively 6-2.

Rovers were now clearly bottom of the League and Dundee second bottom. The feature of the game was that all Dundee's six goals were scored by Davie Brown, a hat-trick in each half.

In other circumstances this would be looked upon as a mighty achievement — and indeed it was — but without in any way wishing to take anything away from Mr Brown, it was a poor Rovers defence cobbled together at short notice depending on munitions industry shifts etc.

Such were the ways of wartime football. Raith's forwards played better, with Sandy Archibald on the right wing impressing everyone, and Alec Lindsay, who had recently joined the club from Dundee Violet, scoring two good goals.

Following the military and naval disasters of 1916 (which propaganda only partially covered up), increasing war weariness was beginning to develop, but a few days ago, David Lloyd George, an unscrupulous and not always trustworthy but certainly very dynamic figure, had organised a subtle non-violent coup to remove Herbert Asquith and take over the running of the war himself as Prime Minister.

December 10 1921

"Fast efficient football" was the honest verdict of *The Dundee Courier* of the game at Stark's Park which ended in a goalless draw, after which Dundee were fifth in the Scottish League Division One and Raith Rovers seventh.

The crowd was a huge 16,000 with a great deal of Dundonian "excursionists", some of whom had arrived in a fleet of omnibuses now parked on the prom rather than the more normal train.

The atmosphere can easily be reconstructed: everyone wearing bonnets, gentle banter being exchanged between sets of supporters, the occasional old friend from the trenches being recognised and greeted, the beggars on the street, the war wounded, the plaintive playing of accordionists and even one or two with a penny whistle, and the small enclosure in front of what there was of a stand where the war blinded were respectfully ushered and introduced to the stentorian voiced volunteer who would provide commentary years before radio did.

No goals to tell them about, but much to praise in the fine half back line of Raeburn, Morris and Collier which broke up Dundee's attacks until about the last five minutes when Dundee suddenly remembered that they had, on the left wing, Alec Troup who began to give Bill Inglis a hard time, but without the support from the rest of the forward line to produce a goal.

This was a clash of the local Titans, and "Dark Blue" of *The Courier* praises both teams, but chastises Walter Bird for his failure to put away an easy chance to win the game for Dundee.

December 11 1965

Today was very much the "down" side of supporting Raith Rovers as they travelled to Coatbridge to lose 0-1 to Albion Rovers.

November had been good for Rovers, but last week's game had been frosted off, and this one came within a whisker of being called off as well, but it went ahead on a bone hard and rutted pitch.

The attendance was miserable, less than 500 huddled together for warmth and some of them trying to light a fire to keep warm until a policeman put a stop to it!

It was actually a low time for Scottish football generally, for on Tuesday Scotland had failed to qualify for the 1966 World Cup in England by losing 0-3 to Italy in Naples.

Given the uncertainty of whether the game would be on or not, it was hardly surprising to find very few Rovers fans at the somewhat primitive facilities of Cliftonhill.

Those who were there suffered a major heartbreak when Reilly ran through a tired Raith defence to score for Albion Rovers at the very end of the game after Rovers had done all the pressing for most of the 90 minutes.

Pat Gardner, Ian Porterfield and Jocky Richardson had all had reasonable chances to score, and a more gullible referee than Eddie Thomson of Edinburgh might have granted us a penalty kick, but as it was, Rovers had a heavy price to pay for their profligacy.

Given the cold, the darkness and the general misery, the journey home was by no means the highlight of a Raith Rovers supporter's life. But Christmas was coming...

December 12 1936

Serious signs of rebellion today at Stark's Park as the Supporters Club ostentatiously refused to sit in their allocated seats or to take up any collection for the club.

Peter Napier, the Supporters Club representative had been upset by a letter he had received from the Board, but this had followed a war of words which had been ongoing for some time.

Basically, the Supporters Club were not going to raise any more funds for the club until such time as the Board agreed to invest some money in trying to buy better players than they had at the moment.

Results this season had certainly been dire. Last week they had lost to Brechin, there had been defeats to Leith Athletic and St Bernard's and a real shocker of a 6-1 defeat from Forfar at home!

Today's game was anodyne and really quite boring. It was a 0-0 draw with Airdrie in which neither side looked like doing anything to warm up the December cold, but as *The Courier* remarked waspishly, "it was an improvement on recent performances".

The crowd, given as 3,000 but in fact looking a great deal fewer than that, spent the game moaning about the Board, talking about the war in Spain now that the Fascists were closing in on Madrid and, more pertinently to recent events, talking about the new King, whose brother Edward VIII had resigned or abdicated on Thursday so that he could marry his American lady friend Wallis Simpson.

December 13 1950

It was a bitter sweet day for Raith Rovers' Willie McNaught.

He played his third International for Scotland this Wednesday afternoon at Hampden in a game that started at 2.15 because of the early December darkness but nevertheless attracted a crowd of 70,000!

McNaught played well by all accounts, but this game was a 0-1 defeat to Austria, the first time that Scotland had lost at home to a non-British country.

It was a sore blow to the country. The only goal of the game was scored by a chap called Melchior (wasn't he one of the Wise Men?) and Austria also had a man called Wagner playing (wasn't he a composer?).

The Press is adamant that the fault lay not with the defence but with the forwards who found it difficult to cope with the fouling tactics of the Austrians.

At one point, apparently the referee called for an interpreter to tell the Austrian captain that the constant handballing was simply not going to be allowed! One has to allow a certain amount for Press bias (this was 1950, and everyone remembered vividly the most famous Austrian of them all called Adolf Hitler!).

What was less acceptable from the Glasgow Press was the insinuation that if Rangers' Sammy Cox had been playing instead of McNaught, things might somehow or another been different! Cox was duly picked for the next Scotland International!

Nevertheless, it was good for Raith Rovers to have a man playing for Scotland.

December 14 1974

As the year 1974 was slowly coming to an end, the predominant mood in the country as a whole and the town of Kirkcaldy was confusion.

1974 had seen a Miners' Strike, two General Elections, the resignation of the American President, apparently uncontrollable inflation, and even strikes by teachers and dustmen!

Rovers were similarly in a confused state. The resignation of George Farm in October after a spectacularly poor start had added to all this, and now Bertie Paton was the manager — a move that would not turn out well, for no-one at this time thought highly of the Directors!

In addition this was an important season for Raith Rovers for the Leagues were to be re-constructed from 2 to 3, and where teams finished up would determine their future.

The remarkable thing was in the middle of all this, Raith Rovers were not a bad team — inconsistent yes, but showing signs of recovering from their bad start. They were capable of producing a good result as here, for example. A John Hislop goal was enough to beat Falkirk 1-0 at Stark's Park, although they were grateful to Murray McDermott in the goal for one or two good saves. Murray, always popular and well-liked by the fans, was one of the few icons of stability in this increasingly unstable world. He seems to have been there for decades (in fact, only since 1970) but he radiated confidence and self-belief. He certainly made mistakes — every goalkeeper does — but they were few and far between.

December 15 2007

Raith Rovers' form had been infuriatingly inconsistent of late (so what was new about that?).

Under manager John McGlynn — who, unlike some of his predecessors, did give the impression of being interested in the club and knowing something about football — there seemed little doubt that things were slowly moving forward, albeit with the odd setback.

As Christmas approached, they were still in the Scottish Cup, something that had not always been the case in the past, and were in a reasonable position to challenge for promotion as they travelled to Somerset Park to play Ayr this dark December day.

A crowd of 1044 was there and although it would have been an exaggeration to say that Rovers were well represented, they did have a knot of supporters in the crowd.

The journey and the money spent was well worth it, for Rovers simply swept the home team aside and won comfortably 3-0, two goals coming from Marvin Andrews and Mark Campbell in the first half.

Then Robert Sloan scored early in the second half to stifle any sort of chance there might have been of a comeback from the home side who were roundly booed off the field at the end by the "honest men and bonnie lasses" of Ayr.

Rovers' star man was Marvin Andrews, now in his second spell with the club. His repeated and excessive talk about his religion did grate a little now and again, but there was little doubt that although now in his 30s, he was still a class act.

John McGlynn

December 16 1922

The vision of Cliftonhill, the home of Albion Rovers, in the middle of December is hardly an appealing one.

When the weather was miserable with mist and rain with a pitch that was cutting up badly, it is not surprising that the report by "Onlooker" in *The Fife Free Press* is a less than happy one.

The picture portrayed is one of football in the raw, although it is important not to despise Albion Rovers who, in the 1920s, were a significant force in Scottish football, having reached the Scottish Cup final of 1920.

But today was another victory for James Logan's side with two goals from Alec Gilmour, the second of then being an excellent header. Albion Rovers fought back in the second half and scored through Walls, but this was a fine Raith side with the immortal half back line of Raeburn, Morris and Collier outstanding, and their victory here meant that they were now recovering from their bad spell in the autumn.

More and more people were beginning to remark on the play of young Alec James. He was a funny little man with a curious run but there was no doubt that he knew how to use a football. Occasionally, it was felt that he lacked a little positional sense and did not always tune in sensibly with the rest of the team, but it was felt that if he could learn to work better with the other excellent forwards that Rovers had, he would be a major player. There was certainly no problem with his ball control.

OFFICIAL MATCHDAY PROGRAMME OF RAITH ROVERS FOOTBALL CLUB   Price 1.50

Raith Rovers
Football Club

Raith Rovers v. Alloa Athletic

Bell's Scottish League Division One
Saturday 16th december 200. Kick Off 3pm.

We all knew that Raith Rovers were an old club, but look at that date! Is that BC or AD?

December 17 1983

It wasn't really cold, but that was about all you could say in favour of this dull, dark and drizzly December day as the faithful trudged their way to Stark's Park.

One would like to say there were loads of them, but that wouldn't be true and even the attendance figure of 680 looked as if it might be an exaggeration.

This was the low-ebb of supporting Raith Rovers.

The week before Christmas is never a great Saturday for attendances at the best of times, and this was far from the best of times for the Rovers with only Alloa underneath them at the bottom of the table.

The club had never survived the traumatic spring of 1981, and people in the town talked more about ice hockey and the Fife Flyers than they did about Raith Rovers as new manager Bobby Wilson tried in vain to make some sort of an impact.

Today saw a miserable 1-3 defeat to Ayr United, ("a dreadful team, but better than us" in the honest opinion of a punter downing his post-match anaesthetic in the Novar Bar) with the solitary goal coming from Colin Harris; the sad thing about it all was that there wasn't really even any great anger or protest.

It was now accepted meekly, and Raith were no longer even the butt of local gallows humour. They were paying the real penalty for letting their fans down — apathy and indifference. And another punter opined "I don't even care about the apathy!"

December 18 1937

The proximity of Stark's Park to the sea was probably what saved this game from the postponements that befell more inland teams today.

Even at that, it was a close call for the pitch was hard and a little slippery occasionally, but nevertheless table-topping Raith Rovers and Alloa served up a nine-goal feast of football.

All the journalists lapsed into the Christmas clichés of it being a "cracker" and how there were a few soft goals on either side which were "Christmas presents from Santa Claus" etc.

"The Judge" in *The Courier* was of the opinion that Alloa played well and were unlucky not to gain something from the game, but he also was full of praise for this free-scoring Raith Rovers side.

Man of the moment was Norman Haywood who scored his second successive hat-trick "Haywood took things coolly and netted three fine goals. His opportunism was a treat" purrs *The Courier;* Rovers fans left the ground happy.

Once *The Sporting Post* came out on the Saturday evening, they would have been even happier, for local rivals East Fife lost at Dumbarton, meaning that Rovers had consolidated their lead at the top of the table which showed a certain Fife domination with Rovers first, East Fife second and Dunfermline third!

For good measure, Cowdenbeath were not all that far away either in eighth position. It looked as if it was going to be a Happy Christmas and New Year, but only a fool would not be a little unhappy and concerned about the worsening International situation. Just what was that Hitler fellow all about?

December 19 1896

Raith Rovers did not yet play League football, so the only games they played were Cup ties or friendlies.

Dunfermline Athletic had given them their "exit ticket" from the Fife Cup a couple of months earlier, but before they had departed for home on October 31, the two clubs had arranged a friendly to be played on December 19.

Dunfermline duly turned up in spite of severe wintry conditions which made things very hazardous, and there was snow on the pitch.

But the snow was a benefit in these dark December days, for it prevented things from getting too murky, and the referee did not need to cut the game short.

Perhaps for reasons of bad weather making travel difficult, Raith had to start the game with only 9 men as Walker and Smith turned up a few minutes late.

A "goodly attendance of spectators lined the ropes" and they saw a very one-sided game in which Rovers were so dominant and determined to avenge the Fife Cup defeat.

Beveridge got a hat-trick, Lambert scored two (one from the penalty spot) Smith got 2 and Walker 1 as the spectators were in danger of losing count, but Dunfermline were not given a "grannie" as they were able to score a goal to give them some self-respect, and to make the score Raith Rovers 8 Dunfermline 1, a score line that was talked about quite a lot among Rovers supporters when they met Dunfermline people!

December 20 1913

Raith came very close today to winning at Firhill for the first ever time, but luck was against them, according to the perhaps slightly biased writer in *The Fife Free Press*.

Raith had put in a good performance against the all-conquering Celtic at Stark's Park last week, and expected to do well today against a team whom they had beaten 3-0 in Kirkcaldy a few weeks ago, but today they came up against the famous Scottish Internationalist Alick Raisbeck, who frankly dominated proceedings.

An encouraging sign for Rovers was the number of fans who came on the train with them to games, sometimes even being allowed to sit with the players and talk about the game.

These fans felt ill-done by today for although Fred Martin scored for Rovers, the Rovers half backs of Logan, Porter and Anderson, normally the mainstay of this very fine side, were a little below their best and Partick Thistle took advantage.

This being midwinter, darkness fell early, but one of the things that one noticed about Glasgow was that the imminence of Christmas seemed to be more of a talking point than in Kirkcaldy with loads of shops illuminated by electric light and advertising cakes and "presents for the lady in your life".

Christmas was not yet a holiday in Scotland and wouldn't be until 1958, and such celebrations as there were seemed to be little other than a rehearsal for the big one a week later of the New Year.

December 21 1996

It was indeed a very bleak midwinter as Rovers went down 0-3 to Hibs at Stark's Park.

The particular disappointment here was that this was far from a vintage Hibs team who were struggling almost as much as Rovers were, and they were one of the few teams that Rovers could realistically hope to catch, if relegation from the Premier Division was to be avoided.

Hibs had sacked Alex Miller as manager in September, and Jocky Scott was in temporary charge, but they were still struggling.

If 68/69 AD was the year of the Four Emperors in Ancient Rome and 1936 was the year of the Three Kings in Great Britain, 1996 was the year of the four Managers at Stark's Park with Iain Munro, still a fairly vague and nebulous figure, now in charge.

Serious and valid questions were now being asked in the national press about what exactly was going on at Raith Rovers, but the team had won three of their last four games and some of the ever loyal and optimistic crowd of 4229 were beginning to hope that the corner had been turned.

They were not without some good players, notably Kevin Twaddle and Tony Rougier, but sadly today Rovers — after holding Hibs for the first half — were simply swept aside in a 20 minute spell in the second half with Darren Jackson scoring twice and Pat McGinlay once.

The Rovers fans, as they drifted away sadly to spend a rather unhappy Christmas were not to know that this was only the start of a dismal festive period from which they never recovered.

December 22 1934

The Fife Free Press pulls no punches about this one.

"The team requires strengthening and until that is done, continued success will elude them".

The writer was referring to a game at Station Park, Forfar where Rovers were 1-0 up until late in the game, but then tired and collapsed woefully to allow Forfar to score three times in the last 10 minutes.

Sandy Archibald had been appointed Manager some six weeks ago, and for a while, as often happens with a new Manager, there had been some sort of improvement with two victories, but now Rovers were back to square one.

The few Rovers fans that were there were dispirited as they trudged across the road to the railway station to get their train back to Kirkcaldy, for their team had started well enough.

George Fulton had scored just on half time, but the whistle had gone, so no goal. However he then scored a beautiful header half way through the second half, and Rovers looked comfortable until Forfar, who had kept plugging away with more determination than skill, scored through Black, Laird and then "Newman" in the very last minute.

It was dreadful midwinter performance from the Stark's Park men, but the game was watched by two famous people. One was James Logan, one-time manager of Raith Rovers and now a hotelier in nearby Kirriemuir, and the other was the Earl of Strathmore of Glamis Castle, a self-confessed Forfar Athletic supporter. Neither of them would have thought very much of this extremely disappointing Rovers performance.

December 23 1961

A good crowd of well over 13,000 were at Stark's Park today to see Celtic, with a huge support with them, beat Rovers 4-0.

The weather was slightly foggy and the pitch was frosty in patches but this was par for the course for the time of the year.

Rovers simply had no answer to the play of this impressive set of Celtic youngsters. Rovers were wearing red that day possibly because they felt that it would show them up better on the TV, for the BBC cameras were there for the highlights at night.

They started off playing well and Bobby Adamson might have scored twice in the early stages, but was thwarted by Frank Haffey.

Then Steve Chalmers scored for Celtic, his impetus on the skiddy surface almost carrying him into his adoring fans behind the goal. Bobby Carroll scored just before half time.

By the second half the game was beyond Rovers, who were going to have a struggle to avoid relegation this year and John Divers scored another two for Celtic.

Celtic fans did not always have a good reputation for behaving themselves in these days, but they were impeccable today as they made their way back to the station, wishing everyone a Happy Christmas and even singing a few Christmas carols.

Their mood was further improved by the news that Rangers had lost 4-2 to Aberdeen, but the team of the season so far, Dundee, had earned a good point at St Mirren. Rovers however were now sixth from the bottom, and the festive period was far from cheerful.

December 24 1927

Christmas in Scotland in the 1920s was by no means the big thing that it later became, but nevertheless Raith Rovers ensured that their fans in the 5,000 crowd would have a Merry Christmas as they beat Airdrie 5-0 at Stark's Park.

It was a sad and chastening experience to listen to the line-ups of both teams, for in the space of three or four years, all the good players had gone — no Hughie Gallacher, no Bob McPhail for Airdrie, no Dave Morris, no Alec James for Raith Rovers, all sold by spineless managements for money.

At least Airdrie had won the Scottish Cup in 1924 with their fine team; Rovers had nothing to show for their success, other than the memories of some excellent players.

Both clubs, situated in mining areas, had suffered badly at the time of the General Strike and its aftermath. In the case of Raith Rovers certainly, and to a lesser extent Airdrie, the asset stripping had occurred before the labour problems, and the impoverishment of the area made it hard for them to rebuild.

Today, however, after Airdrie took the initiative to Raith Rovers and really should have scored several times, Raith took command and scored five goals, two by Bill Birrell and one each from John Beath, Albert Pigg and Bill Allison. The 5-0 score line was perhaps a little unfair on Airdrie, who were not as much out of the game as the score line would have suggested.

Rovers were enjoying a yoyo existence at the moment — relegated in 1926, promoted in 1927 and now struggling to avoid relegation again.

December 25 1920

It was the custom until the 1970s to play football matches on Christmas Day.

In fact until 1958, Christmas Day was not a public holiday, so if Christmas fell on a Saturday, games went ahead as normal.

A distressing sight, however, especially on Christmas Day, was the sight of the beggars outside the ground, some of them maimed, injured or blind, all of them callously neglected by Prime Minister Lloyd George who had promised them a "land fit for heroes to live in"!

It would be a fair bet however that "Townsend" of *The Fife Free Press* did not have a Merry Christmas, nor would many of the Raith Rovers supporters in the 7,000 who saw their team go down 4-2 to Albion Rovers.

Albion Rovers in 1920 were no bad side, for they had reached the Scottish Cup final that year, and all their goals came from the crossing of the veteran winger Alec Bennett, now 39 years old and commonly known as "the artful dodger". He had played for both Celtic and Rangers before the war and had 11 Scottish caps to his credit.

George Waite and John Rattray scored for Raith Rovers, but it was a performance which clearly upset our reporter who said that the defence was as "unstable as water" and while denying that he was a "Jeremiah", the situation was bad enough to "warrant plain speaking" to the effect that the club needed "new players and good players".

It seems to have had an effect on Raith and manager James Logan, for David Morris soon joined the club, and by the end of the season, the club had recorded some fine victories.

December 26 1931

1931 was not a great year for anyone, neither the country of Great Britain — which was suffering severe unemployment — nor Raith Rovers, whose form had frequently been described, euphemistically, as "mediocre" or "disappointing".

Today however, they finished the year with a good 3-0 win at East End Park over neighbours and rivals Dunfermline Athletic with two goals from Joe Cowan and one from Sandy McKenzie.

Cowan took his goals impressively well, nipping in to take advantage of defensive hesitancy for the first goal, then just in the stroke of half time hitting a ball from the edge of the box to ensure that Rovers went in 2-0 ahead at half-time.

The Courier is disappointed with Dunfermline's forwards especially in the second half when no fight back materialised and the three "B"s of the Rovers defence — Andy Bell, Tommy Batchelor and John Beath were always well in command.

The man of the moment was certainly Joe Cowan, a man who had never really made it at Celtic (for it would have been difficult to displace Jimmy McGrory!) but who clearly found Raith Rovers very much to his liking. He had now scored in the last nine games, and with Cowan in form, Rovers now finished 1931 in second place in the League.

The crowd was a slightly disappointing 5,000, something that was poor for a Fife derby but perhaps said a great deal about the grim economic times of 1931.

SCOTTISH LEAGUE PREMIER DIVISION

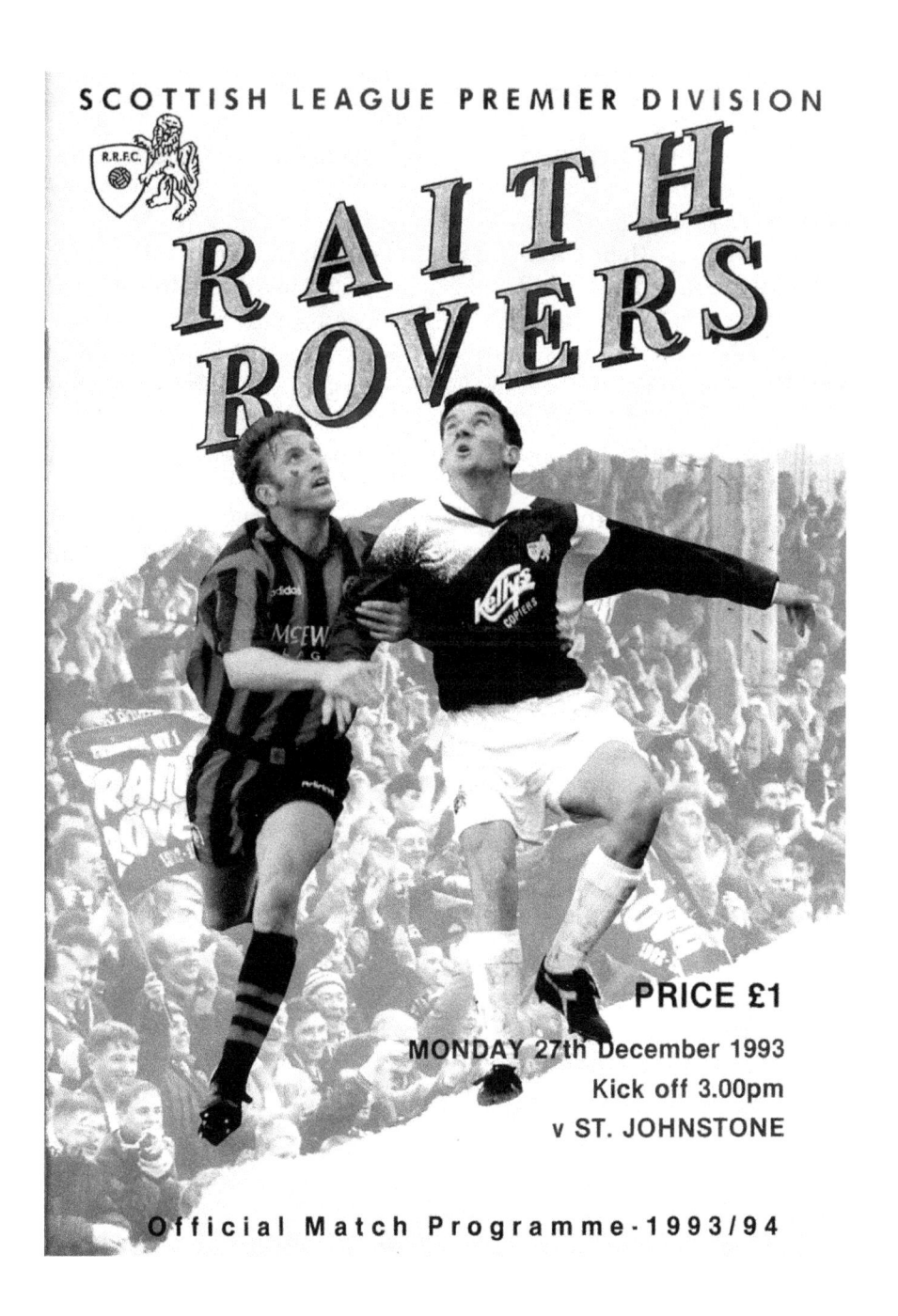

RAITH ROVERS

PRICE £1

MONDAY 27th December 1993
Kick off 3.00pm
v ST. JOHNSTONE

Official Match Programme - 1993/94

December 27 1913

Raith finished the year of 1913 (in which they had reached the Scottish Cup final for the first and only time) with a fine 4-1 win over Dundee at Stark's Park.

They had lost their three previous games in December to Falkirk, Celtic and Partick Thistle and looked like losing this one to the weather, for snow had fallen in Kirkcaldy in the morning and the game kicked off with two inches of snow on the park according to *The Fife Free Press* and snow fell intermittently throughout the game. Players were tough in 1913!

"The ball could not be kicked any great distance on the ground and often it became encased in snow". In spite of this, Rovers stuck to their short passing game. To the delight of the 3,000 crowd, which would surely have been larger but for the snow, scored four goals of "the unsaveable variety" through a Fred Gibson penalty, then a good goal from Fred Martin before Jimmy Scott scored two at the end.

Skene had scored for Dundee, but the Taysiders were outclassed today with Rovers centre half, young Willie Porter having an outstanding game in the centre of the defence.

Perhaps predictably *The Courier's* report of the game concentrates more on the impossible conditions, although it does concede that Rovers were the better side. The conditions had "passed the playable limit" and the reporter seems to think that Dundee were unhappy about being made to play whereas Rovers, with a point to make to their own supporters, were more determined to have a go.

December 28 1901

Rovers' final game of the momentous year of 1901 was played in farcical conditions at Stark's Park.

This was Rovers first (and only) season in the Northern League and their opponents were an Aberdeen side called Orion.

Orion left leave Aberdeen in the early part of the day, so they were without some of their better players, who were still on the fishing boats when the train left the station!

The weather had been bright and sunny but in midmorning, heavy snow fell and although the temperature rose a little, the snow turned to sleet and rain, and the decision of referee Mr Davidson of Arbroath to sanction play was a questionable one.

Rovers started off kicking to the Beveridge Park goal and cheered to sparse crowd with three goals in each half against the totally outclassed Aberdonians.

The goals were shared about — Alec Mackie and Bobby Weir had two each and Jimmy Devine and the immensely talented Jock Eckford one each.

The Fife Free Press praises the spirit of Orion in a phrase that had might not have employed a century later when he says that "Orion did not allow their pecker to drop but kept pegging away to the end in sportsmanlike fashion".

Rovers were now third in the Northern League with games in hand, but for Orion, there were already moves afoot to create a strong football team in the Granite City with an amalgamation of themselves, Victoria United and the team already called Aberdeen to form Aberdeen FC. This happened in 1903.

Raith Rovers 1905-06

December 29 1906

The great Vale of Leven, one of the pioneers of the game in Scotland and winners of the Scottish Cup in 1877, 1878 and 1879 had fallen on bad times with the advent of professionalism and the gradual movement of the best players from villages like Alexandria (from where the Vale sprung) to the larger cities, Glasgow in particular.

Their visit to Stark's Park today was lucky to survive a very heavy fall of snow on Christmas Day and the day after, but a wind had sprung up and blown most of the snow away so that referee Mr Philp of Dunfermline (who would referee this season's Scottish Cup final) was able to allow the game to go ahead.

Rovers played one of their better games this season and won 5-0 with two goals from George McNichol and one each from John Brannigan, James Wilkie and John MacDonald.

The writer in *The Fife Free Press* was quite impressed by the standard of play, particularly because Rovers were obliged to play some time without the injured Brannigan, but like everyone else, he was distracted by a fight among the 1,300 spectators.

It was not clear whether they were locals or men from the west, but the police had difficulties involving "hustling and snowballing" from the crowd before the "delinquents were handcuffed and taken to the police office".

At one point, it looked as if a riot was about to break out, but after the trouble-makers were taken away, the crowd settled down to watch the match. Rovers were now in mid-table of the Scottish League Division Two.

Stark's Park in the 1920s. Pride of place is the new stand, opened on 30th December 1922

December 30 1922

The main stand, which has attracted so much criticism over the years, was opened today.

There could have been a better day for it, for the rain was heavy and the pitch was far from suitable, but Lord Novar was there (although he had lost his voice and could not say much) and the MP Robert Hutchison (who had played for the club in 1902) and Willie Maley, who was there in two capacities, one as President of the Scottish League and also as manager of today's opponents Celtic.

As a result of the weather the crowd was a rather disappointing 8,000. The stand was reasonably comfortable although not quite finished yet, its curious shape explained away by the geographical alignment of Pratt Street.

The admission was 3 shillings and 6 pence to the "chairs" in the bit of the stand near the half way line, and 2 shillings and 6 pence to the corner stand.

Raith lost the game 0-3, a surprise considering that they had players like Alec James and their mighty half back line of Raeburn, Morris and Collier on duty, but it was generally agreed (and not just the opinion of *The Fife Free Press*) that Celtic were lucky.

Their goals came from Johnny Gilchrist and the famous Joe Cassidy who scored twice, but the man of the match was Celtic's goalkeeper Charlie Shaw.

For Rovers, the man who caught the eye was outside left Bobby Archibald, and in spite of the result, it was generally regarded to be one of Rovers' best performances of the season.

December 31 1904

Dunterlie Park, Barrhead, a pitch commonly known as the "Hump" was where Raith Rovers brought down the curtain on their rather depressing year of 1904.

They lost 0-3 to Arthurlie, a major disappointment, for they had beaten them at Stark's Park a couple of weeks ago.

The attendance was a poor one, and the proceeds totalled only £17 with Rovers' share of that barely enough to pay for the train fares.

The pitch was generally regarded as a disgrace and the "Hump" was no exaggeration for the slope from one side to another was like "looking out of a tenement window on the street below" according to one writer whom, one presumes and hopes, was guilty of a little rhetorical exaggeration.

It was on this pitch, however, that the first great upset of Scottish football had been recorded in 1897 when Arthurlie removed Celtic from the Scottish Cup!

Today Rovers' side of Mackie, Inglis and Stewart; Neilson, Phillip and Grierson; MacDonald, Proctor, Wallace, Gray and Bell made absolutely no impact on a very competent Arthurlie team in a game which was "by no means devoid of roughness", a euphemism for what seems to have been a typical Edwardian football game with loads of shoulder charging the goalkeeper and other things not tolerated by modern referees.

Arthurlie scored with a penalty kick, then added another before half time, and in the second half it was no surprise when they scored a third.

Rovers were given a certain amount of praise for hard work, but their kicking and shooting were poor. It was their sheer inconsistency which exasperated the fans, and it was probably just as well that there were not very many there that cold, dark, Hogmanay.

January

Raith Rovers Directors early 1950s

January 1 1955

Raith Rovers opened the New Year of 1955 with a 4-1 win at Stark's Park over neighbours East Fife before a crowd of 12,000 spectators.

It was a traditional New Year Day fixture in the sense of everyone passing around their bottles (alcohol was allowed at Scottish games until 1981) so that everyone (including East Fife supporters) could have a drink and wish each other a Happy New Year.

As far as footballing entertainment went, East Fife were not really in it.

Both teams, currently in the old First Division among the big teams, had enjoyed an up and down sort of season up to now, with Rovers, in particular, plagued by injuries; today saw another injury added to the list — Jimmy McEwan breaking his wrist.

The Courier states that Rovers play was "as bright and crisp as the brand new strip they were wearing", and they took an early lead with a glorious diving header from Andy Young.

Archibald, Copland and Duncan (with a penalty kick) added more for Raith Rovers, but *The Courier* singles out Ian Bain at right half as the star.

East Fife, however, suffered from shaky defenders, a lack of thrust up front and a lack of any fighting spirit. There were of course changed days for East Fife, a team who had won the Scottish League Cup no fewer than three times since its inception in 1946.

Raith, on the other hand, even without Willie McNaught, looked good today, but their form had been hitherto maddeningly inconsistent for the supporters.

January 2 2011

6,534 fans enjoyed the Fife New Year derby against Dunfermline Athletic at Stark's Park.

It was a good tussle, with Raith just edging it and no more, and no quarter sought or given. It was a typical derby fixture in fact, although it did not have any great long term impact on the race for the Premiership, for it was Dunfermline who won the more crucial derby at East End Park in late April.

Today, there were no goals at half time and picking a winner was no easy job. But then early in the second half a Scott McBride inswinging corner kick found Mark Campbell who managed to squeeze the ball home. Scarcely had the cries of triumph died down when Nick Phinn of Dunfermline hammered home an equalizer.

With passions rising and yellow cards becoming frequent, it was Gregory Tade who scored the winner for Raith Rovers, and a fine goal it was as well, driven in from the edge of the box after a pass from John Baird.

So, Happy New Year to Raith Rovers and first blood in 2011, but form was never really consistent enough to win the League — and there were no play-offs in 2011.

It was a funny Division, for the best team by some distance was Dundee, but they had been deducted 25 points for going into administration (not for the first time) and the Pars finished 10 points ahead of Raith Rovers, thus winning the Division and earning promotion — but they wouldn't stay in the top tier for long!

January 3 2000

The Millenium had arrived. It was meant to jigger all our computers with some sort of strange bug, but it didn't.

Raith celebrated the dawning of the new Millennium this Holiday Monday by beating their local rivals Dunfermline Athletic 3-0, to the delight of newly appointed manager Peter Hetherston and their fans in the large crowd of 7463.

The game was a tough encounter which maybe would not have been as much as 3-0 if Owen Coyle of Dunfermline had not argued so much about the non-award of a penalty and got himself red carded in the first half.

Alex Burns scored early and then Paul Browne did likewise before the incident which changed the game or at least prevented a Dunfermline come back.

Coyle may have had a point about the penalty, but holding one's tongue is always a good idea; it was his persistent arguing (with possibly a bad word or two in the middle of it) which led to the red card.

Then Steve Tosh scored a third. It was a good win for Raith, but in spite of this and another Rovers win over them in a game in March at East End Park, it was Dunfermline who were promoted at the end of the season after they ended second.

Rovers simply hit the skids at exactly the wrong time in the month of April.

January 4 1898

For the first and only time in their life, Raith Rovers played a team called Locked Out Engineers.

The details of this fixture are tantalisingly vague but we do know that Rovers won 3-1 and that the game was played at Easter Road in Edinburgh.

The Fifeshire Advertiser mentions it an off-hand dismissive sort of the way. *The Fife Free Press* and *The Dundee Courier* fail to mention it at all, and even *The Scotsman* of Edinburgh has no mention of the game.

It certainly wasn't unique — Dundee North End had met Dundee Violet in a friendly on behalf of the Locked-out Engineers on the day before. They had the support of a procession and a band playing music during the game!

Apart from that, little seems to be known. 1897 had seen a great deal of labour unrest — far more than the Diamond Jubilee of Queen Victoria could cover up entirely — and the engineering industry was gaining a good deal of public support.

But it has certainly been a good start to the New Year for the Rovers — a 9-1 won over one time "World Champions" Renton (the Dunbartonshire men called themselves that 10 years ago after they themselves won the Scottish Cup in 1888 and then defeated English Cup winners West Bromwich Albion) and then another win at Montrose and now this win at Easter Road.

January 5 1925

Football was scheduled this Holiday Monday in both Divisions in Scotland.

The problem was that it was not necessarily a Holiday Monday for everybody and the result was that the crowd for Raith Rovers v Dundee was only about 4,000 when more might have been expected on a Saturday.

This was 1925 and no-one would have dared to take a day off, otherwise they might have found no job waiting for them on the Tuesday!

But the 4,000 who were on holiday saw some marvellous football entertainment in a game which Rovers won 4-3. "So intense was the excitement in the second half that the play was accompanied by an almost incessant roar from the spectators" says "Grenadier" of *The Dundee Courier*.

The score was 2-0 at half time for the home side, both scored by George Miller; one of them was a clear goalkeeping error. Then James "Napper" Thomson of Dundee scored an own goal, to make it 3-0 but then Dundee pulled two back through Jock McDonald and Davie McLean.

It looked all over for Dundee however when Alec James scored a fourth, but Dundee refused to yield and Jimmy Hunter headed a third. With everyone now on tenterhooks, Dundee pressed and pressed, but Raith's goalkeeper Jimmy Mathieson was in inspirational form, and special praise was given to Walter Marchbanks, deputising at centre half for the injured Dave Morris.

It was a wonderful game of football and a good result for Rovers after their otherwise disappointing start to the New Year.

January 6 2018

It was a good day at the office for Raith Rovers as they beat a spirited Forfar Athletic side 2-1 at Starks Park.

This in conjunction with the news that Arbroath had beaten Ayr United meant that Raith were now at the top of the Scottish League Division One, one point ahead of Ayr with two games in hand.

It was a wintry, cold but dry, day and the two teams served up a good game for the 1,575 crowd.

Raith went ahead in the 15th minute when a cross from Ross Matthews found Greig Spence who scored into the Beveridge Park end of the ground. Five minutes later, however, Forfar equalized with a good goal from Josh Peters but then five minutes after that, Forfar's young trialist had the misfortune to concede an own goal from a cross that he might well have let go.

This turned out to be the winner for Rovers, as there was no further scoring in the game. Rovers were the better team in the second half but could not add to their tally.

Yet the cheer from the home fans at the full time whistle told its own story, for Forfar were not without their chances either.

An equally loud cheer arose when the loudspeaker announced the defeat of Ayr United. The Man of the Match was Canadian Dario Zanatta, although many supporters felt that Lewis Vaughan was equally good.

2018 had started well for Raith Rovers!

January 7 1922

The strong-going Raith Rovers made it three wins out of three in 1922 (they had beaten Falkirk and Aberdeen in the New Year fixtures) by beating Hearts 3-1 at Stark's Park today before a large and enthusiastic crowd of 12,000.

As a result of this fine run of form, Rovers were now fourth in the League behind the Glasgow trio of Celtic, Rangers and Partick Thistle. If they had started the season better and not had so many draws, they would have been even higher.

The Sunday Post claimed that Raith were flattered to win, but that was a bit unfair. The difference between the teams was that Rovers were more willing to shoot than Hearts were, and as a result scored three goals through John "Tokey" Duncan, Bobby Bauld and Davie Dawson before Hearts could make their only reply.

"Hawk-Eye" of *The Fife Free Press* conceded that if Hearts had scored again, it would have been not undeserved and would have made for an interesting finish, but he also singles out the work of Raeburn, Morris and Collier in the half back line as the main strength of this Rovers team.

1922 had started well for Raith Rovers, but for the town and the country in general, there was still an unacceptable level of poverty and deprivation with Prime Minister David Lloyd George losing even more credibility every week he stayed in office.

One piece of apparent good news however was the acceptance by Dail Eireann, on this very day, of the establishment of the Irish Free State. More trouble however was coming.

The punters on the old terracing

January 8 1938

The latter part of 1937 had been very good but Raith Rovers had had their New Year spoiled when they were defeated by East Fife.

They had done a little to make it up by beating Airdrie on January 3 and today their season of high goal scoring continued at Firs Park, Falkirk the home of East Stirlingshire.

Poor East Stirlingshire were seriously depleted, when their regular goalkeeper and their regular centre half were compelled to call off at the last minute, and not only that, but a trialist left winger failed to turn up!

They were thus compelled to scour the local junior teams to find a team, and in the circumstances, it was hardly surprising that they had no answer to Sandy Archibald's slick Raith Rovers side.

It was clear that some of the Shire players had never even met each other before the game — they certainly did not know each other's names — and it was no surprise that Raith Rovers were 6-0 up before half time. Tommy Gilmour scored four, Norman Haywood another and John Whitelaw from the penalty spot.

But then East Stirlingshire rallied a little in the second half and even pulled one back, before normal service was restored and Whitelaw and Francis Joyner scored to make the final score 8-1. Rovers might have made it 10, but probably out of compassion stopped at 8.

The crowd was about 2,000 and included several buses of supporters from Kirkcaldy.

January 9 1897

Scottish Cup day, and Rovers travelled to Dumbarton — the team who had won the Scottish Cup in 1884, and had won the Scottish League in the first two years of its existence in 1891 and 1892.

The weather was surprisingly clement for the time of year, and a good game was served up by both sides with Rovers distinctly unlucky not to get a least a replay.

George Ramsay opened the scoring for Raith in what was described as a "soft" goal by *The Courier*.

Crucially, towards the end of the first half, influential centre half John Lambert was injured, and that was significant in the course of the game for Dumbarton slowly asserted control and Mair scored twice for them.

Dumbarton were generally regarded as a class outfit in the 1890s, although the balance of power was slowly shifting to the city of Glasgow where the population was. This year Dumbarton would reach the final of the Scottish Cup but would lose heavily 1-5 to Rangers.

Rovers would now turn to the Scottish Consolation Cup where they would eventually defeat Dunfermline but lose ignominiously to Cowdenbeath.

This day however would see Scottish football's biggest ever shock when Celtic, wracked by internal discord, went down to Arthurlie. When someone told them this score at Buchanan Street Station on the way home, Raith Rovers players would not believe it!

January 10 1981

It had been a long time since the kick-off had had to be delayed to allow fans to enter Stark's Park, but this was precisely what happened here when table-topping Hibs came to town.

10,000 were in position to see Rovers win 2-0 and level themselves with Hibs with games in hand. They thus made themselves favourites for the First Division championship.

Both teams fielded new signings, John Mitchell from Falkirk for Raith Rovers and Alan Sneddon from Celtic for Hibs, and the large crowd saw a great game with Rovers arguably a little flattered by the 2-0 win.

Hibs had chances which they did not make the best use of, and Murray McDermott was in inspiring form in the Rovers goal. Ian Steen scored in the first half, and then Allan Forsyth with a penalty early in the second half to give Rovers the points.

Jim Traynor of *The Glasgow Herald* was surprised to see "Raith's supporters shuffling towards the exits along with the dejected Hibs disciples before the end of the game". He concluded that "old habits certainly die hard in Kirkcaldy".

Maybe however they were just cold and in need of some warming refreshment at the Novar Bar! The game had kicked off late and they had been standing in the cold for a while! And there was also, perhaps, a certain degree of wanting to convince the referee that the game was closer to being over than what it really was!

January 11 1964

Raith's woes continued as they were dumped out of the Scottish Cup by Dumbarton today at Boghead.

The pitch lived up to its name, for it was heavy and wet. It had also in the old days been called "fatal Boghead" because of the tendency of both Celtic and Rangers to lose games there, and today it certainly was fatal for Raith Rovers.

The Scottish Cup had always proved elusive to Raith Rovers. Beaten finalists in 1913, since the Second World War they had reached the semi-final on four occasions including last year in 1963 but had made no further progress, sometimes very unluckily.

Today their exit was comprehensive. A series of bad results over Christmas and New Year had compelled manager Doug Cowie to ring the changes, not so much in personnel as in positions, but the re-jigged forward line of Lourie, Menzies, McGrogan, Bell and Gilpin simply failed to function as Dumbarton raced into an early lead and stayed in command all through the first half.

Then early in the second half *The Evening Times,* in a clear case of "damning with faint praise" said that "for the first time Rovers settled and looked as if they might score".

Not for long though, for Callaghan scored, then Bowie twice for the Sons of the Rock and Dumbarton ran out 4-0 winners. A crowd of 3,200 attended, including a token number of Rovers supporters, who cannot really have enjoyed their trip back home.

January 12 1957

Rovers maintained third place in the First Division behind Hearts and Motherwell thanks to a hard fought 2-2 draw at East End Park.

Such was the current form of Rovers that this result was even considered a disappointment, for Dunfermline were in the lower middle part of the First Division.

East End Park, still a rather primitive location with an old wooden stand that was in desperate need of replacement, was full today; it even looked as if Rovers supporters outnumbered the Pars.

The Kirkcaldy fans had cause to cheer when a Dunfermline player with the unlikely name of Terry Tighe gave the ball away to Andy Young who immediately lobbed the ball into the penalty box for Ernie Copland to run on and score.

But it was the same Terry Tighe a minute later who equalized with a brilliant diving header from an Anderson cross. Rovers now took control of the game, but as often happens, it was the other team who scored, with Charlie Dickson scoring in a goalmouth scramble which should have been cleared up by the normally reliable Rovers defence.

This was just on the point of half time, and a real shock looked on the cards, but it was one of Rovers' lesser known players, Jimmy Carr, playing for the injured Jimmy McEwan, who equalized.

The last quarter of an hour was a great example of what derby football was all about, as both teams battled for the winner that would have allowed what is now known as "bragging rights" in Fife.

January 13 1923

It was a mild, albeit slightly dull January day for the first round of the Scottish Cup, and Fife was the major talking point of Scotland.

It was not so much East Fife's 7-1 victory over Berwick Rangers, impressive though that was, nor Celtic's tight squeeze into the next round by 3-2 at Lochgelly.

It was Raith Rovers' defeat of the Cup holders Morton at Stark's Park before 11,000 spectators. It was a famous victory, yet *The Courier* castigates Raith Rovers for the fact that it was only 1-0 and should have been more, given the pressure that Rovers had.

The fault for all this was the forwards, says the scribe, with Alec James in particular guilty of overdoing the tricky stuff and not shooting on sight. No blame was attached to the half backs — why should there be? — the mighty half back line men of Raeburn, Morris and Collier, nor the defenders, but if the forwards did not take advantage of the opportunities presented, they might live to rue the day.

The only goal that was scored was a rebound off the goalkeeper on which Bobby Bauld capitalised. However, Rovers were now into the next round, and they would be staying at home to play Cowdenbeath.

So Morton, the Cup winners of last year were out. In truth, they did not really look like Cup winners today.

Sadly for the Greenock men, 1922 remains the last time that they won the Scottish Cup. It was however (and stays thus) once oftener than Raith Rovers have ever won it!

January 14 1967

No-one realised it at the time (although the brighter fans might have guessed) that this would be the last time that Raith Rovers would play Third Lanark.

As it turned out, Rovers (as was their right) refused to play the game under the Cathkin floodlights, necessitating an early kick off. One suspects this was a decision which might have pleased Third Lanark as it saved them money on their electric bill!

Rovers manager George Farm, however, was never a fan of floodlights. Promotion-chasing Raith Rovers won 6-1, although some reports say that the game was closer than that.

The crowd was less than 1,000 and they saw John Laurie and Jocky Richardson scoring twice and Pat Gardner and Gordon Wallace once each. That Thirds were in a great deal of trouble was obvious from the state of the ground and the dressing rooms.

The Laws stated that the game had to *start* with a new ball, but at the first throw-in it was replaced (legally, apparently) by an older one!

There were reasons for the imminent collapse of Thirds, mainly the depopulation of Glasgow and their inability to keep up with the big two, but there was also the short-term problem of gross financial mismanagement. Some called it corruption; others, theft.

Formed in 1872 as the 3rd Lanarkshire Rifle Volunteers, they had played a great part in Scottish football, winning the Scottish Cup twice and the Scottish League once and producing great players like Jimmy Carabine, Jimmy Mason, Dave Hilley and Matt Gray. It was sad to see them go to the wall in the summer of 1967.

January 15 1910

It is not often that Raith Rovers feel upstaged in Kirkcaldy, but that was certainly the case today.

Their Scottish Consolation Cup replay against Cowdenbeath was won comfortably enough 2-0 with goals from Jimmy Smith and Jimmy Gourlay, but the talk of the town was Kirkcaldy United who had reached the Scottish Cup proper.

They had been drawn to play at home against the great Queen's Park, still looked upon as one of the giants of the game. But United had sold their ground rights and the game was to be played next week at Hampden.

The United came in for great deal of criticism for this decision with words like "bribery" being freely used, but such was their precarious financial position, they felt they could do nothing else.

And if that wasn't enough to knock Rovers out of the conversation of supporters, there was also a General Election in the offing with the sitting Liberal MP Henry Dalziel taking on a Conservative called Arthur Baumann.

Rovers supporters on their way to Stark's Park passed several posters saying "Arthur Baumann visits Fife, lives in London rest of life" a dig at Mr Baumann's lack of knowledge of Fife but also an unfair one because Dalziel wasn't seen all that often in Kirkcaldy either!

Mr Dalziel duly won the seat, Kirkcaldy United actually drew at Hampden, but lost the replay (also at Hampden!) while Raith Rovers reached the semi-final of the Scottish Consolation Cup before falling to St Johnstone.

January 16 1960

Rovers delighted their 7,000 fans with a remarkable 6-1 win over St Mirren.

It was a result that was totally unpredictable, especially at half-time when the team was 0-1 down to a good Gerry Baker goal.

St Mirren were last year's Scottish Cup winners, but they were never a great League team and were several places beneath Raith Rovers, whose form this year had been patchy and unpredictable.

The game, like all Scottish games, needed a pitch inspection because there had been a frost overnight, but the temperature had risen a degree or two during the day and the game went ahead.

Just as well for Raith Rovers fans! Inspired by Jim Baxter, they simply turned it on in the second half playing football of the type that Rovers fans had not seen for a very long time.

Alfie Conn scored the first from close in, then Willie Wallace scored with a high lob which seemed to be missing and everyone simply allowed it to sail into the goal.

Then Jim Kerray headed home a Baxter lob, went off injured in doing so, came back five minutes later after treatment and then scored again — all in the space of ten minutes!

Late in the game Willie Wallace scored another two for his own personal hat-trick.

This was great stuff, but then Rovers proceeded to lose three games in a row, including their Scottish Cup tie against Queen's Park to the fury and bewilderment of their fans. They finished up closer to the bottom of the First Division than the top.

January 17 1920

The "roaring twenties" had not really started well in Kirkcaldy with a 0-0 draw with Falkirk then a 0-3 defeat to Celtic, but last week had seen a well-worked and unexpected win at Hampden against Queen's Park.

Today saw another welcome, albeit hardly satisfactory, win over bottom team Hamilton Accies at Stark's Park before a crowd of about 8,000.

The weather was dry enough, but with a very strong wind blowing from the "sea" end of the ground, which threatened to play havoc with the game. Rovers won the toss and chose to play with it, but were very disappointed when half-time was reached and they were only 1-0 ahead.

It was a bizarre own goal from Little when he headed back to goalkeeper White who slipped and fell as the ball trundled apologetically into the net.

It was generally reckoned to be one of Rovers' worst ever goals, and fans feared the worst in the second half as they now faced the cold wind. But this was when Rovers half back line of John Duncan, Willie Porter and Scotland internationalist Harry Anderson took a grip of the game, and showed how it is possible to play well against the wind if you play sensibly and keep the ball on the ground.

Rovers forward line had some "fine combination work" but lacked drive and perhaps understandably in the face of the wind, were reluctant to shoot.

Nevertheless, although it was by no means the best game seen at Stark's Park this season, it was a satisfactory result for manager James Logan and it helped to dispel any fears of relegation.

Willie Porter

January 18 1936

When you are down in football and need every break that you can get, that is precisely the time that you do not get one!

Rovers realised the truth of that today when, floundering about at the bottom of Division Two, they went to Tannadice Park to play Dundee United and lost by the odd goal in seven.

Yet Dundonian Don John, the writer of *The Courier*, was at a loss to explain why Raith Rovers were so lowly placed in the League when they could put on such a spirited performance as this.

The entertainment for the 4,000 fans was remarkably good on a slippery surface, and the fans had good value for their money. United were possibly the more composed side, but Rovers deserved loads of credit for their hard work and their goals were scored by Alec Craigie, George Fulton and Bob Allan. Allan's goal came from the penalty spot,

The Courier felt that Rovers might have been worth another penalty in the very last minute as they mounted a frantic attack on the United goal. But it was not to be, and it was more disappointment for the Rovers fans in what was possibly their worst season since their foundation in 1883.

That night, the news bulletins on the radio ("the wireless" as it was called) contained disturbing news of King George V, who was suffering from "cardiac weakness" and whose condition was "giving cause for concern". He would die at Sandringham on the Monday following this game.

January 19 1924

"Are Raith Rovers a fair weather team?" "Have they hit the slide?" were questions asked by *The Fife Free Press* following a rather disappointing defeat 0-2 today at the hands of Partick Thistle at Firhill.

The conditions were adverse in Glasgow, but "Derwent" felt that Rovers should really have done a great deal better with the fine players that they had at their disposal.

Since New Year they had lost to Clydebank and Hibs and drawn with Dundee, although they had beaten Clyde on New Year's Day.

Today however they simply lacked "bite" and "punch" up front with only Alec James and Bobby Archibald showing any sort of form in the forward line.

The Scottish Cup was now looming and Rovers had Broxburn United, a team that they would normally be expected to beat, at Stark's Park, but with this current run of form, no-one was in any way confident.

This weekend however was all about the political crisis following the hung parliament of the General Election on December 1923. If Asquith and his Liberals could not be prevailed upon to lend their support to the Conservatives of Stanley Baldwin (whom he hated), then there was going to have to be a Labour Government under Ramsay MacDonald.

The Press and the Church were all terrified about that. My goodness, MacDonald might even start giving poor people more money! Not only that, but he had been opposed to the Great War. What were things coming to?

January 20 1906

Just what on earth is happening to Raith Rovers these days?

Since a win in a friendly on January 2 against Kirkcaldy United (much boasted about and celebrated in the town, but basically irrelevant) Rovers had managed to lose three League games in a row to Arthurlie, Ayr and now St Bernard's.

Maybe just as well that they were all away from home; the supporters had been spared the sight of these defeats. Although one could make a few excuses about injuries, nevertheless Rovers had suffered the biggest indignity of all in recent weeks, namely not being mentioned at all in local conversation.

The main topic was of course the General Election, which went on for about a month in 1906, and the resultant Liberal landslide.

The reporter of the local papers must have looked at the sparse crowd of about 1,000 and wondered if he was the only Rovers supporter at Stockbridge today to see them go down 2-5 to the Edinburgh Saints.

Certainly the weather was shocking with wind and rain, as Rovers kicked off against the elements towards the Fettes Row end goal of the Royal Gymnasium ground.

Within a minute they were a goal down, and never really recovered, although a couple of breakaway goals from George Dalrymple and Jock Gray made the half time score of 4-2 look a little more respectable than it should have been.

The second half saw only one further goal from St Bernard's, as the two teams obviously tired in the second half. Rovers could not be faulted for lack of effort, but there was a "want of cohesion" in the forward line, as *The Fife Free Press* put it.

January 21 1961

By any standards, this was a shocker.

Raith travelled to Kilmarnock and came back on the wrong end of a 0-6 thrashing.

No real excuse is possible in terms of a poor pitch or bad weather. It was quite simply that Kilmarnock were a very good side, currently second in the League and beaten finalists in both the Scottish Cup of 1960 and the League Cup of this season.

Well managed by ex-Ranger Willie Waddell, Killlie simply swept Rovers aside that day with Andy Kerr notching a hat-trick.

It was clear after this (if it hadn't been before) that Raith Rovers would soon have to recognise the possibility of relegation.

Players had aged, the installation of floodlights had become something of an obsession to the exclusion of a good team, and Bert Herdman, loyal servant though he had been, was becoming increasingly more and more grumpy, moaning constantly about poor attendances at home games.

Yet the fact was that the team was simply not good enough, as today's result proved. Fortunately there had not been a huge contingent from Kirkcaldy to see this disaster.

Black humour abounded in the town, about Charlie Drummond the goalkeeper having a sore back because of bending down to pick the ball out of the net. In fact Rovers did not need a goalkeeper to stop the ball because the net would do that!

The Kirkcaldy Times and *The Fife Free Press* were very depressed this week.

Stark's Park in the early 1960s. Observe the old "cow shed" in front of the railway

January 22 1910

Fresh from the excitement of the General Election campaign (the Liberal Henry Dalziel had been returned to serve Kirkcaldy on Thursday and would now support Lloyd George in his fight against the House of Lords to get his Budget accepted) football returned again to-day.

It had not been the best of seasons for Rovers in Cup competitions (although they were doing well enough in the Scottish League Division Two) and today was the Scottish Consolation Cup for teams who had not made it to the Scottish Cup itself.

Rovers had local visitors in Hearts of Beath, and a good crowd turned up on a cold frosty day to see Rovers win 3-1 on a heavily sanded pitch.

In a sentence which one would not really expect to read in a newspaper report 100 years later, *The Fife Free Press* says that "The Rovers expected that a new half-back would be on trial, but he failed to turn up" They seem to have given him every chance to do so, for the game kicked off ten minutes late.

Hearts of Beath played a good game, but Rovers were better and by half-time Jimmy Gourlay and Archie McAulay had put the home team 2-0 up.

Gourlay then "piloted the ball into the net with a clever header" (unusual imagery perhaps, but then again everyone in 1910 was beginning to waken up to the possibilities of air travel now that Bleriot had flown across the channel) before the Hearts scored a late consolation goal.

Rovers supporters (about 2,000 of them) left satisfied.

January 23 1965

Raith Rovers didn't often go to Inverness, and after today's result, it was just as well.

Today they crashed out of the Scottish Cup even before the First Division giants entered the competition.

Inverness Caledonian (they would not amalgamate with Inverness Thistle for another 30 years) were a Highland League team and Raith were a middle of the table Second Division team.

Rovers travelled up to Telford Street with high hopes of a win, but the weather was frosty and the pitch was hard. Referee Willie Syme, however, had no hesitation in allowing the game to go ahead.

The pitch was a leveller however and Caledonian went ahead in 28 minutes when Grant swept in a Stephen cross. Pat Gardner levelled before half time however from close in. But then McInnes scored for Caley in the second half, and try as Rovers did, they could not get an equalizer.

This was a major embarrassment for the club as well as a loss of money, but there were two saving graces. One was that not very many supporters had gone to Inverness to see them, and the other was that the death of Sir Winston Churchill the following day meant that very few people were talking about football far a day or two.

All this meant however that the Scottish Cup was once again a source of disappointment for the Rovers, especially when the knock-out came from a team they really should have defeated easily.

January 24 1976

Raith Rovers beat Arbroath 1-0 in the Scottish Cup at Stark's Park thanks to a goal from Gordon Wallace in the middle of the second half.

Rovers' team that day was McDermott, J Brown, W Brown, Urquhart, Taylor, Cooper, Hislop, Wallace, Graham (McFarlane), Hunter and Duncan.

The game was technically a giant killing because Arbroath were in the First Division and Raith were in the Second. (This was the first season of the Three Divisions — Premier, First and Second.)

Rovers had been doing well in the Second Division, and in spite of an awful lot of draws, were still unbeaten. There was a sizeable contingent wearing the maroon of Arbroath and the crowd was an encouraging one of more than 5,000.

The weather for January was actually quite good and Rovers, who would win promotion this year, were well worth their narrow victory.

Shortly after the game, Stark's Park became the centre of national attention because the draw was held there for the next round of the Scottish Cup and would be done by the sons of two famous Raith Rovers stalwarts — Bobby Reid and Andy Leigh.

The draw would not contain Celtic who had gone down to Motherwell that day 2-3 after being 2 goals up, but it would contain Rangers and Aberdeen.

Rangers had beaten East Fife 3-0 that day, while Aberdeen, in a game punctuated by some shocking scenes of hooliganism by their own fans, had beaten Alloa 4-0.

However the Raith boys did not exactly produce a plum tie for their club — Montrose away from home, and yes, you've guessed it, Montrose won!

January 25 1969

Raith Rovers exited the Scottish Cup to last year's winners.

This doesn't sound all that bad but when you add that it was a 0-2 defeat at home and that last year's winners were Dunfermline Athletic, it becomes a lot worse!

The truth is that Rovers held the Pars until half-time but then were outplayed by them, the goals being scored by men with Rovers connections in the past and future — Pat Gardner who scored with a header from a Lunn cross, and then Bertie Paton added another as time began to run out on Rovers.

The day was pleasant enough, and the crowd was a respectable one of about 11,000. This being 1969, there was a certain amount of trouble threatened (fortunately only threatened, not actually delivered) by the less academically able young men of both towns.

The Pars supporters seemed to wish Raith Rovers a Happy Birthday. Closer attention to the words, however, indicated that it was "Relegation To You" that they were singing in the old Railway Stand.

They didn't get their wish, at least not this year, but this game was the catalyst for the removal of Tommy Walker from the Manager's Chair.

He was given the Secretary's job as a sop, but effectively he was too old for the job. He had been a great player and then Manager for Hearts a decade or so previously, but was a lot less successful with Raith Rovers. He would be replaced by Jimmy Millar, one time of Rangers.

Raith Rovers v Third Lanark 1950. Observe the rickety railway stand

January 26 1952

Hibs, who would win the Scottish League this season, came to Kirkcaldy to play in the Scottish Cup.

A heavy fall of snow made the game problematic, but an army of volunteers helped to clear the pitch and the game went ahead, albeit in difficult conditions on a very cold but bright winter's day.

The game ended 0-0, which was a lot better than Rovers might have expected, given that they had been on the wrong end of a 0-5 hammering in December from Hibs.

What makes this game memorable is that it was captured on film by Pathé News and is still available on You Tube.

It makes for fascinating viewing, although perhaps the game itself is not quite as exciting as the Pathé commentator makes it out to be!

Nevertheless, there are fascinating shots of the snow being cleared off the pitch, the clearly slippery pitch, the huge crowd at one point swaying behind the Beveridge Park end of the ground (with no shelter and no Balwearie High School!), a good view of the old shed in front of the railway advertising the *Edinburgh Evening News*, and good shots of Willie McNaught, Andy Young, Eddie Kelly and Johnny Maule, not to mention the great Gordon Smith and Eddie Turnbull of Hibs.

This was shown in a Kirkcaldy cinema later that week, by which time Raith had drawn yet again 0-0 with Hibs in the Easter Road replay before eventually beating them in a third game at Tynecastle.

January 27 1974

Rovers played their first ever game on a Sunday.

The country and its Government under the Conservative Prime Minister Edward Heath was in crisis with a Miners' Strike and a Three-Day Week being worked by industry with half the country working on Monday-Wednesday and the other half working Thursday-Saturday.

As attendances were likely to be lower on a Saturday, Sunday football was allowed with an early kick-off so that they would not need floodlights and waste electricity.

Some religious groups objected, but the time when the Churches had any influence over Governments had now long gone.

Therefore Raith Rovers' Scottish Cup game against Morton went ahead at Stark's Park before a healthy crowd of 5,209.

Joe Baker and Malcolm Robertson (with a penalty kick) scored for Second Division Raith Rovers but First Division Morton fought back to equalise late in the game.

It was odd to go to Stark's Park on a Sunday, and there were indeed one or two people there with a billboard protesting at people profaning the Sabbath in this way, but it was a losing cause.

So too was Raith Rovers this year, as far as the Scottish Cup was concerned, for after another drawn game at Cappielow on Tuesday, a third game had to be held next Sunday at Tynecastle and Morton won.

Not long after this, the Government was compelled to call a General Election for February 28, and a minority Labour Government took over.

Bobby Reid

January 28 1967

This was the day immortalised in the history of Scottish football by the defeat of Rangers at Berwick, but Raith Rovers supporters were no less upset by their team's exit from the Scottish Cup.

In our case, it was a heart-breaking last-minute defeat at Hampden Park, of all places, to Queen's Park who had performed a similar deed seven years ago.

It was all the sadder for the Rovers fans in the 3,000 crowd for they had a good team with goalkeeper Bobby Reid, Bobby Evans, Ian Porterfield, Pat Gardner and Gordon Wallace — indeed, they would achieve promotion from the Second Division this year.

Pat Gardner and Jocky Richardson scored for Raith Rovers, but the game seemed to be drifting towards a draw and a Stark's Park replay (by no means the worst scenario in the world, for replays meant money) when Queen's Park scored with a weird goal which seemed to catch Bobby Reid unawares, and was put down to the infamous and capricious Hampden breeze.

But it was simply too bad for Raith Rovers, who were never a great Scottish Cup team, although they had reached the semi-final four times since World War II.

There was an air of unreality about it, though, exiting the Scottish Cup at an empty Hampden to a team who were lower down the League than they were.

And when someone said that Berwick had beaten Rangers, we really thought it was an Alice in Wonderland existence. Even worse, East Fife had beaten Motherwell as well!

January 29 1916

A young and unexperienced Raith side did themselves proud at Tynecastle in extenuating circumstances where it was difficult to get a side together as all sort of last minute snags involving transport made themselves manifest.

To-day's game kicked off at 2.30 pm with about 6,000 spectators present, but after half time there were about 8,000 or 9,000 there, something that says a great deal about the determination of fans to see at least some football in the awful days of the Great War. The additional spectators included some from a late running train from Kirkcaldy.

Hearts of course had enlisted virtually to a man earlier in the war in a brave although possibly foolish move, and were clearly struggling to get a team worthy of the name "Hearts". William Wilson, for example, couldn't get away from his military duties.

Rovers on the other hand had a certain amount of stability, manager John Richardson being able to field the same team for two games in a row (unusual for the times!) but they were all so obviously young lads, in some cases not old enough for military service.

Welsh scored for Hearts but then in a series of shots at the Hearts goal - "a fierce fusillade" - Willie Birrell scored Rovers first ever goal at Tynecastle since they had joined the First Division.

A win was even an outside possibility, but it was Hearts who scored the winner through Graham. The "young Fifers" did well however in what was a fine game of football in difficult circumstances.

What would life be like when conscription kicked in?

January 30 1960

Any hopes that this might at last be Raith Rovers' season in the Scottish Cup were cruelly dashed today at Hampden when the team went out at the first time of asking to Second Division Queen' Park.

It had seemed to be good draw at the time, for Rovers were respectable, at least, in the First Division. Bert Herdman, the Manager. apparently told his players that they were getting a "trial run" at Hampden in preparation for the final in a few months' time!

It was certainly an experience to play at Hampden but the day was absolutely foul with showers of rain and sleet, so much so that the reporter of *The Evening Times* informs us that there was absolutely no-one on the terracing, those who were there having taken shelter under what little there was of the overhang of the old North Stand.

It may be that Rovers took this game too lightly, or there was maybe also the undeniable fact that men like McNaught and Young were now ageing. Leigh had now lost his place to a talented but temperamental youngster called Jim Baxter, and generally speaking, the form of the team was rather unpredictable.

Today a man called Charlie Church scored before half time and "Junior" Omand scored in the second half. Rovers, frankly, never looked like scoring and the small Kirkcaldy contingent in the 2,742 crowd went home very unhappy.

The loss of revenue was considerable, and the loss of prestige even more wounding. It always hurt to lose to Amateurs!

January 31 1951

Raith Rovers made it far more comfortably than the 1-0 score line would have suggested to the next round of the Scottish Cup.

The opposition were Partick Thistle and this was a Wednesday afternoon replay after a 1-1 draw at Firhill on the Saturday.

The crowd was a very respectable 12,000 on a reasonable day for the end of January. Wednesday was Kirkcaldy's half day. In any case, the crowd swelled soon after half time when the schools closed and the pupils from Kirkcaldy High School sprinted or cycled along from the school (where Fife College is now) to see what was left of the game.

The wonder was that it took so long for Rovers to score for they were "all over them" as the phrase went, with Johnny Maule outstanding, but found Thistle goalkeeper Tommy Ledgerwood in inspired form.

The fear began to grow that Rovers might never find the net and that Thistle would run up and score, but then in the 75th minute Les Murray crossed for Andy Young, playing in the centre today, to shoot straight at Ledgerwood but then to net with the rebound.

Partick Thistle, managed by ex-Ranger Davie Meiklejohn, now redoubled their efforts and might have taken the game to extra time, but at the very end, they had a double miss when Stott miskicked with the goal more or less at his mercy, and then Crawford came rushing in and put the ball over the bar.

It was a relieved but happy crowd of Rovers supporters who made their way home that day.

February

February 1 1922

Although Rovers' League form this year had been very impressive, this was a sad day for the club.

They were knocked out of the Scottish Cup by Clyde at Shawfield in this Wednesday afternoon replay. Rovers were the better team in the first game at Stark's Park, but failed to clinch victory and a replay was necessary.

A crowd of 25,000 were attracted to Shawfield on a fine almost spring-like afternoon in Glasgow, and Rovers did not lack support either.

The Fife Free Press was disappointed not so much by the defeat as by the fact that neither team reproduced the form that they had shown on Saturday.

The only goal of the game came some ten minutes from the interval when, bizarrely, a header from Thomson which looked as it was going to be saved by goalkeeper Brown suddenly swerved and hit the post before entering the net.

Rovers tried hard in the second half. Collier came close in the early part of the second half, but the forwards, although better than their Clyde counterparts, seemed bereft of shooting power.

It was a very disappointed bunch of Rovers fans who arrived home at the station that night to be met by the curious and the excited who had no other way in 1922 of finding out the score and the details of the game than by asking spectators.

Otherwise they would have had to wait until the next morning's newspapers. Once again, the Scottish Cup was a disappointment for the Rovers.

February 2 1991

Jimmy Nicholl today made his playing debut for Raith Rovers at Station Park, Forfar.

He had been appointed Manager last November, and it was fair to say that there had not been as yet any great improvement in the standard of play.

Yet there was something likeable about the Irishman and certainly a great knowledge of the game from which it was believed would come great things.

He had always said that he intended to keep playing, but had not done so until today when injuries to other members of the team compelled him to play himself at right back.

It was the time of the First Gulf War with its Scud missiles and so on, and supporters said that Raith got "scudded" every week! This game was no exception, and Forfar (not a bad side in 1991) duly won 3-1 in front of a crowd of 821.

Rovers supporters were not many that day, but those who were there were duly impressed by Nicholl who was called "gaffer" by all his players.

One of the advantages of watching a game at Forfar's ground is that you can more or less hear everything that the players say to one another!

So it was an unhappy experience for Rovers players and fans, but as they often say, the darkest time is often immediately before the dawn and Rovers slowly began to get it together, beating Falkirk, Brechin and Partick Thistle in their next few games.

Peter Hodge

February 3 1912

Having drawn last week in Kirkcaldy in the Scottish Cup, Rovers travelled to Airdrie "under wintry auspices" for the replay, and lost 1-3.

Rovers lost two quick goals in the first 20 minutes before the Special train for Kirkcaldy arrived containing 500 fans.

But "news of their pets [sic] being two goals down proved a knock-out blow to them and they failed to signal their appearance by any outburst of enthusiasm".

Indeed Rovers went another goal down, and although in the second half with the wind and the snow behind them, they pulled one back through Jimmy Gourlay, Rovers were once again out of the Scottish Cup.

But for a spell, they dabbled with the idea of protesting about Dan Rafferty, one of the Airdrie players "for a close-season infringement" which presumably means that he played illegally for some other club.

The protest was lodged by Manager Hodge to Referee Mr Murray at the end of the game, but the Directors thought better of it and withdrew the protest a few days later to allow Airdrie to meet Lanarkshire rivals Motherwell in the next round.

This was Rovers' second year in the First Division, and they were not doing particularly well, so supporters reckoned that a Scottish Cup exit might be a blessing in disguise, the better to allow them to concentrate on the League.

In the meantime people were talking more and more about a new transatlantic liner that was soon to be launched, called the *Titanic*.

February 4 1922

Rovers got over their disappointment of exiting the Scottish Cup on Wednesday by beating Clydebank 3-0 away from home at Yoker and thus maintaining their impressive League form.

They did this however without left half Will Collier, for "Wily Will" as he was called, was away in Wrexham playing for Scotland against Wales.

This was of course a great honour for Collier and indeed for Raith Rovers. He was not the only man with Rovers connections playing for Scotland; Sandy Archibald, ex Rovers player and future Manager, was playing as well.

The result was a disappointment because Scotland lost 1-2 to the home side. The circumstances were exceptional however for Scotland had travelled down on the Friday in steadily worsening conditions, and they arrived at the Wrexham ground on the Saturday to discover it covered in snow.

The game might have been postponed if it hadn't been an International, but Mr Ward, the referee, to his credit, was out there helping everyone to shovel the snow off the pitch, his considerations influenced perhaps by a train load of "fierce looking Caledonians" arriving to see the game more or less at kick-off time, and goodness knows what they might have done if the game had been off.

About 10,000, most of them Scots, watched the game in intermittent snow. The ball was described as a "Xmas pudding covered in white sauce" by the journalist of *The Daily Herald*, and Wales won 2-1.

Collier hardly distinguished himself, but neither did anyone else, and it was a shame that this would be his only cap. He was a good enough player to get another go in better conditions.

February 5 1955

Raith fans travelled more in hope than in anticipation to Greenock today for this Scottish Cup tie; they returned with bigger smiles on their faces than they had had for some time.

Rovers won 3-1 to earn themselves a trip to Shawfield to play Clyde in the next round.

Morton were still a Second Division club in 1955, but one of the more successful ones. They did have a great Scottish Cup tradition, having won it in 1922 and having been in the final as recently as 1948.

Rovers had not had a great January. They had beaten East Fife on New Year's Day, but had since lost three times and had a certain amount of bad luck, with postponements (which are never good for the side), and injuries, particularly to Willie McNaught, who had now been out since early December.

Ernie Copland however returned today. It was Ernie who scored a brilliant hat-trick, which silenced his critics. He had been off-form of late, but that did not excuse the abuse he had been getting from some so called fans. However, Ernie duly shut them up today!

The Courier also singles out left winger Davie Duncan for some fine play and Jackie Stewart at inside right. It was a good day for the Rovers and their supporters, but I don't really suppose that it is possible to go to Greenock in early February without experiencing a little rain! In this respect, there was a certain predictability!

February 6 1982

Raith gave their fans a certain hope that all might not yet be entirely lost from this disastrous season with a 3-2 win at East End Park, Dunfermline.

If it did nothing else, it cheered up the Raith fans in the somewhat disappointing crowd of 2,053.

Neither team was exactly vintage in comparison with what had gone before with, in particular, the great days of Dunfermline in the 1960s looking a very distant memory indeed.

Rovers were still struggling with their credibility problem after the way that promotion had been thrown away last year. The conditions overhead were not all that bad, but there had been a great deal of rain that week and the pitch was cutting up badly.

In point of fact, as often happens with two mediocre teams, a good game of football was served up with Ford, Houston and Gibson scoring the goals for Rovers, and the Pars were never entirely out of it, arguing furiously about one or two refereeing decisions which might have made all the difference.

At the end of this game, however, Dunfermline were ninth and Raith Rovers tenth in the 14 team First Division, something that seemed to indicate that although both teams were safe from relegation, neither was going to make any great impact on the promotion race either.

As the crowd made their way home through the less than totally congested streets, it was generally felt that the Kingdom of Fife deserved a little better than this.

February 7 1914

In what was generally regarded as their greatest performance to date, Raith Rovers beat Hearts 2-0 in the Scottish Cup before 26,000 people at Stark's Park, a record attendance.

Having reached the final of the Scottish Cup last year, the club and the town had clearly been bitten by the "Scottish Cup" bug.

Streets round Stark's Park were sealed off and no horse drawn or motorised vehicles were allowed, although an exception was made when the police were told that a woman was giving birth in a house in Pratt Street and the doctor's car was allowed! (The baby born that day told me that story 80 years later!).

Hearts were a great attraction, having already won the Scottish Cup, their most recent triumph being in 1906, and Edinburgh being close to Kirkcaldy, they were able to bring a fairly large support, some of them holding up a huge heart on which was inscribed "Don't lose this!"

The Courier was ecstatic about Rovers' performance, talking about the "Greatest Triumph of Their Career" and singling out Fred Martin, "the whole hearted leader of the van", who scored the two goals.

The second goal was a great one, and it caused even Kirkcaldy's Provost, the recently appointed Governor General of Australia, to stand up and wave his handkerchief in the air. This was Sir Ronald Crawford Munro Ferguson, Viscount Novar.

At one point a boy was removed from the crowd for his own safety by the constable, The crowd booed, thinking that the child was being arrested! It was a day that would live long in the minds of those who were there.

February 7 1914

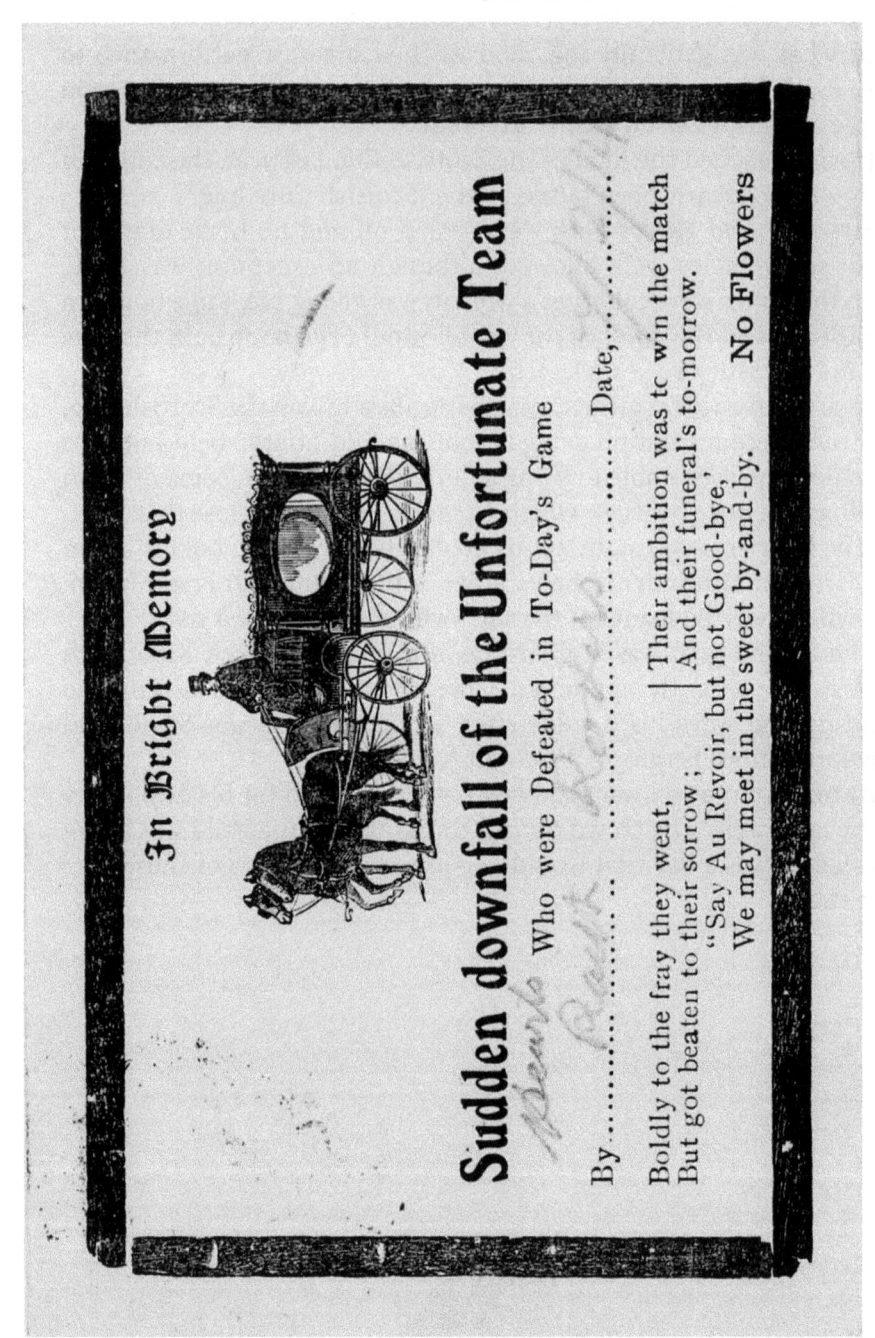

A mock death card signifying the demise of Hearts in 1914. Following the famous death notice of English cricket and the Ashes being taken to Australia in 1880, such things were common

February 8 1996

Snow was covering most of Fife when it was announced that Jimmy Nicholl was leaving Raith Rovers to go to Millwall.

Whatever possessed him to go there no-one can say — only he can answer that question — but if he had bided his time he might have found himself a better club.

Be that as it may, this brought an end to Jimmy's first tenure as Manager of Raith Rovers in which he gave Rovers fans at least as much success as they had enjoyed in the 1920s under James Logan and the 1950s under Bert Herdman.

His big achievement was the winning of the Scottish League Cup in 1994 (still the club's only national trophy against all the big clubs since 1883). At least as impressive as that was the winning of the First Division in 1993, thereby killing the myth which had persisted since the awful spring of 1981 that the club would refuse promotion and even try to avoid it by dropping points!

In addition there was the time when his Raith Rovers team were beating Bayern Munich at half time and he enjoyed the thought that they would all get a "good rollicking" from their Manager!

He would return for a spell between 1997 and 1999 in which he was a lot less successful.

It would be true to say that Jimmy's managerial success has not been replicated anywhere other than in his first spell at Raith Rovers.

It was a shame that he went on this day, for it was a watershed in the club's fortunes. Basically, they have never really recovered.

February 9 1921

Raith Rovers in 1921. Back Row: Brown, Raeburn, Moyes, Jennings, Collier, Brown (trainer); Front Row: T Duncan, J Duncan, Inglis, Morris, Archibald, Bauld. This photograph was taken at Ibrox on February 9 1921, a Wednesday afternoon which possibly explains the poor crowd.

February 9 1952

Rovers played their second game in a week at Tynecastle.

They had defeated Hibs there in a second replay on Monday, and now they were back to play Hearts in the next round.

But in between both visits, the nation had been plunged into mourning with the death of the much respected King George VI. His daughter Elizabeth was now Queen, having been flown back from Kenya.

It was decided however that the normal football programme should go ahead with everyone wearing black arm bands and with a minute of silence for the late monarch. 47,152, the biggest crowd of the day, attended and sang "Abide With Me" before the start.

The Rovers fans, however, were a little disappointed with the performance of their team, who seemed stale and out of sorts after their sterling efforts against Hibs, with wing halves Andy Young and Andy Leigh in particular struggling against Hearts' nippy forward line.

Yet with a bit of hard work they were defending well and looking good for another replay at Stark's in midweek (with cynics naturally noting that there would be a certain pecuniary gain if that happened).

Late in the game the ball cannoned in off the knee of the luckless Andy Young. He simply could not avoid it, and Rovers did not have enough time or energy to mount a fightback.

So Rovers exited the Scottish Cup (never exactly their favourite competition) once again.

February 10 1951

12,000 were at Stark's Park today for the rare visit of "C" Division Brechin City in the Scottish Cup.

Brechin felt that they had been badly treated after the Second World War when the Leagues were reformed with two Divisions of 16, and a "C" Division which included some reserve teams, and from which promotion was difficult.

The weather was good, and the home crowd left happy after a 5-2 win.

Some optimists were convinced that this year was at last going to be Rovers year in the Scottish Cup, a tournament in which they had been less than totally successful since their appearance in the final in 1913.

Yet the part-timers from Angus whose big moment this was put up a brave fight, and it was generally agreed that they would not be out of place in Division "B".

Indeed it took a couple of late Johnny Maule goals to finally settle the issue. Les Murray and Alan Collins had scored for Rovers in the first half to make it 2-1 at half-time; Brechin scored again on the 60th minute mark to make things very dodgy indeed for the home side before Willie Penman headed a third.

Even then the Brechin side did not capitulate until they tired on the heavy pitch in the latter stages. Rangers were knocked out of the Cup by Hibs that day, and Rovers would be rewarded with an away game at Dens Park, Dundee in the next round.

February 11 1950

"Bizarre" and "Freak" were some of the words heard to describe Raith Rovers 3-2 win over Clyde at Stark's Park today in the Scottish Cup.

It also could not possibly be denied that Raith Rovers played very badly, deserved to lose and that Clyde (last year's Cup finalists) were unlucky to be denied at least a replay.

The wintry conditions were worse in Glasgow where the Third Lanark v Celtic game was postponed at short notice, provoking crowd disturbances.

Played in rain and sleet, Rovers managed to win this game 3-2 without scoring a single goal, as all their goals were own goals!

There was one good goal from Alfie Ackerman of Clyde from about 30 yards. Clyde's other goal came from a slack Harry Colville back pass, which was immediately replied to by Rovers in the shape of an own goal from Dudley Milligan of Clyde. (That poor man was also carried off before half time).

It was 2-1 for Clyde half way through the second half until full back Frank Mennie had the double misfortune to put the ball through his own goal twice. To a certain extent, one could blame the slippery conditions for all this, but the 13,180 crowd didn't really care, because Rovers were now in the Scottish Cup quarter final to face Rangers.

A feature of this game was the sight of the two candidates for the General Election (to be held on February 23), Tom Hubbard of Labour and Baillie Robert Bell of the Conservatives sitting together as guests of the club watching the game.

They were good friends and both supporters of Raith Rovers who, they both agreed, were very lucky to get through this game!

Raith Rovers 1937/38. Observe the club linesman with his flag

February 12 1938

Rovers advanced in the Scottish Cup by beating Edinburgh City by the astonishing score of 9-2 today at Stark's Park.

This was a previous incarnation of Edinburgh City, and they are not the team that bears that name today.

They played at New Powderhall, then Marine Gardens and then City Park. They were an Amateur side and had done very well to reach this stage of the Scottish Cup.

They played in all white today at Stark's Park but were unfortunate in two respects. One was that they ran up against the Raith Rovers steamroller which would win the Scottish League Second Division very comfortably. The other was that they had to play the first half against the wind, which was blowing from the Beveridge Park end of the ground.

In fact they were only three goals down at half time, and when MacLeod pulled one back for Edinburgh City, it looked as if there might be a comeback, but Norman Haywood scored soon after, and then Rovers began to show their mettle by playing well against the wind, scoring more or less at will.

Possibly for reasons of humanity, they stopped at nine, not quite reaching double figures, and even Edinburgh City's second goal was an own goal scored by full back John Smith — a goal which raised a cheer from the 7,400 crowd.

Haywood scored his fifth hat-trick of the season, John Whitelaw also got a hat-trick, and the other goals were scored by Alex Glen, Tommy Gilmour and the very impressive youngster from St Andrews called Francis Joyner.

It was an easy win, and Rovers were rewarded with a trip to First Division Partick Thistle in the next round.

February 13 1956

13,280 were at Stark's Park this Monday afternoon to see Raith Rovers beat Hibs 3-1 in the Scottish Cup 5th Round replay and go through to the quarter final of the competition.

The first game had been called off because of weather and then last Wednesday at Easter Road had become Rovers' first competitive game to be played under floodlights.

It had been a 1-1 draw and so all roads led to Stark's Park this afternoon, including a few illegal ones as people took afternoons off their work and school!

The crowd might easily have been doubled if the game could have been played in the evening, so maybe a few people wondered if the installation of floodlights at Stark's Park might not be all that bad an idea.

Hibs floodlights had been very impressive, possibly a little more so than their team who had clearly peaked from their zenith of a few years ago. Of the Famous Five forward line, only three — Reilly, Turnbull and Ormond were playing that day.

Rovers delighted their fans with a great first half display, and went in at half-time leading 2-0 with good goals by Jimmy McEwan and Ernie Copland.

Early in the second half, Copland scored again, and then, although Hibs pulled one back from Lawrie Reilly, they made no further impact on the game as the mighty half back line of Young, McNaught and Leigh, not without cause called "burglar proof", maintained a stranglehold over proceedings, and Rovers were through to play Queen's Park in the quarter final.

February 14 1942

St Valentine's Day this may have been, but the news was dominated by what was happening in the Far East with Singapore on the point of collapse. It would surrender the following day on Sunday 15. Unbelievable British incompetence and arrogance included, for example, having all the defensive guns facing the sea and not the interior of the peninsula!

It was therefore an anxious time for the relatives of the many Kirkcaldy men in the Singapore garrison for whom escape was not a possibility and the horrors of a Japanese POW camp awaited.

However there was a little relief at Stark's Park today when Rovers beat Aberdeen 2-1 to complete a double over the Dons in the North Eastern League.

There was also a touch of sadness in the minute's silence for the memory of the respected James Bogie, one time Chairman of Raith Rovers and Treasurer of the SFA.

Willie Reekie, the manager, had done his usual brilliant job to put a team together in the most difficult of circumstances and he was rewarded by two headed second half goals from Jacky Stewart and Willie McNaught, men who would play a significant part in Rovers post-war history.

A sign of the times was that Aberdeen's consolation goal (a good one) was scored by AN Other, meaning either a junior whom they had picked up on the day of the game or someone from another club unofficially "guesting" for Aberdeen! It would be nice to have known his name or who we was!

February 14 1976

Director and retired goalkeeper Bobby Reid answers the call at Montrose on February 14 1976

February 15 1997

For the first time for a few years, Raith Rovers went to Glebe Park, Brechin for a Scottish Cup tie.

Brechin CITY often seems a misnomer for a fairly small, couthy Angus town, but they are of course correct in that, like Elgin, they do have a cathedral and are therefore entitled to call themselves that.

At one point, they had one of the best cricket teams in Scotland, but no-one would make that claim about their footballers.

The weather was cold but bright, and it was nice to be back in Brechin and see the changes that an ambitious management had made to the ground.

Interesting that it still had the hedge running down the side of the park! Rovers took a good support with them, and they were rewarded with a very good performance by the team and a spirited fight by Brechin.

Iain Munro was now Manager and it would be fair to say that he was struggling to keep Raith in the Premier League with the clear impression that the glory days were evaporating almost as soon as they had arrived.

Today however in the Brechin sunshine was a tonic, because Rovers scored twice through Steve Kirk and Soren Andersen (commonly nicknamed "the Viking" because of his Norse origins) and advanced to the next round where they would be rewarded with a trip to Falkirk.

They were fated to lose there, and Iain Munro would not be able to avoid relegation this year either!

February 16 1985

Big days did not come very often to Stark's Park in the 1980s, a decade which was pretty dreadful for the club and its supporters, but today Aberdeen had been drawn at Stark's Park in the Scottish Cup.

Aberdeen, under Alex Ferguson, had successfully mounted and sustained a challenge to the Old Firm, and were currently both the Scottish League Champions and the Scottish Cup holders.

The success was possibly not entirely unconnected with North Sea Oil which had made Aberdeen a very rich city indeed, but it was certainly a golden era for the club whose supporters had seen and would see in the future a fair amount of heartbreaks.

Not entirely unlike Raith Rovers, in fact. Today the kick-off had to be delayed by five minutes to allow the crowd in, and there looked to be well over 10,000 in the ground.

It was a bright but still cold day with the pitch possibly not giving as firm a grip as the players would have liked. Rovers started well but it was the Dons who went ahead on the 30 minute mark when Frank McDougall (a sometimes under-rated player) scored with a spectacular overhead kick.

The other two goals of the game were both penalties, one awarded to Rovers when Willie Miller handled in the box. Willie was booked (and he was not happy about it!) but Smith converted.

That was the score at half time but two minutes into the second half Donald Urquhart fouled Peter Weir and Frank McDougall converted for his second goal of the game. There was no further scoring, but with a bit of luck, Rovers might have got an equaliser.

Frank Connor, one of Raith's better managers.

February 17 1987

The news that Frank Connor was in negotiation with a view to signing Gordon Dalziel from East Stirlingshire probably meant very little to the supporters of Raith Rovers who were far more interested in their forthcoming Scottish Cup tie with Peterhead.

Dalziel's name was vaguely familiar, for he had played a season or two for Rangers, (winning a League Cup medal in 1981) then had made the disastrous decision to try Manchester City, then Partick Thistle, and now he was on a month to month contract with East Stirlingshire.

Connor however saw something in Dalziel and signed him on today (he was ineligible to play in the Cup ties so it was February 28 before he could make his debut) until the end of the season and might help Rovers to gain promotion from the Second Division.

It was from such inauspicious beginnings that the Raith Rovers career of the man who scored 170 goals was launched. For some reason, he took to Stark's Park a great deal better than his other ports of call and very soon he was instrumental in getting Rovers to the First Division, then in 1993 to the Premier Division and of course it was he who scored the late equaliser in the League Cup final of 1994.

He was more or less a one-team man, and of course long after his playing career was over, he returned as Manager for a spell in which he sometimes appeared to be the only ray of sanity in a crazy house!

Gordon Dalziel

February 18 2017

Is there a chance, the Raith Rovers supporters asked themselves, that the corner may be turned with the new manager?

The last point they gained before today was against Hibs at Easter Road on Christmas Eve, and today they earned another point against the same opposition, but it is fair to say that a lot of water had passed under the bridge since Christmas, much of it muddy and dirty.

The form had been terrible with painful defeats from Dunfermline and Falkirk early in the New Year, and no improvement thereafter. But under new manager John Hughes, Rovers fought well today to gain another point before 4,172 fans, most of them supporting Hibs.

Ryan Stevenson with a crisp half-volley from 22 yards opened the scoring in 52 minutes for Rovers, while Jason Cummings equalised with a free kick on the hour mark. It was a fair performance from Raith and new manager John Hughes pronounced himself satisfied with the point.

Neil Lennon, on the other hand, the manager of Hibs, was far from happy and said that his side, who had appeared in yellow today, were wearing the right colour of jersey for it was a gutless performance. It was not the first nor the last time that Neil would publicly denounce his players — but they did win the League at the end of the season.

It was just as well that he was not the manager of Raith Rovers!

February 19 1938

The war in Spain was going from bad to worse for the Republican Government. All of Europe was looking at Germany with fear and apprehension.

Rovers, now on an increased bonus and playing with tremendous elan, gave their 6,000 supporters a lot to be happy about with a 7-0 hammering of Dumbarton at Stark's Park.

Since the New Year, they had put eight past East Stirlingshire, six past Cowdenbeath, nine past Edinburgh City.

Today's performance with a hat-trick each from Norman Haywood and Tommy Gilmour was quite phenomenal with most of the goals coming in a bewildering spell in the second half.

The Courier talks about "brilliant, incisive football, the likes of which has not been seen at Stark's Park this season" but even that was an under-statement, for there would have been many seasons since anyone saw a goal like one of Tommy Gilmour's when he ran past four defenders before hammering home.

John Whitelaw scored the other one apart from those of the two hat-tricksters. It now seemed difficult to imagine anyone getting the better of Raith Rovers and preventing them re-joining next year's First Division, but the immediate cause of concern was the Scottish Cup game at Partick Thistle next week.

It would be a good indication to how they could cope with the First Division, for those who were never satisfied kept pointing out that this was "only" the Second Division! Maybe so, but it was fantastic entertainment!

February 20 1892

"No small interest" says *The Fife Free Press* "was attached to this fixture at Stark's Park".

It was indeed a remarkable game in the Midland League between Raith Rovers and Camelon and it finished with the astonishing score of 5-5.

"The renewal of winter conditions" postponed quite a few other games, but as both teams had such a backlog of fixtures, it was decided to go ahead with this one, even though in places the snow was about 3 inches deep on Stark's Park.

No attempt seems to have been made to clear the pitch with brushes or spades, even though there was a "goodly" turnout of spectators who might have been able to help.

Rovers were three men short (presumably because of travel difficulties) but managed to recruit two younger men from the second string and a veteran called Nelson at right back.

Very soon it became obvious the conditions were indeed "antagonistic to good play" and that "snow would nullify all efforts at the finer points of the game".

It was actually not bad entertainment - 4-4 at half time and then 5-5 at full time but the writer thinks that in better conditions, Camelon might have won.

The Fife Free Press does not hold back about some players: "Clunie certainly did not distinguish himself in the Rovers goal, and one or two of the points scored against him were rather soft" (He may however have been "benumbed" by the cold). Dall, on the other hand "seemed to take matters rather easy".

February 21 1920

1920 was before the days of penalty shoot-outs to decide Cup ties.

Rovers' game in the previous round had gone as far as four games before Rovers got the better of East Stirlingshire; it was only completed on the Thursday before this game took place.

But today a massive crowd of 20,000 were at Stark's Park to see the next round against Morton, and it was yet another draw.

It was of course not unheard of for people to assume that all these drawn Cup ties were "fixed" for another big gate, but anyone who saw the sheer effort that went into this game against Morton would not have been of that persuasion.

Rovers should have won, and would have done so if their forwards had shot better, particularly if they had shot first time oftener (in the opinion of the writer of *The Courier*).

Jimmy Bauldie scored in the first minute for the home side, and after Morton equalised, they went ahead in the second half when Bauldie was brought down in the box, and Willie Birrell converted.

The game finished in a controversial fashion. Morton managed to score an equalizer when Rovers' goalkeeper Jimmy Dickson was injured and the referee really should have stopped the game.

But Rovers only had themselves to blame, and could have finished the game off on several occasions. But it was Cappielow on Wednesday afternoon, where a tired Rovers side subsided meekly 0-3 before a much fresher home side.

February 22 1908

Foul weather ruined what might have been one of the greatest days of Rovers' history so far.

Having beaten Partick Thistle in the previous round, Second Division Rovers found the mighty Celtic coming to town to play them in the next round.

Celtic had won both the League and the Cup last season and were possibly the best team in the world at this point.

The great Jimmy Quinn and captain James Hay were out injured, but all the rest were there as they disembarked from the train that lunch time where they found a huge crowd of local supporters to greet them.

Raith had commissioned the Local Trades Band to play "Songs of Ireland" for the benefit of Celtic and their fans, but the wind and rain compelled the musicians to give up!

Acting captain of Celtic "Sunny Jim" Young won the toss and chose to defend the north goal (the Beveridge Park end) and therefore had the strong wind and rain at their backs.

The game was therefore over by half time when Kivlichan scored once and McMenemy twice. Rovers fought gallantly in the second half when they had the benefit of the conditions but to no avail.

There was consolation however in the "gate" money of £282 and the 12,000 crowd (which would have been more on a better day) was possibly "as big a crowd as the enclosure had ever seen".

Raith Rovers also had the consolation of winning the Scottish League Second Division that year, while Celtic won every competition they entered.

February 23 1924

A curious sort of a day for Raith Rovers!

Doing well in the First Division, Raith found themselves drawn at home against Second Division St Bernard's (a now defunct team who played in Edinburgh) in the last 16 of the Scottish Cup.

It looked a comfortable win, so comfortable, in fact that, according to the father of one of the players, the Directors were refusing to pay a bonus for a win.

The players, therefore, decided that this game was going to be a draw, and that the "bonus" would come when they had to play the replay in Edinburgh the following week.

Amazingly, the information from this source seemed to be turning out to be correct, for some players looked lethargic and a barrow load of chances was missed.

But if the game was to be a "fix", no-one seemed to have told the Edinburgh men. Late in the game, taking advantage of a slack pass back from Dave Morris, Young scored (breaking his wrist in the process, incidentally) and the incredulous St Bernard's were 1-0 up.

They now barricaded their goal and held out, until in a "cemetery silence" the referee blew for full time.

So what happened here?

Was it a case of a "fix" going disastrously wrong?

Or was it simply a case of St Bernard's having a good day and Rovers a bad one?

Either way, Rovers, their credibility now seriously impaired whether through footballing incompetence or corruption, never recovered for a long time.

Indeed it was the beginning of the end of Logan's great team.

February 24 1923

About 30,000 were at Celtic Park to see the intriguing cup-tie between Raith Rovers and Celtic.

Even in the 1920's, there was talk about who was to be the "third force" in Scottish football to challenge Rangers and Celtic.

Since the Great War, Rangers had done better than Celtic, but had a major problem with the Scottish Cup, whereas Celtic, the better team before and during the War seemed to be on the decline. But no-one else seemed able to challenge on a permanent basis.

Partick Thistle, Kilmarnock and Morton had all won the Scottish Cup since the War, but the team that played consistently well without any great reward for their efforts was Raith Rovers of Kirkcaldy.

Today they had real hard luck against Celtic with Dave Morris winning a few reluctant ripples of applause and admiration for his heading and tackling and in particular his ability to subdue the hitherto all conquering Joe Cassidy.

Morris had been chosen ahead of Celtic's Willie Cringan to play for Scotland against Ireland next week, and the Celtic crowd saw why today.

Unfortunately, though, Rovers lost by 0-1 through an own goal scored when Rovers' David Moyes (no relation to a well-known manager a hundred years later!) and Celtic's Adam McLean went for the same ball and the ball bounced off Moyes' leg.

It was a bitter pill to swallow because Rovers were worth at least a replay, a point conceded in the Glasgow newspapers.

February 25 1961

League form had been atrocious of late.

Rovers had lost their last four games and were now in deep relegation bother.

Still, a crowd of 19,633 came to Stark's Park today to see Celtic in the Scottish Cup. The team was much changed, and took a long time to settle with the big crowd and the big occasion.

Not all of the Celtic support were a credit to their club and on at least two occasions a bottle was hurled from the crowd for no obvious reason. Celtic opened the scoring with a goal from Steve Chalmers, then Willie Wallace pulled a good one back for Rovers.

Things began to look better for Rovers, until veteran Andy Leigh who had been out of the team for a spell, had the misfortune to concede an own goal.

Then Willie Fernie, the man from Kinglassie — and generally agreed to have been one of the best dribblers in his day, who had now returned to Celtic after a spell with Middlesbrough, scored from about 20 yards to make it 3-1 at half-time.

The game was now more or less all over for Rovers, but they kept plugging away without success in the second half. John Hughes, with a header, killed what little hope was left.

And so it was back to the grim relegation battle which was eventually won — but not without a struggle. Celtic were now favourites for the Scottish Cup, but lost in the final — to Dunfermline!

Raith Rovers v Dumbarton 1988. Observe the shelter at the Beveridge Park end of the ground

February 26 1938

Edinburgh was certainly the place to be this Saturday.

Scotland beat Ireland at Murrayfield in the Rugby International thereby strengthening their hopes of the Triple Crown.

More importantly for Raith Rovers, their fine 3-0 win over St Bernard's at the Royal Gymnasium Ground, Stockbridge, in conjunction with other results was very good news for their prospects of a return to First Division football.

The crowd was a worthy 8,000 one of the best seen at the "Gymmie" for a few years, and they saw a fine game in which Norman Haywood (Who else? This was his *annus mirabilis*!) scored first for Rovers with a marvellous drive from well outside the box.

The game was in the balance when St Bernard's were awarded a penalty. Fortunately for Rovers, Grant missed, then Rovers took full advantage scoring another twice through Alex Glen and Tommy Gilmour.

The reporter of *The Scotsman* while singing the praises of Raith Rovers, is now depressed about the prospects of Edinburgh teams St Bernard's and Leith Athletic and tips Airdrie to join Rovers in next year's First Division.

It was a good day for the trainloads of Rovers supporters who travelled to the game from Kirkcaldy.

The result and the excellent rugby score line did a little to take minds off the situation in mid Europe when Hitler seemed determined to take over Austria after he had played his part in demolishing Spain.

February 27 1960

Everyone agreed that Raith's form had been a little inconsistent of late, and also that Clyde were a class outfit (they had won the Scottish Cup twice in the past five years).

Even so, for Rovers to lose 6-1 to Clyde at Shawfield was still a bit of a shock.

It would be safe to say that Rovers did not enjoy travelling to Glasgow for since the New Year, they had lost at Celtic, Queen's Park (in the Scottish Cup) and Partick Thistle.

Next week, they would lose to Third Lanark, and then by the end of March to Rangers as well to make a complete set!

Today, however, Raith were simply swept aside with almost contemptuous ease by a rampant Clyde team who by half time were two goals up through Boyd and McLaughlin.

Ten minutes later, they had doubled that lead through Robertson and McLaughlin again before Jim Baxter, talented but indolent, stirred from his lethargy and released Willie Wallace to pull one back.

Any hopes of an unlikely comeback however were stifled when McLaughlin completed his hat trick and Herd added a sixth.

Rovers were rarely in the game as an attacking force with the forwards more or less totally anonymous. It was as well, perhaps, that not many Rovers fans made the trip to Shawfield, even in 1960 an anachronistic kind of a stadium more suited for greyhounds than football.

February 28 1914

For what was a very important event in football history in Kirkcaldy, there is surprisingly little in the local Press about Harry Anderson, the first Raith Rovers player to play for Scotland.

This happened when Scotland played Wales in a 0-0 draw before a poor crowd of 10,000 at Celtic Park.

Games against Wales and Ireland still tended to be rather undervalued and they were not considered as important as "the" International against England.

A left half, Harry was by all accounts deserving of the honour, the precious "cap" with the tassle on it which meant so much to players.

He also seems to have played competently in what was really rather a dull game, in spite of the presence of Jimmy McMenemy of Celtic, a man generally believed to be one of the best players around.

Anderson did not retain his place for the next International, his place going to James Hay, once of Celtic, but now of Newcastle United.

Of course the Great War broke out in the summer, effectively bringing to an end International football until 1919, by which time Harry was playing for St Mirren. It was still a great honour for the club and for Harry himself.

It was not however a great day for the club. They had been beaten 4-1 last week in the Scottish Cup by Third Lanark, and today they travelled to Greenock to play Morton, and they were defeated 2-1 by the home side.

February 29 1964

It is not often that Raith play on Leap Year's Day, but one such occasion was 1964 when Stenhousemuir came to town and 1815 fans saw a 2-2 draw.

Frankly, it was a fixture that had not a lot going for it, for it was in the old 19-team Second Division, from which Morton actually gained promotion that day, so far were they ahead of everyone else!

Raith and Stenny were in the middle of the table, and the dull day reflected the fare on view.

Rovers' manager was Doug Cowie, who had had a fine career with Dundee as a player, but questions were already being asked about his managerial ability. A dreadful 0-4 thumping at Dumbarton had ended Raith's interest in the Scottish Cup soon after the New Year.

But February had seen a revival with wins over Hamilton, Dumbarton and a very impressive 6-0 win over Alloa at Recreation Park last week.

At half-time Rovers went in two goals to the good, and we were hearing talk about "the new Rovers" and "turning over a new leaf" etc.

Both goals had been scored by Willie Brown who had recently joined the club from Blairgowrie Juniors, and both were made by that character with the lovely name — Felix McGrogan.

Things looked good, but this being 1964, self-destruction kicked in again and Henderson and Dackers scored for Stenny to level the score.

Thus ended a game whose only real distinguishing characteristic was that it was played in Leap Year's Day!

The Rovers team was Reid, Wilson and Stein; Bell, Burrows and McNiven; Lourie, Brown, Park, Gilpin and McGrogan.

March

March 1 1924

Still recovering from last week's shock Scottish Cup exit at the hands of St Bernard's (and with the rumours refusing to go away!), Rovers drew in midweek with Motherwell.

They travelled today to Tynecastle to win 2-1 in front of an 18,000 Edinburgh crowd.

They were without the injured Tom Jennings and Will Collier, while Dave Morris was away at Celtic Park playing for Scotland against Ireland, and he was looked upon as one of the few Scottish successes in an uninspiring victory.

At Tynecastle, the Man of the Match was once again the irrepressible Alec James who had *The Courier* using words like "bamboozled" and "wizardry" and had the Hearts supporters comparing him to their great hero Bobby Walker of the pre-Great War days.

His two goals were particularly rewarding for him, because one of the persistent criticisms of him had been that although he could beat opponents, he was not incisive enough.

Today proved that that was not the case, and, in a rare case of middle class emotion, even the Tynecastle "standites" were seen to rise and applaud the trickery of the wee man.

No less praise was heaped upon Dave Morris at Celtic Park where he played his part in restricting the effectiveness of Ireland's own "wizard", Patsy Gallacher, playing of course on his own ground.

But oh, the events of last week still hurt the Raith Rovers acolytes as they travelled back in the train from Edinburgh that night!

March 2 1963

The big freeze is over!

Football returned today to Stark's Park — but by full time many of the Rovers fans must have wished that it hadn't, as Rovers went down 7-2 to Dundee United.

Rovers' last game had been a Cup tie on January 26 when they had beaten Clyde, but all of February had been wiped out, and some teams in Scotland hadn't played a single game since January 5.

The proximity to the sea had made Kirkcaldy a little more fortunate than some inland areas, and the problem was not so much snow as continuing hard frost.

The pitch was clear of any icy patches, although with the rapid thaw, the pitch looked as if it would cut up. So it turned out, but that was no excuse.

Already well adrift at the bottom of the table before the freeze, it was difficult to see any way to escape a return to Division Two for the first time since 1949.

Today, although Tommy McDonald opened the scoring in the 10th minute and John Caven scored to make a brave attempt to keep Rovers in it in the second half, the defence were simply swamped. Dundee United ran riot with Irvine, Gillespie, Carlyle, Mitchell and Fraser all among the goals to the delight of their noisy fans in the 4314 crowd.

The saving grace was that there were still 13 games left, and time to save ourselves, but Rovers still only had four points and were six behind the team in second bottom place.

Raith Rovers v East Fife 1953. No cover at the Beveridge Park end of the ground, but the half-time scoreboard is clearly visible

March 3 1951

It is not often that Raith Rovers win at Pittodrie, so today was one of their best ever performances in the North-East.

Aberdeen were going strongly for the League Championship (which they had never won) but today two goals by Willie Penman were enough to shock the 20,000 Pittodrie crowd.

Rovers were enjoying a good run in the Scottish Cup (as indeed were Aberdeen) and were now looking forward to next week at Dundee, hoping that this could at last be "our year".

Today the sizeable amount of Raith support saw Rovers go ahead on the half-hour mark. First Willie Penman hit a post, then as Aberdeen's defence failed to clear, the ball came back to him and Willie scored with his second chance.

In the second half, after Raith withstood some incessant Aberdeen pressure, they broke away and forced a corner. George Brander took it and Penman headed his second.

But Aberdeen were not beaten yet and soon after that, their star man, the much travelled and now veteran Jimmy Delaney pulled one back.

Raith however held out, with goalkeeper George Johnstone outstanding, and this result confirmed Rovers in the dizzy heights of sixth in the League table.

A few jokes were made by optimists about a League and Cup double. This was indeed a little too optimistic, but there was little doubt that Rovers, having beaten Rangers last week, were attuning themselves well for an assault on the Scottish Cup.

March 4 1905

Mr Miller, the referee from Edinburgh, must have wondered what the town of Kirkcaldy was all about when he handled the Fife Cup game between Raith Rovers and Kirkcaldy United.

Raith Rovers won 1-0 but that seemed to be almost incidental to the ongoing series of battles that went on throughout the 90 minutes, so much so that *The Fife Free Press* wonders why Mr Miller did not abandon the game altogether.

The repercussions went on for weeks afterwards and the whole business did the game of football few favours.

As all 22 men lived in Kirkcaldy presumably so one can assume that there were certain issues at stake other than just football — perhaps rivalry for jobs or the attention of young ladies?

Raith felt that they represented the west end of Kirkcaldy whereas Kirkcaldy United were the champions of the Pathhead, St Clair Street and Gallatown district of town.

The Fife Free Press does its best not to take sides, and it does seem that one team was as bad as the other.

If there was anyone worse than the others it seems to have been "Brown" the Raith Rovers centre half. "Brown" was not the real name of this trialist, and it is to be hoped that his career did not prosper after that.

Shaw of Kirkcaldy United was sent off, and several others should have been. "Brown" was injured and left the field at the same time as the dismissed Shaw and a "scuffle ensued" which was of the "most alarming nature" as officials of both clubs joined in, and a policeman had to be summoned.

It was the sort of incident that did the image of local football little good.

March 5 1921

Kirkcaldy High Street was a dangerous, overcrowded place on this exciting day.

The previous day had seen a by-election in town, and with a huge crowd gathering for the result, it was widely believed that Labour might have won for the first time in Kirkcaldy.

They had a good candidate in Tom Kennedy and their slogan "March forth on March 4th" had struck a chord with the unemployed and war veterans who had yet to see the country made "fit for heroes to live in" as Lloyd George had rashly promised.

The results were being counted in the Town House (in 2018 Marks and Spencer's) and traffic was at standstill in the heavy rain, such was the throng of people loudly anticipating the declaration.

But football is still football, and when no result came by lunch time, people began to drift away to Stark's Park to see Raith Rovers take on Clydebank in a First Division game.

It was a wise decision for they saw Brown, Inglis and Moyes; Raeburn, Morris and Collier; Rattray, J Duncan, Jennings, Bauld and Archibald beat Clydebank 3-0 with goals from Will Collier, John Rattray and Bobby Bauld.

By the second half the rain had eased, and then the crowd saw a "sandwich-board" man come into the ground and walk round the track. "Sandwich-board" men were often used to advertise raincoats or restaurants, but this one was different.

As he passed each section of the crowd, supporters were heard to cheer and clap, for the sandwich board said on the one side "Kennedy Triumphant" and on the other "Labour Win Kirkcaldy". It was a good day for Labour and Raith Rovers.

Gordon Brown would have enjoyed that — but then again, he would not be born for another thirty years!

March 6 1971

It seemed a long time since Rovers had been to Parkhead — in fact it was only 18 months since they had been beaten 7-1, but now we were in the Second Division.

Today we returned to Celtic Park after two fighting Scottish Cup ties (which had both gone to replays) over St Johnstone and Clyde to play in the Scottish Cup quarter final.

Rovers had not been as far as this in the Scottish Cup for nearly a decade, so it was nice to get once again a certain amount of national attention, but the score was — oh, dear, the same as the last time we were there.

Celtic were, of course, good (European Cup finalists last year and winners in 1967) and their fans were generous (and far better behaved at home that when they were on a day out to Stark's Park, consuming alcohol all the way) but it was a sore experience nevertheless.

Yet, look on the bright side! Roddy Georgeson was by no means the best player ever to play for Raith Rovers, yet he was one of the few who could claim that he had scored a goal for Rovers at Celtic Park and earned a round of applause from the chivalrous and relaxed Celtic fans (who were already four up at the time).

Celtic played in yellow, but without John Hughes. He and Jock Stein had had a dreadful bust up before the game, and guess who won! Rovers got half share of the £32,000 attendance money, and that would be a great help in the now-straitened circumstances of the club.

March 7 1970

David Stirling of *The Evening Times* pulls no punches about this 1-1 draw between Raith Rovers and Partick Thistle.

"It was a woeful match...I can't remember that last time I saw so many miskicks and bad passes in a First Division match ... devoid of ideas on both sides ... lack of urgency ... in some cases there was just no effort".

This is pretty damning stuff, but most of the surprisingly high crowd of 2596 would have agreed with this report, as both teams seems to have given up for the season and accepted that relegation was to be their fate. (In the event, this proved correct. Rovers would rally a little and even beat Rangers and Motherwell but it was too little too late. Partick Thistle would be relegated for the first time in their history).

The weather was cold, the pitch was heavy and this was a totally miserably experience for Rovers' fans, lightened only by a free kick scored late in the first half by Pat Wilson which seemed to take a deflection and left the Thistle goalkeeper unsighted.

Then for a long spell in the second half, Rovers held Thistle at bay and there even seemed to be the glimmer of hope of a victory which would have been the first since December 20, but then late in the game a cross from Bone was missed by several defenders and came to Flanagan who put the ball past Bobby Reid in the goal.

The mood at the end as the supporters trudged disconsolately to their cars was not so much anger as resigned acceptance that next year in the Second Division would give Rovers a chance to regroup.

March 8 1913

SOUVENIR OF THE Fourth Round of the SCOTTISH CUP TIE.
RAITH ROVERS v St. MIRREN
Played At STARK'S PARK, KIRKCALDY Mch. 8th, 1913.

RAITH ROVERS.
M'Leod; Morrison Cumming; Jas. Gibson Logan Anderson;
Cranston Graham Martin Gourlay Fred Gibson

St. MIRREN
O'Hagan; Reid Snoddy; Pearson Burden Stevenson;
Gray Elmore Magner Kyle Sowerby

March 8 1969

It was a pleasant, sunny but slightly windy day at Stark's Park as Raith Rovers welcomed Celtic.

Rovers had had some good results but were basically struggling under new manager, ex-Rangers Jimmy Millar.

They were by no means safe from relegation and every point was vital. Celtic on the other hand were chasing the title.

A crowd of about 15,000 turned up and the game had to be delayed by about 10 minutes to allow the huge crowd in, for the queues at the Beveridge Park end of the ground were particularly congested and dangerous.

When the game started, Celtic took the initiative and Rovers were indebted to goalkeeper Bobby Reid for keeping them in the game.

But it was Rovers who took the lead just after half-time with a goal from Gordon Wallace, and for a spell after that, it looked as if we might have a shock on the cards, but sadly for Rovers, the other Wallace, Willie, who had of course learned his trade in Kirkcaldy before moving to Hearts and then Celtic, equalized.

Then Bertie Auld put Celtic ahead with a 20 yard screamer before Willie Wallace scored just on the full time whistle.

The 1-3 score line was a bit hard on the Rovers who had fought hard, a point acknowledged by Celtic's Manager Jock Stein, who expressed the view that Rovers. on that showing at least. were not relegation material.

March 9 1907

Probably for the first time in their history, Raith Rovers made Scottish football "sit up and take notice" with a spirited 2-2 draw at Tynecastle against Hearts in the Scottish Cup quarter-final.

Hearts were of course the holders of the trophy and had won it on four occasions, but today Rovers gave as good as they got, and several newspapers were of the opinion that Rovers were decidedly unlucky not to actually win the tie.

A crowd of 15,000 was reported to be at Tynecastle with a strong contingent from Kirkcaldy, some of them making their first ever trip to a ground other than Stark's Park.

Snow actually fell intermittently throughout the game, but it never threatened the chances of the game being completed, for the pitch was firm.

Hearts were actually two goals up shortly after half time, but one of them came from a debateable penalty awarded by English referee Fred Heath (from Birmingham) after the famous Scotland International Bobby Walker had been brought down, apparently just outside the box.

But Rovers, winners of the Scottish Qualifying Cup, fought back taking advantage of Hearts suffering from a couple of injuries, and first George McNicoll pulled one back, and then Henry Mitchell with a "fine slanting shot" after a "spanking run" levelled matters.

The last quarter of an hour was thrilling stuff and both teams might have scored, although Hearts probably had more of the play.

Nevertheless when Mr Heath "signalled retreat", a draw was a great result for Raith Rovers and Kirkcaldy fans looked forward to the replay at Stark's Park in a fortnight's time.

March 10 1951

It was a fine spring day at Dens Park with a crowd of over 40,000 dangerously packed in, "like herring in a barrel" according to one spectator.

They would see a great Rovers victory in the Scottish Cup quarter final against a strong Dundee side, which contained at least one world class player in Billy Steel and several others who were almost as good.

Rovers plan was to play in a strong formation with only three forwards in George Brander, Willie Penman and Johnny Maule while the other two would be deployed to keep an eye on Steel.

This plan, the brainchild of Bert Herdman, worked although *The Courier* singles out Harry Colville at centre half and Willie McNaught at left back for praise in their defensive role.

The two goals came from Willie Penman. One was early in the game from a George Brander cross, and the other was when he was just simply on the spot (with his striker's instinct) to score what turned out to be the winner.

Dundee had equalised in the first half and almost did likewise at the death when Ewen had a double chance but fortunately for Rovers, missed the pair of them.

It was a great win for Rovers, and they were now in the semi-final of the Scottish Cup for the first time since before the First World War, and Dundee's manager George Anderson was gracious in his best wishes for the Raith team in their semi-final.

March 11 1995

This was a terrible game for Raith Rovers.

Airdrie dumped them out of the Scottish Cup 4-1 and thus gained a little revenge for Rovers having knocked them out of the League Cup in October.

Rovers had also beaten then at Broadwood on the previous Monday in the League, but this was Airdrie and manager Alex MacDonald's revenge.

Thus any chance that Rovers might win the Scottish Cup to join the League Cup vanished.

There was more than just a 4-1 defeat from their bitter rivals. Some idiot threw something at a linesman, and two Rovers players Shaun Dennis and Stephen McAnespie were given red cards when the game was over.

It was a very chastening experience for Rovers and their fans.

Rovers were two goals down at half time with Shaun Dennis having a personal nightmare, first knocking a throw-in straight into the path of Jimmy Boyle and then being outjumped by Steve Cooper who knocked the ball down to John Davies to score a second.

In the second half Kenny Black killed the game with a penalty and then Paul Harvey scored a fourth before Colin Cameron scored a consolation almost at the end.

Airdrie would go on to reach the final of the Scottish Cup that year, before losing to Celtic. This was the season in which they were "homeless" and having to play their home games at Clyde's Broadwood.

Alex MacDonald made the strange comment that they actually preferred to be away from home because there was more atmosphere!

March 12 1949

In what was their first ever Cup final at Hampden, Raith Rovers, chasing promotion from Division "B", lost the League Cup final to Rangers, but were decidedly unlucky to do so.

The crowd was a slightly disappointing one of 57,450 to see Rovers (in red jerseys presented to them by the Supporters Club) take on Rangers, now famous or notorious for their "Iron Curtain" defence.

Rangers were represented by Brown, Young and Shaw; McColl, Woodburn and Cox; Gillick, Paton, Thornton, Duncanson and Rutherford while Rovers had Westland, McLure and McNaught; Young, Colville and Leigh; Maule, Collins, Penman, Brady and Joyner.

The referee was Mr W G Livingstone, Glasgow. Both teams were without key men.

Rangers were without Willie Waddell. Young Andy Leigh discovered only on the morning of the game at the Kenilworth Hotel that Ernie Till had called off injured and that he was playing.

Rangers won 2-0, but that was not anything like the full story. Near the end of the first half, with the scores still level, came a moment which some veteran Raith Rovers supporters recall to this very day. Willie Penman himself would regale admirers with it for years.

He seemed to take about three steps forward to pick up a Collins cross-field pass and to hammer home a brilliant goal, only to find the goal disallowed.

The Press, with surprising unanimity, declare that this goal was legitimate.

The League Cup was won and lost in the early part of the second half when Willie Thornton made two goals, one scored by Gillick, the other by Paton.

But *The Courier* felt that Raith Rovers should have had at least two penalties — one was when Andy Young was held when about to shoot, and the other was when Penman was pushed off the ball!

Willie Penman, more commonly known as a goalscorer, proves his versatility by saving a penalty kick against Leith Athletic in

March 13 1965

Raith Rovers today made the trip to Kilbowie Park to play a team with the unlikely name of East Stirlingshire Clydebank.

The name was of course a geographical absurdity, and the club was a result of an amalgamation between the two sides.

The amalgamation did not go down at all well with the fans of East Stirlingshire, who found that they had a long way to travel for a home game!

Yet this hybrid side was doing better in the Scottish League Second Division than Rovers were, for this was a far from vintage season for us.

The attendance was given as 1,728. It was frankly, sparse for all sorts of reasons — Raith Rovers supporters had little to encourage them, East Stirlingshire supporters were in a sulk, there were hardly any Clydebank supporters at the best of times — and it was a day of very heavy rain.

Andy Roxburgh, who would one day become Scotland's manager, scored for the home side and, a few minutes later, Jones made it two.

ESC were denied a fairly obvious penalty and Rovers were lucky to get to half-time only 0-2 down. But to their credit, they fought back, and in the second half, Jimmy Murray got then back into the game, and then George Lyall equalised later in the half.

Rovers' best player was Pat Gardner, and they deserve some credit for fighting back to earn a 2-2 draw and a valuable point, but it was still a miserable day.

March 14 1925

A trip to Somerset Park, Ayr was the order of the day for Raith Rovers.

It was the first game for the club without Tom Jennings, the prolific centre forward who had been sold to Leeds United in midweek.

Tom had been in great form this season, having scored a hat-trick against Bo'ness United in the Scottish Cup about a month ago. Leeds United had not been his only suitors.

It was of course part of the process of asset stripping which went on at Raith Rovers at this time, not all of it explained by the general economic situation of the town in the 1920s.

There was more than a little greed and pocket lining as well, the supporters felt.

With all due respect to George Chapman, who took his place, Jennings was badly missed as Ayr United beat Rovers 3-2.

It was a good game however and one of Ayr's better results of the season, but Rovers were not disgraced with Davie Morris again showing just why he was the captain of Scotland and Alec James scoring a brilliant goal, beating two men on his own before netting.

The Cassandras of the Raith support (Cassandra was the Trojan princess who always predicted bad news) wondered how long it would be before Morris and James were also transferred. (Before the year of 1925 was out, as it happened!)

Raith's other goal came from an impressive young left half called Jim Miller.

March 15 1917

The Ides of March was the date of the assassination of Julius Caesar in 44 BC. Today's March 15 was a serious blow to Raith Rovers.

At a special meeting of the Scottish League in Glasgow, Raith Rovers, Dundee and Aberdeen were asked to discontinue their membership of the Scottish League as from the start of next season in August until such time as the War came to an end.

This was naturally seen as some sort of west of Scotland conspiracy to keep eastern teams out, but it was only realistic. The problem was not so much shortage of manpower — for, although conscription was now in force, there were always enough players on leave or engaged in war work in the vicinity — as problems of transport.

As players were meant to work a half day shift in a "war related" industry on a Saturday morning, it was not always easy to get a team to Paisley or Greenock for a 3.30 kick off, and of course in winter the games had to start a great deal earlier.

Some financial support was to be given to the three excluded teams from the rest of the League, but oddly enough, Raith Rovers do not seem to have been represented at this meeting — possibly logistic transport difficulties — but Mr McIntosh of Dundee and Mr Phillip of Aberdeen argued against the motion.

The motion was carried by 16 votes to 2 with Falkirk and Raith Rovers being recorded as absent. Rovers would now join for next season an Eastern League where the problems of transport would, theoretically, be less acute.

The Footballers' Batallion of World War I containing Jimmy Todd (second left, back row), George McLay (second right, back row) and Jimmy Scott (extreme right, front row). All three of them perished in the conflict.

March 16 1935

With Raith Rovers more or less on their knees and the crowd reduced to a pitiful 500 or even less, the picture suddenly brightened with a devastating 6-0 defeat of Morton.

Symbolically, the skies brightened and it was a nice spring day as Raith Rovers (in an unlikely headline) "put six past Kirkaldy" as Bob Kirkaldy was the name of the luckless Morton goalkeeper who conceded six.

And how the faithful few enjoyed this! It was the first home win of the year, and of course *The Fife Free Press* went into overdrive — talking about "invincible forwards" and "100% improvement" on recent displays and how the policies of the new Manager, Sandy Archibald, (who had only been in harness a few months) were now beginning to take effect.

It all happened in a purple ten-minute patch before half-time when George Fulton, Jimmy Wilson, George Denholm and Alex Main all scored, and then Jimmy Scott and Fulton again in the second half made it six.

It turned out to be a false dawn, for next season would prove to be worse than this one, but at least this season ended on a happier note than appeared likely in midwinter.

The quality of the goals was what enthused the support and the Press as much as anything else — there were no simple tap-ins, they were all good goals with Denholm scoring from fully 25 yards, and both of Fulton's goals being spectacular ones as well.

Cynics however (who abounded in the town in 1935) said that Morton must have been a terrible team to lose to Rovers in this way!

March 17 1962

Considering just how much was at stake at both ends of the table, today's attendance at Stark's Park was a little disappointing.

Raith Rovers were still struggling to avoid relegation, and Dundee were still entertaining hopes of their first ever League title, even though recent defeats at Partick Thistle and Celtic had given the edge to Rangers.

Rovers, on the other hand, were locked in a battle with teams like Falkirk, Stirling Albion and Airdrie, the traditional relegation strugglers.

Today, however, they shocked Dundee by taking an early lead through Bobby Gilfillan when he headed home a peach of a cross from Bobby Adamson. Alan Cousin, who doubled as a teacher of Classics when not playing for Dundee, equalised through an amazingly soft goal which goalkeeper Thorburn clearly thought was going past.

Rovers then had a good claim for a penalty kick turned down when Ian Ure appeared to handle, before Gilfillan again put Rovers into the lead early in the second half after some sloppy play from the Dundee defence.

The Dundee support were now totally depressed especially with news coming through that Rangers were hammering Falkirk (something that was actually good news for Raith Rovers).

Then the team showed that they were title challengers after all with two goals from Andy Penman, the equaliser being a good header but the winner a somewhat lucky deflection. But it was enough to keep Dundee in the race for the title, and further hard luck for Raith Rovers.

March 18 1972

Raith Rovers were not enjoying the best of form in the Scottish League, but they were enjoying a good Scottish Cup run.

They had defeated Brechin City, Dunfermline and Dumbarton. Today in the quarter finals a crowd of 10,815 arrived at Stark's Park to see Kilmarnock.

Manager George Farm would have preferred Celtic or Rangers, no doubt, but Kilmarnock were a strong First Division team, albeit not as well supported as they deserved to be.

Long queues were still visible as the game kicked off, and people made the justified point that clubs, Raith Rovers not least, moaned about fans not going to games, and then when they did get a good crowd, they could not cope with it!

Raith started well, and when Kilmarnock got their first goal, it was definitely against the run of play, a goal scored by Cook with his head off a rebound from the bar. In the second half a great 20-yard goal from Maxwell put Killie two goals up. Things looked bad for Rovers but Dick Staite, a man who had played many years for Partick Thistle and Clyde at centre half, headed them back into the game, and with the crowd in an uproar, it looked as if Rovers were about to earn themselves a replay. But then, sadly, it was Kilmarnock who got the decisive goal and won 3-1.

It was however an indication of how a well-motivated Raith team in front of a good crowd, could play, and showed that things did not need to be as depressing as they had been for the past few years.

Stephen McAnespie and Davie Sinclair with mascots

March 19 1969

A crowd of over 3,500 were at Stark's Park this Wednesday night to see Raith Rovers win a grim relegation battle against Aberdeen 3-2 on a heavy pitch.

There had been some unseasonable snow in the vicinity but it tended to be rain in Kirkcaldy.

Aberdeen, managed by Eddie Turnbull, had had better sides in the past, and this season, along with Falkirk, Raith Rovers and Arbroath were fighting a battle for survival.

Yet they were still in the Scottish Cup and were due to play Rangers at Celtic Park on Saturday in the semi-final. Eddie Turnbull was blamed by the sizeable Aberdeen support for not playing his talismanic but moody star Jimmy "Jinky" Smith, whom he was keeping for Saturday and did not want to risk him on the heavy pitch.

The red-and-white-clad supporters also turned on goalkeeper Ernie McGarr whom they blamed for the loss of all three goals. This was unfair and did less than justice to the goals scored by Gordon Wallace, Alan Millar and veteran Davie Sneddon (who had served Kilmarnock for so long before joining Rovers), Sneddon's winning goal in particular being a memorable one.

Jimmy Millar, the recently appointed manager of Raith Rovers was delighted with the result, although it would have to be said that Raith's defending was not always of the best, and Aberdeen's second goal in particular came from a slack pass back from John Bolton.

Nevertheless, it had been a thrilling game, and Raith fans went home happy after this rather unexpected victory.

March 20 1971

Things had changed radically for Raith Rovers in 1970, and most supporters felt that it would be a long time before they would take a turn for the better.

Rovers today, however, kept alive their slim hopes of promotion with a narrow 1-0 win over Queen's Park at Hampden in a feisty encounter before a small crowd.

The Hampden bowl was due to host Celtic v Ajax in the quarter final of the European Cup on Wednesday night. There was of course more than a hint of the ridiculous in a huge stadium hosting a small crowd, but the quaint and somewhat anachronistic amateurs owned the ground.

Dave Gray scored a late winner in a game where each side had had a man sent off — Mackay of Queen's Park and Jimmy Lindsay of Raith Rovers. This was Rovers' first season in the Second Division after four years upstairs. Many of the support were clearly missing the big time and the top class opposition, hence the disappointing travelling support today, which nevertheless outnumbered and outshouted the home support.

Rovers were now sixth in Division Two, and nothing is ever really impossible in football, until it becomes a question of mathematics, so the optimists were out in force. But there had simply been too many dropped points in the earlier stages of the season.

East Fife were at the top of the table, but Partick Thistle, in their first ever season in the Second Division, had games in hand and looked likely to catch them.

March 21 1925

The equinox was quite a day in Scottish sport.

It saw the opening of the new Rugby ground of Murrayfield, an event which Scotland celebrated by defeating England to win the Calcutta Cup.

Across the railway line from Murrayfield, Tynecastle was also packed to see the semi-final between Dundee and Hamilton Academical.

Meanwhile in Glasgow in the Scottish Cup semi-final at Hampden, the first ever 100,000 crowd to watch a non-International fixture, saw Celtic beat Rangers 5-0.

Not to be outdone by these events, Raith Rovers on a fine spring day, also "went nap", a phrase which meant they scored five goals, in a League game against Partick Thistle at Stark's Park.

What made it particularly rewarding was the play of the new left wing of Willie Deuchar and Tommy Turner who created four of the five goals.

And yet it was Partick Thistle who scored the first goal through Grove, but then Rovers took a grip of the game with left half Miller taking advantage of a Turner cross. The followed an astonishing goal from right back George Barton who punted an aimless ball up the field and as goalkeeper Ramsay "stooped to gather the sphere", the ball "passed between the custodian's legs" to the consternation of the Partick Thistle players and the bewilderment of Barton himself.

Before half time, Deuchar scored from a Turner cross, then a similar thing happened in the second half to make it 4-1 before right on time Alec Ritchie headed home yet another Turner cross.

It was an excellent performance from Rovers whose supporters left the ground in a rare state of euphoria.

March 22 1924

A bitter sweet experience for Raith Rovers today at Stark's Park.

On the one hand it is always good to beat Celtic 1-0 (and it should have been more according to "Derwent" in the *Fife Free Press*,).

On the other, the turnout was very disappointing, with less than 5,000 there for a game which might have attracted four times that in other circumstances.

There were several reasons for this. One was that the weather was dire after several dry weeks. Another was that Celtic were not enjoying the best of seasons, and fewer than normal brake clubs had made their way from the west.

The main one was an unofficial boycott by Rovers supporters after "recent events for which the Rovers have not yet earned complete forgiveness" — a coy reference to the circumstances of the defeat by St Bernard's in the Scottish Cup a month ago.

It was a pity that so many people absented themselves for it was one of Rovers' best performances even in this great era, and the Press unanimously singled out one player from each side.

"I scarcely know who to eulogise most" says "Derwent". One was Alec James for his trickery — it was Alec who scored the only goal of the game, and as the other was Celtic's goalkeeper Charlie Shaw, that says a great deal about how the play went.

Celtic's great star Patsy Gallacher had a poor game; that talks volumes about Jimmy Raeburn and Davie Morris.

March 23 1938

1938 saw heady days in Fife.

The country may have been slowly sliding into another war now that Hitler had organised his Anschluss with his native Austria.

The war in Spain continued to horrify with its casualties, but the big talk in Fife was the form of the local sides Raith Rovers and East Fife, who were now locked together in the Scottish Cup.

They had drawn 2-2 at a packed Bayview on Saturday (and had not been above doubling the entrance prices!) and now the game returned to Stark's Park on the Wednesday afternoon.

Possibly fearing a backlash from their supporters, Raith Rovers pegged their prices at the normal, and, like Saturday, made it an all ticket game lest there was an influx of supporters which would be too much for the ground.

Even though it was a Wednesday afternoon, the crowd was an astonishing 25,000. It was half day in some shops, and some firms simply bowed to reality and gave their workers the afternoon off, or at least made a public statement that, although they would not be paid, they would be exempt from the possibility of dismissal! Or they could make up their hours some other time!

The game was a thriller with East Fife just edging it 3-2 thanks to couple of penalties, one them very late in the game scored by their classy left half Alec Herd, the final one at the very death.

Both teams went on to greater things that season — East Fife won the Scottish Cup but Raith Rovers won the Second Division championship establishing a British record for goal scoring in the process.

March 23 1938

Raith Rovers v East Fife in the Scottish Cup replay

March 24 1956

58,643 were at Easter Road today to see the semi-final of the Scottish Cup between Raith Rovers and Hearts with the crowd in places swaying dangerously on the terraces.

The Evening Times stated that this was the biggest day of the year for sport with two Scottish Cup semi-finals, the Grand National and the University Boat Race all on, and the Boat Race was on television.

The Forth Road Bridge was still several years in the future.

Although a few cars went round by Kincardine to Edinburgh, the only real method of transport was the train; packed Football Specials carried fans throughout the morning to Edinburgh in what was Raith's biggest day for many years. Increasing prosperity of the 1950s meaning that more and more people could afford to go.

The huge crowd at Easter Road saw a great game in a rather troublesome wind with the action swinging to and fro, but there were no goals, thanks basically to the mastery that Willie McNaught held over Willie Bauld, Hearts charismatic centre forward.

For Rovers goalkeeper Stewart was a hero, but many Hearts supporters were of the opinion that left back McLure was lucky not have had "an early bath" for several coarse tackles on Alec Young.

Still, a draw was generally agreed to be a fair result and everyone would re-convene at the same venue on Wednesday.

Elsewhere, Celtic beat Clyde 2-1 in the other semi-final but the sensation of the day was in the Grand National at Aintree where Devon Loch, the Queen Mother's horse, was clear and running home yards ahead of anyone else, then suddenly and inexplicably sat down!

March 25 1972

Any good will that may have been engendered by the Cup run of this spring — which culminated in a defeat by Kilmarnock last week — was dissipated by this awful performance against Brechin City at Stark's Park.

The Cup run had at least shown that the good times weren't necessarily gone forever, but one would have found it hard to be cheered up by this unfortunate performance watched by a crowd of little more than a thousand on a pleasant spring day.

Brechin City were often the butt of jokes made by those with a sense of insecurity about them — they were called Brechin Village and if they were really poor, Brechin Shitty, and their star men were men called Trialist, Newman and Junior.

On this occasion, the joke was on Raith Rovers, for early on "Junior" did in fact score for Brechin City, and hard though Rovers tried (men like Gordon Wallace, Jim Dempsey and Malcolm Robertson were no slouches normally) they could not break through a defence which was rugged and rustic but did not disdain the ugly but effective boot up the park.

The more the second half wore on, the more we began to hear the boos, the catcalls and even on one occasion an outburst of laughter at a particularly inept piece of play when a man waltzed through the defence and then shot tamely at the goalkeeper.

It was as if the players were exhausted and demotivated after their Cup run. Six more League games remained, but it was now the end of the season.

March 26 1977

Raith Rovers' wretched season continued today at Links Park, Montrose when after a lucky break they failed to capitalise and lost two second half goals.

The few Rovers supporters in the sparse crowd at the trim provincial ground of Montrose were thoroughly despondent.

It was now impossible to avoid using the R word of relegation, something that now in the late 1970s would involve Rovers playing the third tier of Scottish football.

Those supporters who recalled the days of 20 years ago when they were more than a match on occasion for teams like Celtic and Rangers found that very hard to accept.

It was clear now that Rovers, although still having some good players were woefully deficient in some areas of the field. Today for example late in the first half they got a goal which some newspapers put down as a goalkeeper's own goal when goalkeeper Gorman of Montrose made a terrible hash of a harmless Andy Harrow lob.

Having been given such a break, it might have been hoped that Rovers would capitalise, but they allowed an anodyne Montrose team back into the game, and goals from Bobby Street and then Derek Daun saw the Angus side turn defeat into victory.

Rovers and their supporters were condemned to a miserable weekend, not the least unhappy aspect being the sight of Rovers players openly shouting at each other on the field.

A difficult end of the season now awaited manager Andy Matthew and the Kirkcaldy men.

March 27 1957

Raith lost their Scottish Cup semi-final replay against Falkirk 2-0 at Tynecastle.

Falkirk were possibly just the better side but Rovers fans left Edinburgh with a feeling of injustice after what looked like a good equaliser had been disallowed.

As they had similar feelings in the first game on the Saturday, the trains home that night were sullen, angry places!

25,300 fans were there that day, and it appeared that at least 10,000 of them were from Kirkcaldy on several special trains.

Quite a few fans faced the prospect of an embarrassing moment or two explaining to their employers tomorrow why they appeared not to be at their post the previous afternoon.

Falkirk's first goal was a beauty from Doug Moran. Having previously hit the post, he then picked up a back heeler from George Merchant before beating Charlie Drummond.

But Rovers were mystified as to why Bernie Kelly's 36th minute goal was disallowed for offside when the ball almost certainly came off a Falkirk defender.

In addition, a reasonable penalty claim was turned down by referee Hugh Phillips, and there was a bizarre loss of three minutes when the referee ordered the goal line to be redone with sawdust!

Yet Falkirk were that wee bit faster to the ball than Raith and their victory was confirmed late in the game when Eddie O'Hara gave the Bairns a place in the final against Kilmarnock who, when all this was going on, were beating Celtic at Hampden.

Raith's team was Drummond, Polland and Bain; Young, McNaught and Leigh; McEwan, Kelly, Copland, Williamson and Urquhart.

March 28 1956

Rovers disappointed their fans in the huge crowd of 54,364 by going down woefully 0-3 to Hearts in the Scottish Cup semi-final replay at Easter Road.

The first game on the Saturday before had been tight, and a good case could have been made out for Rovers being unlucky.

This could not be said tonight as Tommy Walker's Hearts side simply turned it on to the delight of their fans in the crowd.

Amazingly, it would be Hearts' first Scottish Cup final for almost 50 years, and their opponents would be Celtic, the same team that they had met in 1907.

Rovers only excuse was a bad injury to Malcolm McLure which eventually reduced Rovers to ten men. Although that happened early in the game, Hearts were already ahead through Jimmy Wardhaugh who had scored in the first minute when some of the vast crowd were still thronging the inadequate turnstiles in an attempt to get in.

Wardhaugh scored again 17 minutes from time, by which time Hearts were well on top and then to settle any remaining doubt, Ian Crawford scored a third.

The Glasgow Herald was less than sympathetic to Raith Rovers. Andy Young was singled out for engaging in a perpetual feud with Wardhaugh and Jimmy McEwen was spoken to three times by the referee - "twice too often" in the opinion of the writer.

Raith Rovers supporters, no strangers to heartbreak and disappointment, had an excuse in the injury to McLure but could do nothing other than hold up their hands and admit that they had been beaten by a better side who would in fact, deservedly, go on to win the Scottish Cup that year.

March 29 1913

For what was Raith Rovers biggest game to date, "shoals of supporters" travelled to Edinburgh to Tynecastle o see Rovers take on Clyde in the semi-final of the Scottish Cup.

From as early as 9.00 supporters left Kirkcaldy to "make a day of it".

Some, *The Fife Free Press* says, had difficulty distinguishing the teams by the time the game started, although their vocal support for the Rovers was very pronounced.

Credit was paid to the staff at Kirkcaldy station for the way that they coped with the huge crowd, and ensured that of the 20 or so trains that left Kirkcaldy that morning, not one was a minute late.

It was generally agreed that although Rovers had done very well to get there, Clyde the Scottish Cup finalists of 1910 and 1912 would be just too good for Rovers in the semi.

It was Rovers who took an early lead through Jimmy Gourlay and held on to it until virtually the very end as excitement mounted at the thought of Rovers reaching the Scottish Cup final.

But Rovers' shooting had been woeful and they had been unable to add to their lead, and as was always likely to happen, Geordie Reid equalised for Clyde with minutes to go.

Then Clyde might have won the game but Ebenezer Owers shot wide. A draw was the result and "the treasurers smiled" said the cynical *Fife Free Press,* for it meant another big payday next week at the same venue.

The crowd was given as 28,000 with an estimated 10,000 from Kirkcaldy. In the other semi-final at Ibrox, Falkirk beat Hearts.

March 30 1963

Raith Rovers, anchored at the foot of the First Division and heading inexorably for relegation, nevertheless pulled off an amazing result today in the Scottish Cup quarter final when they beat Aberdeen 2-1 at Stark's Park.

Rovers, like everyone else, were still trying to recover from the bad winter which had paralysed so much football from January until early March.

They were trying to play off a backlog of fixtures without any great success, and the Scottish Cup came as a bit of light relief.

Aberdeen were similarly struggling but nevertheless brought a goodly crowd of supporters with them to form a 5,000 crowd who saw a game that was high on effort and excitement but a little low on basic ball-playing skills.

Aberdeen had had a few good results in the Scottish Cup and were looking for a good Cup run to recoup some of the dreadful financial losses that they had sustained.

Today was all about a hitherto underperforming character at Stark's by the name of Bobby Gilfillan who had been re-introduced by manager Hugh Shaw.

He opened the scoring by hooking a ball over the heads of defenders and into the net in the 15th minute.

Aberdeen came back with a strange goal which hit goalkeeper Thorburn and bounced another two or three times before it entered the net.

To their credit, the pace never slackened in the second half, but it looked as if we were heading to a replay at Pittodrie on Wednesday night, especially after Billy Wilson had a penalty saved by "Tubby" Ogston, but then Bobby Gilfillan popped up again in the last minute to give Rovers fans a victory and a happy Saturday night, something that had been rare in 1963.

March 31 1951

The heavy rain had stopped but it was still a dull damp day.

84,237, probably the biggest crowd that Raith Rovers had ever played in front of, were at Hampden Park to see a thrilling Scottish Cup semi-final between Raith Rovers and Celtic.

Although Celtic won 3-2, everyone from Kirkcaldy was convinced that Celtic's winning goal was a foul on goalkeeper George Johnstone, who was impeded from jumping.

Most people agreed that Rovers were worth a draw, the only difference being the sublime play of Charlie Tully.

Jock Weir opened the scoring for Celtic, but then Rovers equalised when a shot from Les Murray went in off Alec Boden. John McPhail then scored for Celtic just before half time.

Then Willie Penman scored one of his great goals. Willie McNaught took a free kick and found George Brander who sent the ball across for Willie Penman to head home. It was a classic "three card trick" goal.

A minute later, however, came Celtic's winner. It may have been a foul, but the ball came to the ever alert Charlie Tully.

Even after that, Rovers had hard luck hitting the woodwork twice in the last ten minutes when Willie Penman hit the post and Joe McLaughlin the bar.

It was hard luck for Raith Rovers, but *The Evening Times* felt that Rovers might have done better if they had utilised the talents of Johnny Maule a little oftener.

In the other semi-final played that day, Motherwell beat Hibs, but it was Celtic who won the Scottish Cup that year beating Motherwell 1-0 in the final.

April

April 1 1981

Raith Rovers' "mensis horribilis" of April 1981 commenced this Wednesday night at Dens Park with an unlucky 1-2 defeat to Dundee.

This was a re-arranged fixture of a postponed match from earlier in the season.

Although one will never convince some supporters to the contrary, there probably was no deliberate throwing away of promotion to the Premier League in this dreadful month.

The main feature of April 1981 was bad luck, certainly in this game, and then the growing negative momentum throughout the month of the belief that it was not going to happen anyway.

6,500 were at Dens tonight to see a couple of bad mistakes. The hitherto excellent goalkeeper, Murray McDermott, watched an easy overhead kick drift over his head into the net; then after Chris Candlish had scored a fine equalizer, McDermott saw a shot squirm under his body to restore the lead for Dundee.

Credit must of course be given to Dundee, but for Rovers who had faltered a little in March (when Dundee had also beaten them) the decline now intensified.

Possibly the important feature was the belief of the supporters that it was all being done deliberately because they would never have afforded the Premier League.

It was all so unfair on the players, who were trying so hard to get out of the whirlpool of devastation, but it would be many years before Rovers would regain the respect of some of their supporters.

April 2 1960

Raith Rovers today travelled to Pittodrie to play Aberdeen in front of a low crowd of 6,000.

Aberdeen supporters, going through one of their frequent periods of depression with their team, seemed to have abandoned them to relegation.

Yet only last year they had reached the Scottish Cup final!

Rovers, on the other hand, although clearly past their best of a few years ago, also had several players now missing.

Only Andy Young of the great half back line of Young, McNaught and Leigh was playing today. They were nevertheless a respectable mid-table outfit whose season had been satisfactory at least.

A few Rovers supporters travelled up in the train to Pittodrie and they saw not a bad game.

The Dons played with the "desperation of necessity" as a newspaper put it and won 4-2, although it was only late in the game before they scored the two vital goals.

One of the Rovers' goals was an own goal scored by George Kinnell off an Andy Young cross which was clearly intended for someone else, and the other was a penalty sunk by the very impressive Willie Wallace.

Yet the game seemed to be heading for a 2-2 draw before a long range effort from Archie Glen found the net.

Then in injury time Billy Little scored to make it 4-2, a cruel result for Rovers who deserved more, but it did at least remove a few torn faces from the chronically unhappy Aberdonians.

April 3 1982

A pitiful crowd of 365 (one for each day of the year!) turned up at Boghead on what was not a bad spring day to see the visit of Raith Rovers.

Boghead was one of the grand old ladies of Scottish football, but her day had passed many years ago.

Of the 365 crowd, not many would have come from Kirkcaldy, one would have imagined, for the form of the team had been generally mediocre in season 1981/82.

Still suffering from the hangover of promotion-blowing last year, crowds had been disappointing.

There were some good players around — Ian Ballantyne, for example, who scored two good goals today for Rovers to win the game 2-0 and Donald Urquhart.

There was the occasional good game e.g. a 3-2 win over Dunfermline, but generally it had been a poor season.

Meanwhile Forfar, (yes, Forfar!) were playing in the Scottish Cup semi-final against Rangers and earning a 0-0 draw, something that proved that there was no real excuse for Raith Rovers, but even that was not the main topic of conversation.

The House of Commons was today sitting in emergency session on a Saturday — a very rare event indeed — for Argentina had yesterday invaded the Falkland Islands. Not everyone knew very much about the Falkland Islands, but Mrs Thatcher with ill-disguised glee told everyone that she was going to get them back.

It was one of the few times in her Premiership that she had the support of the majority (not everyone, of course!) of the British people.

April 4 1925

Raith Rovers were not playing today, and yet it was possibly their best ever day.

Today at Hampden, Scotland, captained by Raith Rovers' Dave Morris, beat England 2-0 to win the British Championship. They had beaten Wales 3-1 and Ireland 3-0, both under the captaincy of the same Dave Morris.

This year, the SFA had taken the brave decision to restrict selection to those who were playing in the Scottish domestic League, rather than Anglo-Scots.

This meant that there were three from Rangers, two from Airdrie, and one each from Celtic, Aberdeen, Ayr United, Hibs, Partick Thistle and of course the captain from Raith Rovers.

It says a great deal for Dave Morris that men like the brilliant but temperamental Hughie Gallacher, "the wee blue deil" Alan Morton, and the respective captains of Celtic and Rangers, Willie McStay and Davie Meiklejohn, were willing to take orders from the handsome young giant from Kirkcaldy.

One man, elderly and lucky enough to have seen Morris play, said that "Davie could heid a ba' further than maist guys could kick it". Morris and Raith Rovers had every cause to hold their heads up high that night, but it would not last long. Morris was never capped again, incredibly, and by the turn of the year both he and Alec James were playing for Preston North End, while Raith Rovers themselves were well on their way to relegation.

Both goals were scored by Airdrie's Hughie Gallacher.

April 5 1913

Rovers reached their first ever (and to date only) Scottish Cup final today.

They beat Clyde 1-0 at Tynecastle in the semi-final replay before 20,000 spectators, the only goal of the game coming through Fred Martin from a Tom Cranston cross.

The Dundee Courier is ecstatic at the thought of a Fifeshire team in the Scottish Cup final for the first time, as it talks about the team's "bustling qualities".

> *Never with them is an opportunity gone. It is followed up persistently and the opposition defence is worried and harassed until an advantage, however slight it may be, is gained. It is the real fighting spirt they display. Determination, the offshoot of enthusiasm, carried them through against Clyde, and (who knows?), may be their means of triumph against Falkirk.*

The game was "crammed with incident" and "never for one moment was the attention of the huge crowd allowed to stray".

It was agreed that this was one of the better semi-finals and a lot better than the first game last week, and the "Kirkcaldy trippers" were in rare good humour as they came off their trains at the station.

The only thing that could possibly dampen their enthusiasm was the news which had arrived "on the wire" from London that in the International that day, England had defeated Scotland 1-0 at Stamford Bridge.

But the main topic of concern in Kirkcaldy that night and indeed the rest of the week was whether they would be able to afford the trip to Glasgow next week to see the Scottish Cup final at Celtic Park.

April 6 2014

John Baird scored the goal that won the League Challenge Cup over Rangers.

April 6 2014

Winners of the League Challenge Cup in 2014

April 6 2014

Raith Rovers won the second major national trophy of their existence when they beat Rangers 1-0 at Easter Road in the final of the League Challenge Trophy.

The League Challenge Trophy was played for by all Scottish teams other than those in the Premiership.

It was not, perhaps, the most prestigious of tournaments and certainly a step or two below the Scottish League Cup which they won in 1994, but it was nevertheless a great honour for the club.

The opponents in the final were Glasgow Rangers — who had gone into administration in 2012. Currently in the First Division of the Scottish League, they were trying to fight their way back to the Scottish Premiership, from which they had been deposed as a part of their punishment for going bankrupt.

Today's game was a good one in front of a crowd of 19,983, although it would have to be said that Rangers had the bulk of the chances.

But Grant Murray's side, backed up by about 4,000 fans, held their nerve and by the end of the 90 minutes were at least the equals of Rangers.

But no goals came, and the extra time period looked similarly barren, and a penalty shoot-out looked inevitable.

But then a series of errors in the Rangers defence gave Raith Rovers the Cup. They were unable to clear the ball, and Greig Spence's drive was only parried by goalkeeper Cammy Bell.

The ball rolled to John Baird who finished the job and earned his special place in Raith Rovers history. It was a great day in their history, second only, perhaps, to November 27 1994.

April 7 1984

Even in the worst of seasons (and 1984 was, by most people's reckoning, pretty bad) there are the occasional games when things do not seem to be quite so dire.

Today was one such game.

A pleasant, albeit slightly blustery Stark's Park where a diehard crowd of 839 (whom no-one could accuse of being glory hunters or bandwagon jumpers) saw their team suddenly turn it on.

They thrashed fellow strugglers Ayr United 5-0, leading to wild speculation that the spectre of relegation which hung over Stark's Park might yet be banished.

Jimmy Kerr opened the scoring in the first five minutes, then converted a penalty before setting up Keith Wright to give Rovers a scarcely credible 3-0 half time lead, before Paul Smith and Jimmy Marshall scored in the second half to make it 5-0.

An Ayr United man called Armour (whose ancestor may or not have fallen in love with a Mr Burns a couple of centuries previously!) was sent off as well,

The small Raith crowd had a rare chance to boast about their team, at least for a day or two. Sadly, however, not for long.

Three feckless defeats followed.

Although there was a late desperate rally, events earlier in the season meant that the Four Horsemen of the Apocalypse — Incompetence, Poor Crowds, Poverty and Relegation came calling at the end of the season.

1984 was thus for Raith Rovers fans every bit as bad as George Orwell had said it was going to be.

April 8 1939

Doomed Raith Rovers at least put up a show of defiance today by beating Aberdeen 3-2 at Stark's Park before a crowd of 4,000.

It was not only Raith Rovers who seemed doomed, however.

Western civilization seemed in the same boat. The defeat and surrender of Republican Spain the previous weekend hammered another nail in the coffin for those who thought that a world war could be avoided.

But at least the country was now prepared for the inevitable with much talk of air raid shelters being built and gas masks being procured.

The football season was now coming to an end and Rovers' five defeats earlier in the spring meant that there was now little hope, yet the writer in the *Aberdeen Press and Journal* was at a loss to understand why Rovers had got themselves in that position.

An own goal gave them the lead, and after Aberdeen had equalised through a goalkeeping error, Ernie Till and Willie Dunn made it 3-1 until George Hamilton pulled one back for the black and golds.

The reporter is also highly critical of Aberdeen who now seem to have blasted their chances of finishing runners up to Rangers.

For Rovers fans, it was a small moment of happiness in an otherwise gloomy outlook. There was still a theoretical chance of avoiding relegation, but in fact they lost their last two League games.

But looking at the world situation, did it matter?

A sign of the Premier League in 1993, a TV box!

April 9 1921

This was the day that Raith Rovers showed to the world that they were as good as anyone, for they beat Celtic 2-0, thereby killing off what little chance Celtic had of winning the Scottish League.

The game was unfortunate in that it took place on the same day as Scotland beat England 3-0 at Hampden.

It didn't get as much prominence as it deserved.

It was also the day that John "Tokey" Duncan scored the goal that earned him immortality in song. "Oh, Chairlie Shaw, he never saw, whaur Tokey Duncan pit the ba'".

The tune was the very current and politically subversive "Red Flag", and although Rangers supporters copied it and made it into Alan Morton, it was definitely Raith Rovers who got there first!

It was a tremendous shot from well outside the box, and it was the opinion of *The Courier* that no goalkeeper on earth could have stopped it.

That was his first goal, and his second was from a goalmouth scrimmage of the sort that earned him his nickname "Tokey".

Celtic pressed hard, and indeed earned a penalty kick but goalkeeper Jimmy Brown managed to save from Willie McStay.

Celtic had a few injuries that day and Patsy Gallacher was away playing for Ireland, but Tommy McInally, their unpredictable boy wonder was held well in check by Morris.

Rovers side was the immortal Brown, Inglis and Moyes; Raeburn, Morris and Collier: T Duncan, J Duncan, Jennings, Bauld and Archibald.

The crowd was a massive one of nearly 20,000.

With Ireland currently in open rebellion against Great Britain, strong measures had to be taken against flags, banners or any political demonstrations.

April 10 1993

It was pay-off time for Raith Rovers and their supporters, particularly those 4893 who attended Stark's Park this spring Saturday afternoon.

Normally by now interest in football has flagged with everyone talking about the imminence of the Links Market, and the need to cut the "gress" (as one's lawn is eccentrically called in Kirkcaldy).

Not this year, for Rovers beat Dumbarton 2-0 to gain promotion to the Premier League and win the Championship at the same time.

Craig Brewster, who had had a good season, scored the two goals, but it was a great triumph for all the team who were quite clearly the best team in the Division.

It was the first time that Rovers had been in the top tier since 1970, and for a proud club like Raith Rovers, 23 years was a long time, with the year 1981, a particular horror story.

But the ghost of that year had now been exorcised, and nothing but praise was due for Jimmy Nicholl and his men. Nicholl admitted to having been a little overwhelmed by the emotion of it all.

Since the start of the season when Rovers beat St Mirren 7-0, they had stayed on top more or less all season. There was a wobble or two at Kilmarnock in January and one strange reverse at Clydebank in a midweek game in December, but apart from those few odd blips, it had been consistent good play all the way through the season.

Next year with the big boys would be a different matter altogether, however...

April 11 2010

A disappointing crowd of 16,671 were at Hampden to see Raith Rovers' first Scottish Cup semi-final since 1963.

The game was equally disappointing because Dundee United beat Raith Rovers 2-0.

The Scottish Cup had never been Raith's favourite trophy, but it was felt that this year might just do it, given that in the other semi-final the previous day, Ross County had beaten Celtic.

The weather was fine as the supporters' buses left town and everyone else prepared to watch the game on television.

It had hardly been a vintage season for the Rovers.

They were struggling to avoid relegation from the First Division and had suffered the misfortune of having lost an awful lot of games to the weather in the hard winter.

They had done well in the Scottish Cup, beating teams like Aberdeen and Dundee who had both fallen on hard times.

They also had, most unusually, the support of 10 Downing Street for PM Gordon Brown, although unable to attend, sent his best wishes to John McGlynn's team.

Sadly, they were to no avail, for Dundee United put on a slick performance, scored twice.

David Goodwillie finished an excellent Danny Swanson pass, and Andy Webster headed a second, and United finished the game comfortable winners.

Rovers' only real chance was a glancing header from Jamie Mole, and they failed to raise their game in the second half when they were two down.

For most of the players and some of the supporters, however, it was a rare chance to savour the Hampden atmosphere — such as it was!

Raith supporter Val McDermid who also writes crime stories

April 12 1913

Raith Rovers travelled to Celtic Park, Glasgow to play in the Scottish Cup final against Falkirk.

It was an unusual Scottish Cup final, the first for both teams.

More unusually, the Cup final did not feature a team from Glasgow, the first time this had happened since 1896.

There had been an unseasonal fall of snow in Glasgow overnight, and Celtic's Manager Mr Willie Maley had to organise a party to clear the pitch.

It being April, the snow melted anyway and a wind sprung up, but it was an east wind and therefore still a little on the cool side.

The crowd was 45,000; it was rather pleasing to note that the Glaswegians did in fact support a final between two provincial sides, when pessimists predicted a crowd of about half that.

Both teams normally wore dark blue, but Rovers won the toss to keep their own colours and therefore Falkirk came out wearing white.

Rovers side was McLeod, Morrison and Cumming; J Gibson, Logan and Anderson; Cranston, Graham, Martin, Gourlay and F Gibson while Falkirk were represented by Stewart, Orrock and Donaldson; McDonald, Logan and McMillan; McNaught, Gibbons, Robertson, Croal and Terris. Referee T Robertson, Queen's Park.

Rovers fought well but lost goals at key times in each half — Falkirk scoring through Jimmy Robertson in the first half, and then through Tommy Logan, their attacking centre half in the second.

After that, Rovers mounted some sort of a fightback but it was not enough. Soon after the final whistle, a wire was sent to *The Fife Free Press* with the bad news, and a man put a placard in their window in Kirk Wynd.

It remains to this date the only time that Rovers have reached a Scottish Cup final.

April 13 1963

Raith, apparently doomed to relegation, lost 2-5 to Celtic in the Scottish Cup semi-final at Ibrox.

The day was sunny but still a little cold and certainly windy — there had been snow in Glasgow the previous day — and it was generally regarded that this was a poor game for the 35,681 crowd, with a sizeable presence from Kirkcaldy.

Yet Raith Rovers put up a reasonable fight and the balance of play was probably a lot closer that the score-line would suggest.

With a strong wind blowing from the west, Celtic won the toss and decided to play with the wind. John Divers opened the scoring for Celtic, but then Tommy McDonald equalised before half time taking advantage of an awful clearance by Frank Haffey.

Things look promising for Rovers, given that they now had the wind behind them, but then crucially they conceded two penalties — correctly awarded by referee Bobby Davidson — and Dunky MacKay scored them both.

But yet, the plucky Rovers were still not defeated for Bobby Gilfillan pulled one back before, sadly, Steve Chalmers and Frank Brogan finished the job for Celtic.

The Glasgow Herald, while admiring the pluck of Raith Rovers, is compelled to state that they were "not endowed with much subtlety or elegance".

In the other semi-final on the same day, Rangers beat Dundee United by a similar score 5-2. Although we were now in mid-April and the Links Market was imminent, there was still a lot of football to be played because of postponements caused by the big freeze-up of January and February 1963.

April 14 1923

Most of the country was enthralled by the Scotland v England International at Hampden today (Scotland drew 2-2 which was enough to give them the International Championship).

Meanwhile, Raith Rovers were quietly going about their business by beating Partick Thistle 1-0 at Stark's Park, their goal coming from the somewhat under-rated Peter Bell.

Peter scored in the 6th minute, and the rest of the game was a grim battle for midfield supremacy but it was Raeburn, Morris and Collier who took charge.

The crowd was 6,000, not a bad crowd for 1923, but it might have been more if some fans had not gone to Hampden or chosen to hang around the office of *The Fife Free Press* awaiting news of the big game.

1923 was not to shape up as such a good season for Rovers as 1922 had been, and the main problem seemed to be how to harness the immense talent of the diminutive Alec James and develop it to the good of the team.

To this intent, Rovers came out with a different formation in the second half with Tom Jennings at outside right and Bell and Miller in the centre while James played slightly further back almost as an extra midfield man.

It did not yield any further goals but any victory is a victory, and the fans were satisfied at that.

As the crowds dispersed, rumours spread that Scotland had beaten England 4-0, and counter rumours said the opposite, but 2-2 it was, and that was also a satisfying performance.

Naturally, all Kirkcaldy was convinced that if the Scotland half back line had read Raeburn, Morris and Collier, the score line would indeed have read 4-0.

April 15 1967

Raith Rovers were entitled to claim their share in Scotland's famous 3-2 win over England at Wembley to-day.

There was no game for Raith Rovers today, and many supporters had taken themselves off to Wembley, leaving on the train at 11.00 on the Friday night and returning (not always in the peak of condition!) on the Sunday.

They saw what turned out to be a famous victory for Bobby Brown's men. Denis Law scored in the first half and Jim McCalliog and Bobby Lennox scored in the second half.

The two Rovers old boys Jim Baxter and Willie Wallace did Kirkcaldy proud with Jim Baxter's famous keepy-uppie being shown time and time again on TV.

It was England's first defeat since they won the World Cup at Wembley the previous year.

For Willie Wallace this was merely a stepping stone on to further glory with Celtic in the European Cup the following month.

Rather sadly, this game was probably Jim Baxter's swansong, for his career had not prospered since he left Rangers in 1965 and his subsequent performances were disappointing, particularly when he returned to Rangers in 1969.

All this was in the future, however. It was time to celebrate.

Meanwhile back at Stark's things were heating up nicely in the promotion race. On the Tuesday night after this game, Rovers went to Stenhousemuir and won 4-0 with three goals from Pat Gardner and one from Tommy Mackle.

April 16 1927

A remarkable day for Fife football.

At Hampden Park, East Fife fought against Celtic in the Scottish Cup final.

Raith Rovers found their way back to the First Division by beating East Stirlingshire.

Bo'ness had won the Second Division and the fight was on for second place. All Rovers had to do today was win.

The game at Stark's Park before 3,500 spectators was a remarkable affair, punctuated by barracking in the first half after Rovers had failed to score in the first 20 minutes!

This extraordinary phenomenon can only be explained by the common cynical perception widely believed in the linoleum factories in town that they "were not wanting to go up" for financial reasons.

A more charitable explanation could have been nerves on the big occasion, but in any case Rovers shut everyone up by scoring four goals in five minutes and then eventually winning 6-3.

Even then the Press used phrases like "unconvincing display" and "staggering to safety", but the bottom line was that the team were now back in the First Division, the goals having been scored by Alec Ritchie (2), John McNeill, Hugh Todd, Owen Dorrans and an own goal, and that was after East Stirlingshire had scored first.

And if Rovers fans had any further need for happiness, it came when the news came through to *The Fife Free Press* building in Kirk Wynd that Celtic had won the Scottish Cup 3-1, and that there would be no need to thole any boasting from along the coast!

April 17 1937

Little more than 1,000 were at Stark's Park today to see Raith Rovers bring down the curtain on their rather ordinary season.

They finished 8th in the Scottish Second Division.

Today they beat King's Park of Stirling 3-1 with George Fulton scoring a hat-trick.

It was a good enough performance but it failed to excite the spectators too much, and in some ways it was typical of the season, although there were a few things which led one to believe that better days might just be around the corner.

For example there was a young left winger on trial from St Andrews United and he had looked good. He was called Francis Joyner.

But two other things were exercising the minds of the spectators. One was the news — and how it got there no-one knows, for there was no such thing as a portable radio — that Scotland were beating England at Hampden.

This was certainly true for Scotland won 3-1 in front of a record and scarcely believable crowd of 149,407. That would, in part, explain why the Rovers crowd was so low that day — loads of supporters had been seen getting on the train for Glasgow that morning.

But the other thing that was the topic of conversation was what was going on in Spain. People with pamphlets had stood outside the ground urging young men to join the International Brigades to save Spain from Fascism.

The argument was that a World War was coming soon anyway, so maybe better fight Hitler now rather than later. A few from Kirkcaldy and Cowdenbeath had already gone.

April 18 1981

It was one of the least pleasant return trips on the train from Edinburgh for Rovers supporters.

They had just seen their team lose 0-2 to Hibs, with goals on either side of half-time, in a game which meant that Hibs were now the winners of the First Division, and they were duly presented with the trophy at the end of the game.

No disrespect to Hibs, who were worthy winners and deserved their return to the Premier League, (so confident was Manager Bertie Auld that he had actually gone on holiday that week!), but what on earth had gone wrong with Raith Rovers?

Ian Paul of *The Glasgow Herald* likened their fall to that of Devon Loch in the 1956 Grand National (a horse which was well clear, and then sat down within sight of the finishing line!)

They had already beaten Hibs twice that season and had looked good for the First Division Championship themselves until about the middle of March.

Two defeats to Dundee and one to St Johnstone, along with feckless draws with Clydebank and Falkirk had seen a serious dip in their promotion chances, but even worse, a loss of credibility in the eyes of their support, some of whom were now saying openly that Raith did not want promotion.

The local press stopped short of saying that, but nevertheless joined in the general amazement of how there could be such a total loss of form.

Donald Urquhart's injury was certainly an unfortunate factor, but the pall of gloom that now settled over Stark's Park was very tangible, and for the next few seasons, attendances would drop alarmingly.

It would be a long time before Rovers would win back the respect of their fans.

April 19 1930

Perhaps "good neighbours" was putting it a little strong, but thanks to Raith Rovers' comprehensive 6-2 defeat of Albion Rovers, East Fife were promoted to the First Division.

They themselves beat Armadale 3-0, but needed Raith Rovers to beat Albion Rovers as well.

East Fife's achievement was much hailed in *The Courier* where Don John likened it to their reaching the final of the Scottish Cup in 1927.

It was not necessarily greeted with unbridled enthusiasm in Kirkcaldy, but there was a grudging respect, particularly as Raith could claim a share.

Raith had nothing at stake in this game other than a desire to avenge the events of December 14 1929 when they were on the receiving end of a severe 0-7 tanking at Coatbridge.

Albion Rovers were late in arriving, delaying the kick-off a little. They soon shocked Raith Rovers and the meagre crowd on this cold, rainy day by scoring two early goals.

Rovers however rallied and by means of a hat-trick from Fred Panther, a goal from Willie Birrell, another from Jackie McLaren and an own goal, ran out winners by 6-2.

Along at Bayview with their own game over, East Fife fans lingered on the park to await the news from Stark's Park. Telephone communication in 1930 was somewhat primitive but eventually the reporter of *The Courier* was able to get through to his office, and his Sports Editor told him the good news.

Raith Rovers had thus earned promotion for East Fife!

Some 29 years later in 1959, there was a parallel to this event when Celtic beat Hearts, thereby winning the League for Rangers!

April 20 1954

The funeral was held today at Dysart Cemetery of Will or Bill Collier, one of Raith Rovers greatest ever players.

Aged 61, he had died three days previously in the Bridge of Earn Hospital.

Sometimes called "Wily Will" by his fans and part of the immortal half-back line of Raeburn, Morris and Collier, his career was marked by its quality and its brevity.

He only really started playing after the Great War by which time he was well into his twenties, making his Rovers debut on April 17 1920. (Ironically he died on April 17, some 34 years later).

He won one cap for Scotland against Wales in 1922, and quite a few people thought that he might have won more with a bigger club than Raith Rovers.

He suffered a serious injury at Pittodrie on December 1 1923, and effectively never really played well for Raith Rovers again.

He was transferred to Sheffield Wednesday in 1924, but he was no great success there, and moved to Kettering and then as player-manager to Dartford.

When his footballing days were over, he entered (like so many ex-players) the licensing trade. But he was always Bill Collier of Raith Rovers.

He was at Stark's Park for less than five seasons, but they were probably the best five years of their history.

His funeral was attended by many of those who had played with him and against him as well as those who had cheered him on. He was survived by his wife and son.

Raith Rovers 1922 in front of the old stand which was shortly to be demolished

April 21 1962

In a rather surreal atmosphere at a desolate Celtic Park, Raith Rovers more or less confirmed their First Division status by beating Celtic 1-0 in what was, frankly, a dreadful game of football.

It would now take an odd combination of results to relegate Raith Rovers.

They owed this victory to a piece of opportunism from Bobby Adamson to take advantage of some hesitancy between Jim Kennedy and Frank Haffey.

Credit had to be given to manager Hugh Shaw for saving Rovers from relegation, and the man of the match was veteran Andy Leigh, still doing his bit for the Rovers and keeping Steve Chalmers and John Divers quiet.

Rovers also took advantage of the fact that Celtic were now demotivated. The crowd on this damp day was given as 12,000 whereas a mile away at Hampden Rangers were beating St Mirren 2-0 in the Scottish Cup final before a crowd of over 120,000.

Celtic and their supporters found this hard to take, and such was the standard of the fare on offer here that quite a few of them drifted away in the second half or even transferred their allegiance to Raith Rovers, recognising that here was a team who had fallen on hard times but were at least battling.

Their own team wasn't even doing that! When Bobby Davidson blew for full time, the small knot of Raith Rovers supporters celebrated loudly in the empty stadium, as the Public Address system tactlessly told everyone that Rangers had won the Scottish Cup.

April 22 1967

Raith Rovers today took a large step towards promotion with a competent 3-1 win over Hamilton Academical at Douglas Park.

This result combined with the news that the game at Cappielow between Champions Morton and Arbroath had ended in a goalless draw meant that Rovers were now level on points with the Red Lichties, but had the crucial advantage of a game in hand.

The crowd at Hamilton was a poor one of 1,291. Hamilton supporters had clearly given up for the season, but the crowd was supplemented by a few extra bus loads from Kirkcaldy.

They saw their team, talented but infuriatingly inconsistent sometimes, go into an early lead with a Pat Gardner header following an Ian Porterfield free-kick in the sixth minute.

Towards the end of the first half Rovers doubled their lead with a goal from Gordon Wallace following good work from Ian Lister.

Things turned even better in the second half when Small of Hamilton had the misfortune to concede an own goal. Although Hamilton pulled one back, Rovers, with Bobby Evans, in command never looked like losing.

The small band of supporters were anxious however. In the absence of any reliable information from the radio or anywhere else, mischievous rumours were spreading about how Arbroath were beating Morton.

However full time brought a loud speaker announcement to the effect that the game at Cappielow had finished goalless.

Rovers now had two games left — away to Montrose on Wednesday, never an easy ground to visit — then a home game against Queen of the South on Saturday.

April 23 1949

Close to 10,000 shared the tension at Stark's Park today as Rovers took on St Johnstone in one of the tightest ever promotion races to the "A" Division.

Stirling Albion, who had played all their games, were already there, but Raith Rovers, Dunfermline and Airdrie were still battling it out for the other spot.

Because Raith had been involved in the League Cup, they had games to play and this was one of them.

Accounts of the game are all unanimous in saying that as a football spectacle, it was a dreadful occasion with words like "scrappy" and "nervous" used all the time, as a defeat would certainly kill Rovers chances and a draw would not be a great deal of use.

Next week was scheduled the game against Dunfermline Athletic — a huge occasion at the best of times - and absolutely vital, as long as the Rovers won today.

St Johnstone had nothing really to play for, but were out to dent the Rovers. Half-time came to an eerily quiet Stark's Park with no score, and no-one really looking like scoring.

Then just after half-time, Rovers' star man of the season, Willie Penman, got a goal. Like the rest of the game, "scrappy" was again the word; as the ball rebounded back off a post Willie was on hand to prod home.

But another goal did not come in spite of the increasing dominance of men like Andy Young, and with supporters counting the minutes to full time — trains passing often gave an indication of how long to go "that one usually gets in at 4.25" — goalkeeper Doug Westland was called upon to keep everything calm.

But eventually the full time whistle came and it all meant that Rovers would be promoted if they beat Dunfermline next week!

April 24 1909

The Fife Cup is often seen as an irrelevance today, and sometimes even suffers from the indignity of being ignored and not even competed for in some seasons.

Not in 1909, however, when a huge crowd in lovely weather descended on the neutral venue of North End Park, Cowdenbeath to see the Fife Cup final between Raith Rovers and East Fife.

Special trains ran from both Kirkcaldy and Methil. The police and the authorities were more than a little edgy, for the previous Saturday had seen the Hampden Riot at the Scottish Cup final, and they feared something similar here.

No disturbances, however, other than a few brave Suffragette ladies distributing pamphlets and enduring the coarse taunts of some of the supporters.

Rovers, to the delight of their fans, won 3-0 with two goals coming from Tom McAinsh and another from Davie Axford. The crowd of 2,900 yielded net receipts of £58.

The Fife Cup thus joined the Stark Cup on the sideboard, and in a few days' time the Penman Cup would also be accrued, but important as these things were, they were not the main issue as far as Raith Rovers were concerned.

This was the ongoing campaign to become members of the Scottish League First Division. It was not in 1909 a question or promotion and relegation.

It was a question of "knocking on doors" and impressing the other teams that a county like Fife deserved some sort of representation at the top table of Scottish football. Days like today would certainly help.

April 25 1914

Raith Rovers played their last home game of the season before 4,000 fans at Stark's Park and beat Queen's Park 1-0 thanks to a Fred Gibson penalty kick.

The score should in fact have been a lot more over the lowly amateurs who were third from the bottom of the League. Nevertheless, Rovers fans were happy with the season, which once again confirmed them as a respectable First Division club.

The season had lacked the excitement of last year when Rovers reached the final of the Scottish Cup, but there had been a few good moments.

Certainly there were some good players, notably a very strong half-back line of James Logan, George McLay and Willie Porter.

This season had also seen International recognition when Harry Anderson had been capped for Scotland at left half, although he was now playing today at inside left!

Today's big match was the English Cup final at the Crystal Palace — an all Red Roses of Lancashire affair in which Burnley beat Liverpool and captain Boyle had the trophy presented to him by King George V.

In Scotland, a League and Cup double had been won by an inspired Celtic side, but the great day had been a few weeks earlier when Scotland beat England at Hampden.

The cricket season had already started and everyone was looking forward to the balmy days of summer.

It was as well that no-one had the slightest inkling of what lay ahead. If anyone talked about politics at all, it was of the endless complications of Irish Home Rule or of these tiresome Suffragettes.

The main entrance to Stark's Park until the 1990s

April 26 1967

These were heady days for Scottish football.

Last night Celtic had reached the final of the European Cup, tonight Kilmarnock had reached the semi-final of the Inter Cities Fairs' Cup and next week Rangers would try to reach the final of the Cup Winners' Cup.

And we were all still on cloud nine after the win at Wembley 11 days ago.

Small wonder then that Montrose 1 Raith Rovers 1 did not really make the national headlines.

Yet it was a crucially important result for Raith Rovers, in that it meant that all Rovers had to do to ensure promotion to the First Division was to win on Saturday in their final game against Queen of the South at Stark's Park.

Their fate was now in their own hands and it did not matter what anyone else did. It had been a long time since Links Park, Montrose, a pleasant but mundane ground, had seen such a crowd especially on a Wednesday night.

Of the 2,657 crowd it would be reasonable to say that 2,000 were Raith supporters, but for a long time, they were frustrated.

A draw would give Rovers the initiative in the promotion race, but Montrose had gone ahead through young Bobby Livingstone, a man who would became a Montrose Great over the next few years, and then Raith simply could not score with the cynics of the "they're not wanting promotion" persuasion beginning to make their voices heard.

But then with time running out, they scored.

What can only be described as a scrappy goal by Pat Gardner went in off the post.

That made it 1-1, and Rovers were now ahead of Arbroath.

Oh, Arbroath! Maybe that explains why some of the Montrose guys weren't exactly in tears at the end!

April 27 1968

We all know that Raith Rovers supporters are emphatically not narrow-minded, insular, selfish, bigoted sort of people, don't we?

Heavens, no! Perish the thought!

So there was a great deal of rejoicing (there was, wasn't there?) in Kirkcaldy when Dunfermline won the Scottish Cup today beating Hearts 3-1 in the final.

In fact, there was a lot to be happy about, for not only was the manager of the Pars, George Farm, an ex-Rovers man stolen from us last summer, but all three Dunfermline goals were scored by ex-Rovers men — one from Ian Lister and two from Pat Gardner.

In fact it was the second year in a row that ex-Rovers men had scored two goals in the Scottish Cup final, for Willie Wallace had done likewise last year for Celtic.

(It was a pity they couldn't score two goals in a Scottish Cup final for Raith Rovers, wasn't it?)

There was further cause for happiness (of the Schadenfreude variety admittedly) when Rovers fans learned that Rangers had blown up and lost the League that same day, for they had been incredibly lucky to get the better of Rovers at Stark's Park two weeks ago in a very tight 3-2 game.

Rovers themselves had finished the season reasonably happy to have avoided relegation, something that did not look at all likely round about the turn of the year, particularly New Year's Day when they lost 0-6 to Dunfermline.

Aagh! (But that was on a hard pitch and the game should have been off!)

April 28 1945

It wasn't just the football season that was coming to an end today.

So too was the 1,000 year Reich with the Russians last reported to be a few streets away from Hitler's bunker, and news was expected at any minute of "unconditional surrender".

Hitler himself was still believing in phantom armies that were going to rescue him, but it was only a matter of time.

Meanwhile, on a rather windy day in Kirkcaldy, with people quietly optimistic about good news, Raith Rovers were taking on Falkirk in the North Eastern League at Stark's Park.

Form had been unpredictable, (as was always likely to be the case in wartime circumstances) but it looked as if Rovers would end up round about the middle of the table.

The crowd was about 3,000 (it was a fallacy to suggest that war time football attracted poor crowds) and they saw a good game won 5-1 by Raith, the star man being Andy Young of Celtic (playing on loan for Rovers, and looking like it might be a good idea for Rovers to try to buy him).

They also had a player with the name (appropriate for the times) of Willie Montgomery, who had a good game, but two goals were scored by left winger Willie Penman, who looked particularly sharp.

The crowd cheered, but every time the loud speaker spluttered into action, there was a noticeable sudden pause.

Everyone knew that "they had a wireless in there" and really important news might be coming, especially for those whose "laudies" were in Germany, the Far East or on the High Seas.

April 29 1967

It was a great day at Stark's Park.

A crowd of 5,921 — maybe a little disappointing in the circumstances — turned up to see Raith Rovers regain promotion to the First Division from which they had been absent since 1963.

The Second Division had been won deservedly by Morton. For Rovers to pip Arbroath for second place, all they had to do was beat Queen of the South, and this they did with a degree of ease, beating the Doonhamers (for whom this was a meaningless end of season game) 7-2.

Gordon Wallace, signed from Montrose earlier in the season, scored a hat trick, Bobby Stein scored two and Pat Gardner and Ian Lister one each as Rovers sailed into the First Division to the great joy of all concerned.

The pitch was invaded at the end by boys determined to congratulate their heroes, and great praise was heaped on manager George Farm, that sometimes brusque and outspoken character who did not suffer fools gladly but who had done a great job for the club.

This was believed to be the day that Sam Leitch said "they would be dancing in the streets of Raith", but one often feels that that story, often attributed to David Coleman, may be an urban myth and owes a little to romantic exaggeration!

There was no exaggeration, however, in the romance one felt for Bobby Evans, now almost at the end of a great career — he had been playing since 1944! — and being instrumental in the return of Raith Rovers to the First Division.

His old team Celtic also did well that day, winning the Scottish Cup by beating Aberdeen 2-0 and both goals were scored by ex-Rovers favourite Willie Wallace.

April 30 1949

For the Division "B" Championship decider between Raith Rovers and Dunfermline, Stark's Park was absolutely crammed today with an attendance given as 24,150.

Those who were there insist that there was an awful lot more than that. People were seen scaling the walls and even, incredibly, entering the park via the railway line.

A draw would have been enough for the Pars but Rovers needed to win. This they did by the barely credible score line of 4-0.

One would have to agree with Dunfermline supporters that a key moment came early on when, following an accidental collision with Willie Penman, their goalkeeper Jimmy Michie was carried off, leaving (in these pre-substitute days) Dunfermline with only 10 men and an outfield player having to act as goalkeeper.

This proved to be an insuperable handicap.

Although Willie Penman (who had scored an incredible amount of 58 goals in all competitions this season) did not score, he was enough of a decoy to allow Allan Collins and Jimmy Stirling to score two each.

With a defence like Westland, McClure and McNaught; Young, Colville and Leigh, there was little hope that 10-man Dunfermline could score, and long before the final whistle, the celebrations had started.

Considering that the team had also reached the final of the Scottish League Cup that season as well, one would have to say that 1949 was a great year for Raith Rovers, and the following year in Division "A" was looked forward to with a great deal of relish.

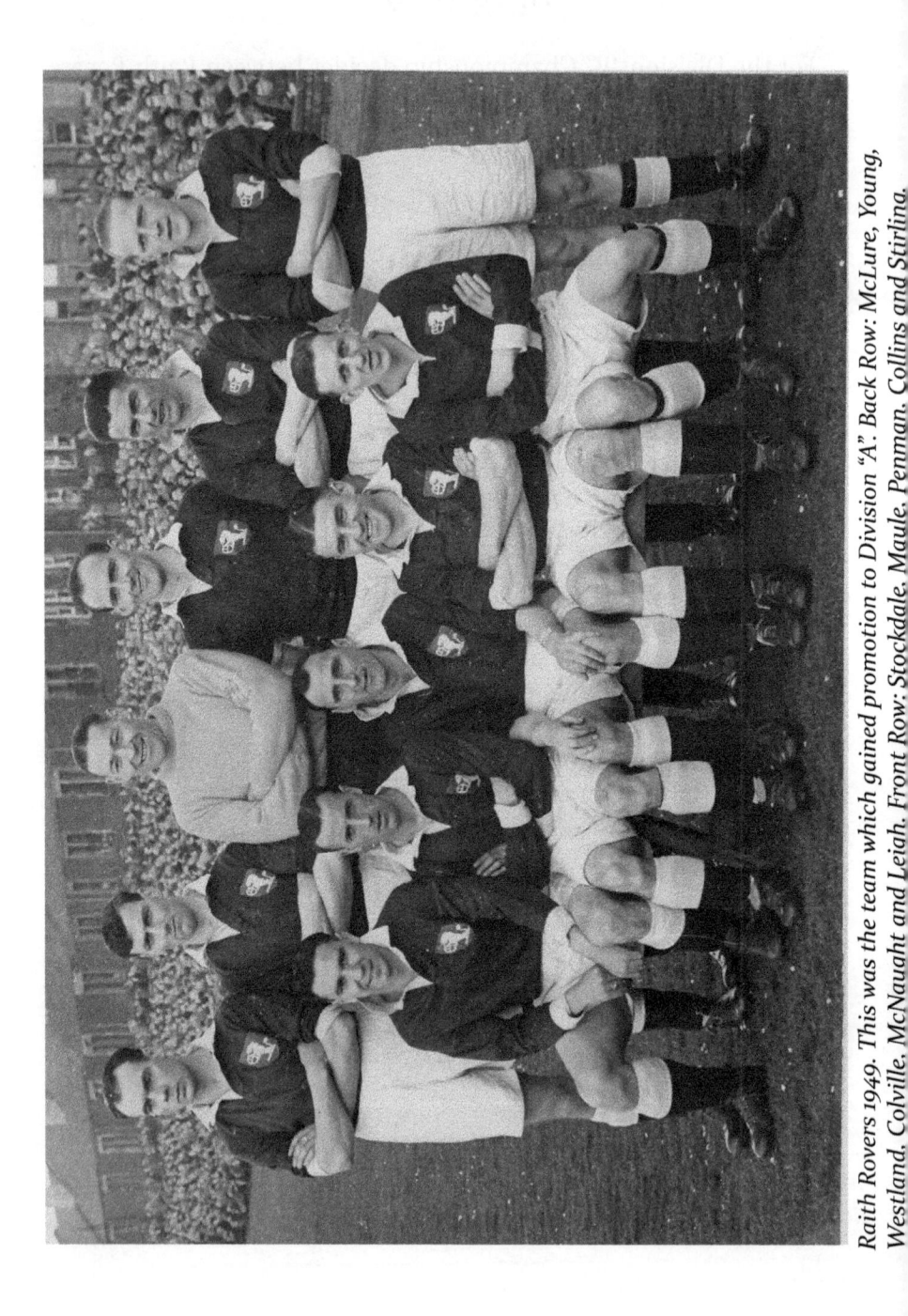

Raith Rovers 1949. This was the team which gained promotion to Division "A". Back Row: McLure, Young, Westland, Colville, McNaught and Leigh. Front Row: Stockdale, Maule, Penman, Collins and Stirling.

May

Raith Rovers Football Club
IRN BRU Scottish 2nd. Division
CHAMPIONS
2008 - 2009

May 1 1926

A truly awful season for Raith Rovers came to a fittingly dreadful end today at Methil.

They went down 0-2 to East Fife in the Fife Charity Cup.

The crowd was meagre, and there certainly were very few from Kirkcaldy who went along the coast. Asset-stripping had brought its own reward in the shape of relegation.

It really was astonishing the speed with which this fine side, as good as any in Scotland from 1922-1924 had now morphed into an under-performing, poor, side with little hope of regaining any kind of eminence in Scotland any time soon.

But Rovers' decline was not entirely unconnected with events on a broader stage. May 1 1926 saw football pushed to one side by the imminence of the General Strike called by the Trade Union Congress for Monday.

The origins lay in the coalmining industry and, of course, affected Kirkcaldy intimately. The coal owners were attempting to lengthen the working day and to lower wages while still clearly making huge profits.

The National Union of Miners had appealed to the TUC for support, and it had been given.

Supporters of East Fife and Raith Rovers were united in their support of the strike, while the Press were talking hysterically about "anarchy" and "revolution" fearing that what had happened in Russia in 1917 was about to happen here.

In the event, after a few spectacular days of the country being virtually immobilised, the whole thing fizzled out — apart from the miners who continued their strike in awful circumstances until the autumn.

May 2 2015

One presumes that the writer on the BBC website did not have his tongue in cheek as he talked about an "end-of-season thriller" at the Dumbarton Football Stadium, as it was called in 2015 but has changed since.

In fact Rovers' season had probably ended weeks ago and this draw brought to an end a dismal run of five defeats in a row, something that failed to upset the support overmuch, because they had now all but given up.

Admittedly two of the defeats had been to Rangers and Hearts, but Rovers (like Dumbarton) were in the comfortable place of the middle of the Championship, not affected by play offs at either end.

It had to be looked upon as a successful season in that regard, and today the two teams served up a reasonable game for the meagre crowd of 801.

The Sons of the Rock scored first with a rebound off the post which came back to Jordan Kirkpatrick, but then Rovers equalised and went ahead in a ten minute spell in the second half when first Mark Stewart equalised, then Lewis Vaughan with a deft lob caught the goalkeeper napping after a poor kick-out.

With time running out, and Rovers looking as if they were heading to their 13th League win of the season, Scott Agnew equalised for the home side with a curling shot which deceived goalkeeper David McGurn.

An over fussy referee booked three players, but it wasn't really that kind of game.

May 3 2008

This was another sad end to the season as Raith Rovers drew 2-2 with Airdrie United at the Shyberry Excelsior.

This meant that the First Division play-off semi-final had ended 4-2 in favour of Airdrie.

The damage had really been done in the first leg at Stark's Park on Wednesday night when Airdrie had won 2-0, but today's result was slightly misleading as well in that Rovers had equalised only in the final minute when the tie was over and many of the fans had already made their way to the exits.

Airdrie had opened the scoring, but then Graham Weir had netted a penalty awarded for hand-ball to give Rovers a theoretical chance.

A few chances came Rovers way but they were squandered.

At 1-3 down, the tie ended for Raith Rovers when Iain Davidson made a mistake and allowed Bobby Donnelly to put the tie beyond reach.

Graham Weir's late goal was an irrelevance.

Raith's manager John McGlynn would claim that all Airdrie's goals over the two legs were defensive errors, but the truth was that Airdrie were the better team.

In any case Raith's form over the season had not always been impressive, and the team would probably not have lasted long in the First Division.

Airdrie in fact lost the play-off final to Clyde, but were promoted anyway because Gretna went bankrupt, leaving two places.

Airdrie had, of course, themselves gone bust a few years earlier as Airdrieonians, but had now resurrected themselves as Airdrie United. This was a great triumph for them.

May 4 1996

The curtain came down on an acceptable season.

Rovers consolidated their Premiership status even though Jimmy Nicholl had inexplicably abandoned them in favour of Millwall (yes, Millwall!) in February.

The last game of the season, with Jimmy Thomson in charge, was at a half-built Celtic Park on a pleasantly warm but possibly rather too windy a day.

The pitch, as often happens at the end of the season, was fiery and a little bare, and Rovers did not give any great impression of being bothered at the 1-4 defeat.

Celtic themselves, with not even a theoretical chance of catching Rangers, scored some good goals (two through Jorge Cadete, and one each from Stuart Gray and Peter Grant).

Peter Duffield scored Rovers only goal.

Rovers finished sixth (fifth equal if one discounts goal difference) in the Premier League, and this must go down as one of their better seasons, holding at least their own against the weaker teams like Falkirk and Partick Thistle.

Ironically the venue for the final game of the season, Celtic Park, was also where they had exited from both Cup competitions.

For their Premier League survival this season, a great deal of credit was owed to Jimmy Thomson who took over in unfortunate circumstances but inherited a reasonably good squad and introduced a few good buys himself, not least Peter Duffield, the scorer of today's goal.

Ian Porterfield

May 5 1973

It is a shame that so many of Raith Rovers' triumphs are done by proxy, as it were, for a different club.

Rovers fans had cause to be happy with events at Wembley today when Second Division Sunderland beat the favourites Leeds United 1-0 to win the English Cup.

The only goal of the game was scored by Ian Porterfield, ex Raith Rovers, in the 32nd minute.

A fine goal it was, too, as he found room for himself in the penalty box to turn and shoot past Leeds goalkeeper David Harvey.

Ian, although he was officially called John, had been with Rovers between 1964 and 1967.

He had of course been heavily identified with the promotion season of 1967, but had sadly not stayed around for long enough to make an impact on the Scottish First Division with the Rovers.

He was a fine midfield player, very strong in the tackle and with the ability to take a goal or two, as he proved today, creating one of the few highlights in the sadly underperforming history of the Mackems.

The final is also remembered for the fine double save by Sunderland's goalkeeper Jimmy Montgomery, and it is a comment on the times that each team had four Scotsmen playing for them!

The success of Sunderland was not really maintained, however, and Porterfield had a couple of seasons as manager of Aberdeen, but found Alex Ferguson a hard act to follow.

May 6 1967

To Raith Rovers supporters already on a high after winning promotion last week, this game came as an added bonus.

They won the Fife Cup by beating East Fife 5-1 at Stark's Park today.

The Fife Cup, once a mighty tournament with great prestige given to the winners, was not always taken seriously these days with weakened teams and the final being held over to the following season and things like that.

But not this year, for in spite of the incessant rain, over 2,000 appeared to see a great second half performance after what had been a fairly pedestrian first half.

It was as if someone had pressed a switch with Gordon Wallace netting a hat-trick and the other goals coming from Ian Lister and Pat Gardner.

As the trophy was duly presented at the end, the wet and bedraggled fans thus celebrated for the second Saturday in succession at Stark's Park, for last week had been the famous 7-2 defeat of Queen of the South to gain promotion to the First Division.

Things looked good for Rovers fans, for there was the First Division to look forward to next year, and there seemed to be a decent team in place.

Meanwhile in Glasgow, Celtic were drawing with Rangers to win the Scottish League with both teams having European Cup finals to look forward to.

And as it was only three weeks since Scotland beat England at Wembley, it wasn't a bad time to be alive!

May 7 2016

A major disappointment today for Raith Rovers at Easter Road.

They went out of the quarter final play-off for admission to the Premiership.

Rovers had had a reasonably good season and finished fourth in the Championship. This meant that they qualified for the play-off quarter final against Hibs, and hopes were high that they could progress after a 1-0 win at Stark's Park with a goal scored by Harry Panayiotou.

Alas! Hopes were dashed today, when Hibs simply upped a gear and were too good for Rovers. They got a bit of luck when John McGinn's shot took a bit of a deflection in the eighth minute and entered the net via the crossbar.

11,133 mostly Hibs fans then became animated, and four minutes later, Hibs went ahead in the tie, with a fine header scored by Darren McGregor from a Liam Henderson cross, McGregor rising high and heading low.

This seemed to knock the stuffing out of Rovers, and although there was well over an hour and a quarter to go, no meaningful fightback game from a team who simply "froze".

Realists in the support said that possibly the Premiership was a stage too far for Ray McKinnon's side in any case, but it was still a disappointment.

Hibs, managed at this time by Alan Stubbs, themselves failed to qualify, going down to Falkirk, although they had a major compensation in the shape of the Scottish Cup a fortnight later.

They had been waiting for it since 1902, so no-one could really grudge them it. But it was to be the Championship once again for both Hibs and Rovers.

May 8 1979

A pretty dreadful season came to an end tonight at Dens Park, Dundee.

The home side won 2-0, more or less guaranteeing themselves Premier Division football next season.

The home fans certainly thought that, for they invaded the field at the end, even though promotion was not yet a mathematical certainty.

They had certainly defeated Raith fair and square, and Gordon Wallace congratulated Tommy Gemmell on his achievement at the end.

For Raith Rovers, it had been a long and painful season. A bad winter had caused loads of postponements, explaining why the season was taking so long to come to an end.

Rovers had also changed managers at the end of January with Gordon Wallace taking over from Willie McLean.

Wallace had been able to avoid relegation, but it was clear that some major surgery would be required.

There were some good players like Murray McDermott, Chris Candlish and Donald Urquhart, but the team had been cursed by inconsistency, and sagged alarmingly towards the end of the season.

Nevertheless, there was an example here in Dundee of how things could go well even after a few bad seasons, and hope was expressed, as always, that things might be better next year.

The system of the three Divisions had been in place for four years now, and Rovers had been in both Division One and Two, but had yet to taste the fruits of the Premier League.

Those who recalled the visits of the big teams in the 1950s and 1960s missed that.

Frank Connor

May 9 1987

Raith today gained promotion from the Second Division in remarkable circumstances.

In the first place, they did so at Stair Park, Stranraer, and then, they did it when no-one expected them to.

Meadowbank had won the Division.

Rovers had battled hard all season but seemed to be just a little short when they drew their third last and second last games against Ayr United and St Johnstone.

But there was still a ray of hope. Raith had to win at Stranraer — and manager Frank Connor kept telling the Press that this would indeed happen — and Stirling had to beat Ayr at Somerset Park.

An attendance of 625 does not suggest that the Raith Army marched south in any great numbers, but there were at least a couple of buses and a few carloads, mainly of the diehard "never miss a game" sort of fan, not the Johnny-come-latelies who appeared, for example, at the League Cup final in 1994, talking knowledgeably about the club as if they had watched them all their life.

The game at Stair Park started off poorly, but then Rovers took a grip with Gordon Dalziel on song and scoring twice in what was eventually a 4-1 victory.

But Ayr were going to win at Somerset Park, weren't they? Well no, for Stirling Albion found themselves 3-0 up and things looked great.

A local radio station called West Sound was giving a commentary with poor reception and a hysterical commentator, but more reliable information came from BBC Radio Scotland who told us that Ayr had pulled one back, then another and were now only one more goal away from promotion.

But Stirling held out and Rovers were promoted!

May 10 1922

Raith Rovers about to embark to Denmark for a summer tour in 1922

May 10 2017

Glebe Park, Brechin was the destination this Wednesday night as the troops headed northwards to see the Championship play-off (or play-aff, as some supporters put it!).

Raith had of course ended up second bottom of the Championship thanks to some appalling football in mid-season and indeed if they had not rallied a little towards the end, they might have finished up rock bottom instead of Ayr United.

But here we were in the play-offs alongside Brechin, Alloa and Airdrie. The crowd was just a little over 1,000, obviously Brechin's best crowd for a while, and it owed a lot to the Raith Rovers supporters.

It was a good game tonight. Brechin took the lead with a penalty just on half time, but then Declan McManus equalised for Rovers halfway through the second half.

It was a fair result, Rovers fans all felt, as the cars sped home via Forfar and Dundee. There wouldn't really be any problem in beating them in the second leg on Saturday, would there?

Then again, of course, we would have to kill it early, and if we didn't, well you never know what could happen with a penalty shoot-out, do you?

But no, surely not, the Championship is for teams like Raith Rovers from fairly large towns and with good supports, not for the likes of Brechin who, although technically a City, are really little more than a village, are they not?

No, no, we will win on Saturday nae bother, and then Alloa will be similarly disposed of, and we will retain our Championship status!

May 11 1901

Disappointingly, Raith Rovers lost their opportunity to play Scottish Cup winners Hearts in the final of the East of Scotland Shield.

They lost today to Leith Athletic by the only goal of the game in the semi-final at Easter Road, having drawn 0-0 the previous week at Tynecastle.

This was a blow to the club which now had aspirations to reach the Scottish League, and indeed would play in the Northern League next year.

Feelings of jealousy however prevailed in the town and not everyone was unhappy at their discomfiture, for lovers of other local teams felt that Raith Rovers were getting "above themselves".

Rovers were however a good side and had a good following — as had been evidenced by the large numbers of supporters who had gone with them on the train to Edinburgh to see both semi-finals.

The 1901 season had been a successful one with the winning of three trophies — the Wemyss Cup, the King Cup and the East of Scotland Qualifying Cup, and the club was ambitious.

Scottish League entry was clearly desirable, but could not necessarily be achieved by results alone — a certain amount of what was called "jobbery" was needed in the shape of bribery, sycophancy or "quid pro quo".

Yet a thriving town the size of Kirkcaldy could surely support a Scottish League team, and as the team had now played in successive weeks at Tynecastle and then Easter Road, they had a taste of the big time.

But today's result was a disappointment, and the season had now ended.

May 12 1926

Kirkcaldy was maybe not exactly paralysed but was nevertheless deeply affected by the General Strike which had now been going on for a week.

There had been the odd outbreak of violence on picket lines elsewhere in Fife, but Kirkcaldy generally was quite calm and peaceful.

News however emanated from Stark's Park to the effect that manager James Logan had resigned.

This news would be carried in tomorrow's *Dundee Courier*, which had managed on some days to produce a newspaper and other days not.

The news travelled quickly through the town. Many people were hanging around idle, and the weather was actually very pleasant.

The main mood was one of sadness, for Logan had done so much for the club, which had now been dismantled by the selling of star players to England, and of course the team had been relegated.

It was time, one felt, for a new start and a rebuilding.

Logan's big failure was that he had not won anything. Kilmarnock, Partick Thistle, Morton, Airdrie and St Mirren, teams of similar status had all won the Scottish Cup, but Raith, although arguably having a better team, had not actually won a trophy.

It was also clear by this time that the General Strike was fizzling out. The Government had stood firm and essential supplies had been delivered, and workers were beginning to ask why they should not go back to their work?

The Trades Union Congress would indeed capitulate, leaving the miners isolated. The miners would stay on strike for another few months in conditions of dreadful poverty before being compelled to return in the autumn.

By that time, Raith Rovers would be experiencing life in the Second Division.

May 13 1995

For the second time this season, Rovers and their supporters returned from Glasgow in triumph.

The circumstances were however quite different.

Rovers travelled to Firhill to play not Partick Thistle but Hamilton, who were temporary lodgers at Firhill because they were in the throes of moving to New Douglas Park.

Jimmy Nicholl's men knew that a draw would be enough to win the First Division Championship, as they had drawn 0-0 with Dunfermline last week.

As it happened today, both nearest challengers, Dunfermline Athletic and Dundee, won, Dundee quite handsomely, but it did not matter as long as Raith did not lose.

Hamilton had "only professional pride to play for" and did not seem to pose any threat, but neither really did Raith Rovers, and the two sides played out the most dull 0-0 draw anyone was ever likely to see on a dry, bumpy pitch which had had an awful lot football played on it all season.

The crowd was 5333 and seemed to consist more or less entirely of Raith Rovers fans looking at their watches and willing the minutes to pass.

They duly did, and full time saw great celebration at the return to Premier League football after only a year downstairs.

The men who bore Raith Rovers to triumph that day were Thomson, McAnespie, Broddle, Narey, Denis, Raeside, Nicholl, Dalziel, Dair (Wilson), Cameron and Sinclair.

There was distinct feeling of anti-climax, but the job was done.

Jason Dair

May 14 1898

The Fife Free Press was of the opinion that the weather was a "trifle too warm" for this local encounter at Newtown (sometimes written Newton) Park between Raith Rovers and Kirkcaldy in what was Rovers' final game of the season.

This was the "second test match" (according to the writer who possibly felt that they should have been playing cricket instead) for the Kirkcaldy Cottage Hospital Cup, a trophy given by the Nairn family.

The report of the game is duly respectful (some might use the word "sycophantic") about the Nairn family, for we are told that both Miss Nairn of The Priory and Miss Nairn of Dysart House were in attendance along with various crawling Town Councillors.

The game was as one-sided as the 8-0 score line would suggest (it had been 6-0 the week before) and this was really a very fine Raith Rovers side, now clearly, if there had ever been any doubt before, the best local side.

It was slaughter in the sunshine with 7 goals being scored into "the railway goal" in the first half, and the second half a long bore in the intensifying heat.

Davie Walker scored three, Jock Eckford and Andy Blyth two each and Jimmy Neilson the other one.

At the end, one of the Miss Nairns presented the trophy and gold medals to the players, and then everyone called for three cheers for everyone else, with the loudest ones being called for Miss Nairn — just in case the Kirkcaldy working class were going to forget who their masters were.

May 15 1982

The curtain was brought down on a very disappointing season.

Raith Rovers went down 0-1 to St Johnstone at home in front of a diehard crowd of slightly over 1,000.

Even that must allow for a fairly large contingent of St Johnstone supporters, who were there in reasonably large numbers, although their season had been similarly bereft of anything to get excited about.

The weather was pleasantly warm, something which was nice to see after a hard winter with snow and hail as recently as two weeks ago.

The poor crowd showed that Rovers were still paying the price for what happened last year and the perception, difficult to eradicate from the support, that promotion to the Premier League last year could have been achieved with a little more effort.

It was difficult to persuade spectators to attend in season 1981/82, and in spite of Gordon Wallace's efforts the team finished third bottom, just above the relegation spot.

Next year, we trusted, would be better but in the meantime there was the World Cup to look forward to.

There was however a problem about that, and that was the Falklands War in the South Atlantic. Argentina had occupied the Falkland Islands at the beginning of April, and Great Britain had sent a task force to remove them.

The British forces would in time do that just as the World Cup was starting, but in the meantime it was as well that Scotland or England did not meet Argentina.

The refereeing would have had to be good in these circumstances!

May 16 2017

The club today issued an important statement.

There has been a day of important meetings at Stark's Park today. The board of directors met this morning to consider the financial implications of our relegation from the Ladbrokes Championship. This was followed by a meeting between the board, players and football support staff as a group, and then a series of meetings with individual players and support staff to discuss their own personal contractual situations and options for the way forward. Finally the board met again to review the findings of the day's discussions and agreed to continue to work towards achieving the objective of retaining full time football for season 2017 / 2018. A further progress report on this work will be issued as soon as possible, and in the meantime the board will take its time to identify a new manager.

All this was in the wake of what had happened on Saturday.

In a distinctly traumatic couple of hours for Raith Rovers supporters, the team saw the loss of its Championship status, in a penalty shoot-out to Brechin City, and the more or less immediate departure of the manager, who did not stick around.

The team had had a poor season - a bright start, a gradual decline and then an awful spell from the end of October until the beginning of March when not a single game was won.

The prospect of First Division football (the third tier) failed to live up to the expectations of the supporters, but at least the supporters could console themselves with the thought that it was nothing really new!

May 17 2017

The trauma of Raith Rovers supporters continued.

Just four days after the play-off defeat by Brechin and following yesterday's vague and unsatisfactory announcements about the future of the club, it was announced that French centre half Jean-Yves M'Voto had turned down a another year's contract and had decided to move to Dunfermline Athletic.

While logically no-one could blame a man for going to a more successful club and one that was to play in a higher division and which also had a manager in place, Raith fans were bitter about M'Voto who was blamed disproportionately for the Brechin disaster.

M'Voto himself was honest enough to admit he had made two mistakes to allow Brechin to score.

This tends to ignore the fact that he had had a good season for the club, a bulwark when everything was collapsing all about him.

He had even scored a goal for the club in the play-off, and a good one it was as well!

M'Voto, a man of many clubs, probably played as well for Raith Rovers as he had for anyone else, and it would have been nice to see him at Stark's Park under better circumstances than the chaotic 2016/17 season.

He wished Raith Rovers well and said he would understand it if the Rovers fans booed him if they ever met again.

Raith Rovers fans were probably a great deal less charitable about him, but now had to turn their attention to the rebuilding of their team in their new and straitened circumstances.

Summer and no football was a relief.

May 18 1930

On the same day (a Sunday!) that Scotland beat France 2-0 in Paris in one of the first overseas internationals, Alec James who, many believed, should have been playing for Scotland made a public gesture of gratitude to one of Raith Rovers Directors Robert Morrison.

James had just won the English Cup with Arsenal on April 26 and James had scored the first goal as the Gunners beat Huddersfield Town 2-0 in the final.

The game was made memorable by the appearance overhead of the German airship the Graf Zeppelin.

Incredibly it was Arsenal's first-ever major honour and only the third time that a London team had won the English Cup.

James had been presented with his medal by King George V but now decided that he should give it to Mr Morrison, the Raith Rovers Director who had discovered him playing for Bellshill Athletic and then Glasgow Ashfield and who persuaded the other Directors that James was worth a go.

When he came to Kirkcaldy, Morrison had also encouraged James to read books (something that he had not done very much of) and also befriended him when the crowd turned on him (as they did sometimes when they thought he was overdoing the trickery).

Even before the English Cup final, Morrison, now an old man, had written to James wishing him all the best.

James, in donating his Cup medal to Morrison, showed how grateful he was to Morrison in particular and to Raith Rovers in general for giving him a great start in his football career.

May 19 1922

Raith Rovers set off home from Denmark after a very successful post-season tour.

They had played three games in Denmark, but only won one of them.

This may have been looked upon as a disappointment, considering the fact that the team had finished third in the Scottish League, but one must make allowance for them adapting to different conditions.

The team had set off on Wednesday May 10, and had played their first game of the tour on Sunday May 14, a Sunday game being something that would have shocked quite a few people back home in the town, notably Rev John Campbell of the Old Kirk.

The Courier praises the team and says that it was a happy tour, but there were other perceptions as well.

Some of the Danish Press accused Raith Rovers of dirty play and singled out Bill Collier who was "near to taking the life from" a Danish player in a somewhat melodramatic piece of writing.

In the last game, Dave Morris was greatly admired for his heading ability and Bobby Archibald was given a round of applause all to himself.

But the whole thing was a great experience for the Kirkcaldy men, who probably would have had no other opportunity of visiting the continent other than with the football team — or if there were to be another war!

The journey across the North Sea passed in very fine weather and took two days, and *The Courier* tells us that they docked in Leith early on the Sunday morning.

May 20 1926

It was two suitably chastened Raith Rovers representatives who attended the AGM of the Scottish Football League at 6 Calton Place, Glasgow.

Rovers had now, of course been relegated to Division Two for the first time since their promotion before the Great War, and the club was still facing a large amount of criticism in the local press, normally of the sarcastic "Congratulations on your relegation" variety.

The main shaft of the criticism was for selling good players and buying "duds" but this was not always fair because the dire economic circumstances of the time compelled them to do such things.

Another sign of the times came at the AGM today with the news that the Third Division had imploded because too many clubs had gone bankrupt and had been unable to fulfil their fixtures.

The Third Division was therefore abolished and two ex-Third Division clubs were voted into the Second Division, namely Bathgate and Forfar whose applications were supported by Raith Rovers.

The demise of Division Three was a timely reminder to Raith Rovers, for there was no guarantee that Division Two might not go the same way one day.

In the meantime, Rovers had a job to do, for although some players had signed for next year, others hadn't and Rovers still did not have a manager or a trainer following the resignation of James Logan and Willie Smith.

And there was still not a great deal of money in the town for the miners were still on strike, and unemployment was unacceptably high.

May 21 1963

Raith Rovers were on their knees in summer 1963.

The weather was good, but the position of the club was gloomy.

Relegation, which had threatened for a few seasons, had now come a few days ago. Pessimists used words like "finished", whereas optimists said "they'll come again".

The optimists were given a certain boost with the news that Rovers had appointed a man called Doug Cowie to be new manager.

His remit was to be nothing more and nothing less than promotion.

It seemed to be a good choice, for Cowie, originally from Aberdeen, certainly knew enough about football. He was 37 and had played for Scotland 20 times.

He had been the mainstay of Dundee throughout the 1950s and with Tommy Gallacher and Alf Boyd had formed the mighty half-back line of Gallacher, Cowie and Boyd which Dundonians even claimed to be better than Young, McNaught and Leigh.

He had won the Scottish League Cup twice in the early 1950s with Dundee, but was just a little too old to be part of their League winning side of 1962, by which time he was playing out the last days of his career with Greenock Morton.

His appointment was greeted with enthusiasm in *The Courier* and *The Fife Free Press,* but of course a good player does not always make a good manager, the pessimists pointed out, and in any case there was an awful lot that needed to be done.

May 22 1954

Today's *Fife Free Press* carried the sad news of the death of Tommy "Tucker" Turner, who played for Raith Rovers in the 1920s.

He was only 46 and had been in poor health for about two years.

He died in Glasgow Royal Infirmary and would be buried in the Arkleston Cemetery, Renfrew.

He had played for Rovers in the late 1920s, at a time when Rovers had reached their peak and were on the decline.

Nevertheless Tommy was a good left winger with an ability to beat a man with apparent ease and to send over a good ball for his centre forward.

When Rovers were relegated in 1929, he and Leslie Bruton were transferred to Blackburn Rovers, and he played for them for several years.

In the meantime in 1954, Scotland's football players were not idle.

They had beaten Norway at Hampden, then drawn with them in Norway and were now preparing to play Finland in Helsinki.

All this was in preparation for Scotland's first ever participation in the World Cup in Switzerland in a month's time.

Not everyone was excited about this idea — indeed the SFA were distinctly half-hearted about it — but there was a rumour that some games might be on the new medium of entertainment — television.

Those lucky few who had been able to see the English Cup final at Wembley between West Bromwich Albion and Preston North End on that funny box had been impressed.

May 23 1908

John Manning, one of the heroes of the great 1907 team, and who had been transferred to Blackburn Rovers at the end of that season, paid a somewhat inglorious return visit to Kirkcaldy today.

The general consensus was that he was a better football player than he was a cricketer.

The English football season having now finished, Manning was back in Fife and playing for the strong Burntisland Cricket Club team against Kirkcaldy at the Beveridge Park.

The game was played in glorious sunshine and attracted a crowd of about 2,000 (the norm for a good day) although as people came and went from cricket matches, it was difficult to give an exact figure.

Quite a few supporters turned up to see their former hero. John (inevitably called "Jock" by the English fans) had not had the greatest of seasons down south — he had only featured in a handful of games — and it was put to him by one persistent fan that he might have been better staying with Raith Rovers!

He laughed at that, and took it as a compliment! But today he was playing cricket. He batted no 10 but did not last long, being bowled for a duck by Kirkcaldy's professional Henson.

In spite of that, Burntisland reached 217 for 9 declared and Kirkcaldy came nowhere near to that with the game being drawn at 115 for 5.

It is a practice that is frowned upon nowadays, but it used to be quite common for footballers to play cricket in the summer as a way of keeping fit.

May 24 1902

The Fife Free Press appeared as usual this Saturday morning with the town still all aglow with the achievements of Raith Rovers.

They had won the Northern League, admittedly in a play-off.

Hard on the heels of that came the Scottish League AGM, in which it had been decided to increase the League to two Divisions of 12.

Raith Rovers and Falkirk would now join Airdrie, Hamilton, Motherwell, Ayr, St Bernard's, Leith Athletic, East Stirlingshire, Arthurlie, Clyde and Abercorn in Division Two.

The problem would be an increase in travelling to teams in the West of Scotland, but that was compensated by the increase in prestige. The Directors were obviously happy, for in a rare bout of generosity, they announced that they would strike gold badges for their players who had won the Northern League.

The Fife Free Press, however, deplores the fact that everyone will now talk incessantly throughout the summer about football rather than giving cricket a chance.

Cricket had started and everyone was excited about the destination of the Ashes, but on a local level Kirkcaldy had lost heavily to Burntisland.

In the meantime news from South Africa continued to be good with the imminent prospect of a Boer surrender.

The town, like every other town, was preparing itself for the Coronation of King Edward VII in a month's time, although there were rumours circulating that the King's health was not too good.

May 25 1967

Raith Rovers played a part in Scottish football's greatest day.

Celtic beat Inter Milan 2-1 to win the European Cup, and there was an ex-Rover playing for them in Willie Wallace who had played for Bert Herdman's side in seasons 1959/60 and 1960/61.

Willie had been a great player, but was obviously destined for greater things and soon joined Hearts where he was a star and won the Scottish League Cup in October 1962.

Then Celtic bought him in December 1966 and he scored the two goals which won Celtic the Scottish Cup in 1967.

Willie always spoke highly of his time in Kirkcaldy with a particular fondness for Bert Herdman.

There was another connection as well in that Celtic's trainer was Neil Mochan, who had played the final games of his illustrious career for Raith Rovers.

Raith supporters, themselves still on a high after their promotion from Division Two, were delighted with the result for it meant that they would have a chance to play against the European Champions next year.

They were also happy for the general health of Scottish football and joined in the euphoria and merriment after the full time whistle blew at 7.15 pm on that never to be forgotten night.

Some local Celtic supporters from Kirkcaldy had gone to Lisbon.

It made it a great summer for football, because Scotland had also beaten England at Wembley in April with two ex-Rovers in the side, Jim Baxter and the same Willie Wallace!

Happy Directors in 2003 when promotion is achieved.

May 26 1982

It cannot be often that a Kirkcaldy-born man wins the European Cup, but it happened tonight in Rotterdam as Aston Villa beat Bayern Munich 1-0 to lift the trophy.

This was Ken McNaught, the central defender, who was born in Kirkcaldy on January 11 1955, the son of the great Willie McNaught.

Willie played five times for Scotland and played for Raith Rovers more often than anyone else.

It was often felt that Ken McNaught was good enough to play for Scotland, but the call never came. He had started off with Everton and played for them in the English League Cup final of 1977 against Aston Villa.

Aston Villa won but were so impressed by McNaught that they signed him soon afterwards, and they won the English League in 1981, and now the European Cup this year, a game watched avidly by the McNaught family and indeed a large number of Raith Rovers supporters who recalled his father.

The game was not a great one (European Cup finals seldom are) but McNaught played well as central defender to stifle the threat of Hoeness and Rummenigge, particularly after Peter Withe scored the only goal of the game.

Allan Evans and Des Bremner were the other two Scotsmen in the team.

The result — unexpected, for Bayern Munich were a powerful team and expected to win — was greeted with great joy in the town of Kirkcaldy.

Meanwhile, the British Army was clearly winning the Falklands War, and everyone was looking forward to the World Cup.

May 27 1939

Manager Sandy Archibald had been busy, even though Raith Rovers' season was well and truly over, and even the junior football season finished today.

He had signed a young goalkeeper called Houston from a Dundee junior side.

This man also played cricket for Cupar, reminding everyone of Tom Crosskey of a few years ago, who was actually the professional for Carlton Cricket Club.

Houston would, apparently, be a "Jock Brown" type of custodian who "filled the goal". (Jock Brown being the goalkeeper of the great team of 20 years ago).

But two players had now been released — Bob "Piper" MacKay and Johnny Buist, neither of whom really made it at Stark's, even though MacKay had been there for about 18 months and had played a few games in the great 1938 season.

They were given free transfers. No other signings had been made and *The Fife Free Press* feels compelled to remind Raith Rovers that further recruitment is necessary.

But it is another form of "recruitment" that everyone is talking about. This is 1939, and unlike 1914 when everyone was taken by surprise, very few people honestly thought that war could be avoided.

The one hope would have been a treaty with the Soviet Union but Chamberlain refused to enter into such an alliance, as Hitler continued to rant and rave, now turning his attention to Poland.

May 28 1932

The Cowdenbeath Cup final was played today at Stark's Park between Rosslyn Juniors and St Andrews United.

It was a poor game but Rosslyn Juniors were to be congratulated on their first ever winning of the Cowdenbeath Cup in which they triumphed 3-2.

The Cup final attracted a reasonable attendance as Cup finals did then, but there were distinguished guests there as well in Mr and Mrs Alec James, and another ex-player in Sandy Archibald, now of Glasgow Rangers.

Clearly revelling in being back in his old haunts, James told everyone at length about what it was like to play at Wembley in the Wembley Wizards team of 1928.

If he had been playing for the Gunners in this season's English Cup final (he had been passed fit but then injured himself in a photo-shoot!) it would have been a different story, he said. Newcastle would never have won, even with the benefit of the dodgy goal that they were given.

He told everyone that the first result he looked for in the evening paper was that of Raith Rovers, and that went down very well!

Sandy Archibald, less extroverted and more thoughtful, was also very sociable telling everyone about life at Rangers, but also saying that he still loved Raith Rovers.

He would, of course, come back to Rovers as a manager one day, but he still had a couple of years of his playing career to run at Rangers, even though he was now in his mid-30s.

May 29 1929

Football may have been enjoying a well-deserved break, but there was plenty of other things going on in Kirkcaldy and Scotland, particularly the General Election campaign.

This Wednesday night in fine weather, Tom Kennedy Labour MP held his eve-of-poll rally in the open air at the Port Brae.

It was well attended, and Kennedy was duly returned the following day with a substantial majority, not least because the Conservative candidate had a hyphenated name and was supported by Michael Nairn and Lord Novar, neither of them beloved by the Kirkcaldy populace.

It was the first General election in which all women over the age of 21 were allowed to vote, and it became known as the "flapper" election, because of the way young women dressed.

In addition, the Church of Scotland and the Free Church of Scotland decided to settle their differences and re-unite, but Kirkcaldy's two cricket teams were having a lean time, Kirkcaldy CC having lost to Leith Franklin and Dunnikier to Falkland.

All this helped to take everyone's mind of Raith Rovers' rather disappointing season for they had had been relegated again for the second time in four years.

The future did not look bright for Willie Birrell and his men, not least for the fairly obvious reason that the club did not have any money!

The better players found employment elsewhere, and rumours swept the town periodically about insolvency and the need to become an amateur club.

May 30 1936

The Fife Free Press appears this Friday with an interesting story that James Logan, who has twice been manager of Raith Rovers will be interviewed for the managerial job at Lincoln City.

The reporter than talks nostalgically of Logan's great forward line on 1922/23 of Bell, Miller, Jennings, James and Archibald and how a great English team offered a phenomenal amount for all five of them, possibly about £50,000.

The club in question was supposed to be Millwall. The same report says that Logan played in Rovers' only Scottish Cup final appearance in 1913 (by error, the newspaper says 1911).

There being little other football news at this time of year, the paper says much about Schools Football — Abbotshall School won the League this year and their vice-captain was a J Urquhart, (who would do well for Raith Rovers in the future).

At secondary level a youngster called J Maule (similarly destined for great things) of Viewforth was attracting attention, even though Kirkcaldy Schoolboys went down 0-3 to Cowdenbeath Schoolboys at Beatty Crescent in the Fife Cup final.

They would also be involved in the East of Scotland School Cup final against Falkirk next week.

In the meantime, the cricket season had started but was doing little to fire anyone's imagination with Kirkcaldy drawing with Murrayfield after the Edinburgh side had taken two and a half hours to reach 111, and Kirkcaldy's batting being similarly uninspiring. Dunnikier also earned a draw with Leith Albion.

May 31 1895

The season came to an end tonight with a visit from Glasgow Celtic. It was Celtic's first visit to Stark's Park.

They had only been in existence for seven years but had already won the Scottish Cup once and the Scottish League twice.

Last week they had won the Glasgow Charity Cup beating Rangers 4-0 in the final, and a hat-trick had been scored by Sandy McMahon.

Celtic arrived in the afternoon and spent the afternoon visiting the linoleum works of John Barry, who had been an Irish Nationalist MP and a great admirer of the Glasgow Irishmen who had done so much to revolutionise the game.

They then went to the Crown Hotel on the High Street for their tea, and attracted a large crowd of admirers as they walked down.

Raith Rovers had not had a great season, but their Committee were praised for bringing "top level football" to the town.

Over 2,000 (a large crowd for the 1890s and containing quite a few local Celtic lovers) appeared at Stark's Park on a pleasant evening to see the giants of the game.

It was a disappointing 1-1 draw, Rovers scoring in the first half through Jimmy Walker and Celtic equalizing late in the game through Sandy McMahon.

Because the Celtic party needed to get the train at 8.38 pm the game was reduced to 35 minutes per half and half-time was simply a quick turnaround.

The teams were — Raith Rovers: Grieve, Kay and Oag; Suttie, Lambert and Cowper; J Walker, Blyth, D Walker, Eckford and Neilson.

Celtic: Cullen, Reynolds and Doyle; Dunbar, Kelly and O'Rourke; Blessington, Madden, McMahon, Divers and Campbell.

Referee A Hall, Hearts.

June

Can you spot the Prime Minister and the writer of detective fiction in the Directors' Box?

430

June 1 1953

Everyone was preparing, especially in London, for the Coronation of the new Queen, Elizabeth II.

The mood was upbeat and excited, but for fans of Raith Rovers, there was one sad piece of news today in that Alec James died in the Royal Northern Hospital in London at the age of 51.

He had played for Raith Rovers, Preston North End and Arsenal, had won eight caps for Scotland, four English League medals with Arsenal and two English Cup medals.

He was best remembered for his play in the "Wembley Wizards" International of 1928 when Scotland beat England 5-1, but Raith Rovers fans felt that he had played best for Rovers in Kirkcaldy between the years of 1922 and 1925.

There were of course still a great number of Rovers fans still alive in 1953 who remembered him for his trickery and generally brilliant play for the team.

Those who gathered around the various bonfires held throughout the town to celebrate the Coronation would exchange reminiscences about "wee Alec", "the little genius" or "Jimmy".

Letters flooded into *The Fife Free Press* for weeks from fans who told their favourite stories about the little star with the baggy pants under which, on a cold day, there were small hot water bottles to minimise the rheumatic pain which plagued him all his life.

Those who saw Alec James play would not acknowledge any counter-argument to the contention that Alec James was the greatest Raith Rovers player of them all.

June 2 1945

The European war had been over for almost a month now.

Some of the luckier soldiers were given a few days leave, and treated themselves to a day in Aberdeen to see Rovers play in what was called the Mitchell Cup.

It was not yet quite "fun and laughter and peace ever after" as Vera Lynn had promised them all.

There was still the Japanese War, civil wars in places like Greece and the continuing uncertainty about the erstwhile allies in the Soviet Union, but the main task had been completed.

8,000 were at Pittodrie to see what was a rather disappointing game; both sides were still unable to field their full sides because so many men were still required in the forces.

The city of Aberdeen in particular had so many men whose whereabouts were still unknown, for many of the Gordon Highlanders had been captured in the fall of Singapore and were, apparently, in Japanese POW camps.

Johnny Pattillo scored twice for the Dons and they were three up before Willie Penman pulled one back in the closing stages.

The forward line of Kelly, Young, Weatherspoon, Glassey and Penman was "generally ragged" although "Glassey and Penman did some adroit moves".

Rovers left half was called Willie Montgomery. When his name was read out over the Public Address system, it received a loud cheer from the Aberdeen crowd, but of course he was no relation to the Field Marshall!

This game signalled the end of Raith Rovers in the Second World War, where the administration had coped heroically in difficult, almost impossible circumstances.

Next year would be different!

June 3 1944

It was hardly the biggest secret in the world that something big was about to happen in Europe.

Every available soldier and sailor was stationed in the south of England awaiting the signal, and, more discreetly but still hardly with any secrecy, nurses were also mobilised to hospitals in Portsmouth and the south coast to await casualties.

The only question was where exactly and when, although everyone knew it would have to be summer to take advantage of daylight and good weather.

Meanwhile, advances were being made in Italy with the allies more or less at the entrance to Rome.

On a more mundane level at Stark's Park, Raith Rovers were playing Morton in the first leg of a Summer Cup tie.

It attracted a crowd of 4,000 (killing any idea that war-time football had no popular attraction) and *The Sunday Post* is convinced that Rovers of the North Eastern League were just as good as their Southern League opponents even though Morton had a marvellous player called Billy Steel playing for them.

Steel would of course become a legend for Dundee.

Both goalkeepers are singled out as well — Willie Bruce for Raith Rovers and Jimmy Cowan for Morton, (a man who would do well for Scotland after the war) but it was Morton who won 2-1.

Rovers' goal was scored by Willie Penman although *The Sunday Post* reporter adds caustically that he "had more speed than football".

433

Malcolm McLure of Raith Rovers and Billy Steel of Dundee at Stark's Park

June 4 1926

Raith Rovers today announced the appointment of George Wilson to be their Manager in succession to James Logan.

It was a hard act to follow, and Wilson had the misfortune to take over the club when it was in an impoverished position and with embittered supporters who took ill after all the successes of a few seasons ago to be back in the Second Division.

Arguably, Wilson was the best ever player to become Manager of Raith Rovers, for he won six caps for Scotland between 1904 and 1909, a Scottish Cup medal with Hearts in 1906, an English Cup medal with Newcastle United in 1910 and an English League medal the year before in 1909 with the same club.

He played for Raith Rovers for a few years in the First World War when he was over the age of 30 and a little past his best.

He was a fast and tricky left winger, but was toughness personified, something that was put down to his grim Lochgelly background. He was known as "smiler" because he seldom did that!

But he was welcomed by Raith Rovers supporters as one of their own, and it was largely through his gritty determination (it was alleged that some of his players were frightened of him!) that Raith Rovers regained their First Division status in 1927.

But he struggled in the First Division in the first half of season 1927/28 and resigned in December of that year with the team in trouble.

June 5 1920

It now seemed likely, according to the Press, that Harry Anderson was to leave Raith Rovers, for ever this time.

He was to go back to St Mirren.

He had been allowed to play for St Mirren in the latter stages of the Great War for he had been based in the west of Scotland, and regulations about player availability and registrations were a great deal looser in war-time.

Indeed he had played for St Mirren in the team which won the Victory Cup in 1919.

For season 1919/20 he had returned to Raith Rovers, where he had played a little below the standard of what fans remembered of him before the War.

Towards the end of the season he had been replaced by Will Collier.

Harry Anderson was of course the first player from Raith Rovers to earn a cap for Scotland, something that he had done against Wales at Celtic Park on February 28 1914.

It was a goalless draw, and Harry can be proud of the fact of his part in ensuring that the great Billy Meredith failed to score against Scotland.

He was not however chosen to play in the "big" game against England, and of course the outbreak of war in August 1914 meant that there would be no more International games for the duration.

Harry had also played in the Scottish Cup final of 1913 and been regarded as one of the successes for Rovers that day.

He would play for St Mirren for a year or two, then finish his career with Clydebank.

June 6 1891

Even for 1891, June 6 was a fairly late day for the end of a season, but this was the replay of the Fife Charity Cup between Raith Rovers and Dunfermline Athletic which "came off" at Newton Park, which seems to be where near where Ava Street is now.

The first game, which had been held in Dunfermline a couple of weeks previously on May 23, had finished in disgraceful scenes after a crowd invasion following a disputed goal.

What had upset a letter writer to the newspaper was that these riotous scenes had all happened in the name of "charity".

Fortunately there was no repetition today There was a "goodly concourse" of spectators present as well as a few constables with their "cudgels of office" to be used when and if necessary, but the game passed peacefully.

They saw the Rovers win 5-2 with a hat-trick from Alex Bogie and one each from William Cowan and John Leitch.

Thus ended an interesting season for Raith Rovers who, in addition to the Fife Charity Cup had also won the King's Cup.

Not only that, but the development of the Beveridge Park meant that Rovers would be "flitting" from Robbie's Park to a ground nearer the sea called Stark's Park for next season.

Nationally this had been the first season of the Scottish League, shared between Rangers and Dumbarton, but the Scottish Cup had reverted once again to Queen's Park who had now won the trophy on nine occasions.

Raith Rovers 1887, believed to be the earliest photograph ever taken of the club

June 7 1961

James Henry Logan died in Edinburgh of a coronary thrombosis in his home in Edinburgh at the age of 75.

Thus perished one of Raith Rovers' greatest sons.

He had played for the club before the First World War including an appearance in the 1913 Scottish Cup final.

He was a tall, large striding centre half who could also play at wing half.

He then joined up for the War in the Royal Scots, gained promotion fairly rapidly but was badly injured on the first day of the Battle of the Somme and had to be invalided home to his house in David Street, suffering from shellshock and deafness.

He eventually returned to the front, and reached the rank of Captain. In 1919 he became manager of the club, and it was under his leadership that the club reached its acme of achievement, ending third in 1922 and fourth in 1924 in the old Scottish First Division, with loads of great players like John "Tokey" Duncan, Alec James, David Morris and Will Collier.

He left the club in 1926, having been compelled through economic pressures to sell his best players such as Dave Morris and Alec James.

After that he became "mine host" of the Airlie Arms Hotel in Kirriemuir, but returned to Raith Rovers to be manager again but for a less successful spell between 1930 and 1933.

He bought a tobacconist's shop in the High Street and was a well-known character in town.

He was also manager of Wrexham for a spell.

June 8 1910

This morning's edition of *The Courier* contained the news that all Kirkcaldy had been waiting for!

After many years of trying, Raith Rovers have been elected to the First Division.

There was no automatic promotion in those days, and it all depended on the Scottish League AGM, which was held in Glasgow yesterday.

Raith had done well in the Scottish League Division Two for the past three years (first equal this year) and because they had a good ground and a sound financial footing, they felt they had a good chance.

They had also a good record in the Scottish Qualifying Cup and represented a wide area of Fife which was well served by railways. They also very successfully courted Willie Maley of Celtic (who tended to get his own way in such matters) and defeated the new club Ayr United by 13 votes to 2 for the vacant spot left by Port Glasgow Athletic.

Abercorn of Paisley and Dumbarton were also unsuccessful.

Possibly what swung it was that the Scottish League needed to be a little wider than Glasgow and the surrounding area, and the two Edinburgh teams, Dundee and Aberdeen were strongly in their favour.

The decision had repercussions of course because, as the local papers argued, the whole idea would be pointless unless an effort was made to strengthen the team.

Moreover, when the two big teams from Glasgow and the two big teams from Edinburgh arrived, Stark's Park might struggle to hold the crowd.

Nevertheless the new season was now awaited with great anticipation.

June 9 2017

Last season may have ended in heartbreak, but new manager Barry Smith seemed determined to fight back as the Raith Rovers web site announced today the signing of three new players, although one of them was very familiar to Raith Rovers supporters.

This was Greig Spence who, of course, played a large part in the capture of the League Challenge Cup in 2014.

He had been with Alloa, Celtic and Cowdenbeath in a fairly widely travelled career for a 24 year old.

But his travels were nothing compared to those of 23 year old Euan Murray who had actually played in the Solomon Islands (and not many people could say that!) as well as Motherwell, Stenhousemuir, Southport and Barrow.

Making up the threesome was 32 year old Liam Buchanan who joined the club from Livingston.

His furthest port of call had been Sligo Rovers, and he had also had spells with East Fife, Dunfermline, Ayr United, Airdrie and Alloa Athletic.

Quite clearly there was a wealth of experience there, and loads of goal scoring, but it remained to be seen whether Barry Smith, who had impressed by his enthusiasm, could make everything tick as Rovers embarked on their quest to return to the Championship, the place which most people regarded as the natural habitat for a team from a town with the size of population of Kirkcaldy.

It would be a funny Division One next season, for five teams out of ten began with the letter A — Ayr United, Albion Rovers, Airdrie, Arbroath and Alloa!

Raith Rovers 1903/1904

June 10 1927

The mood was upbeat tonight at the meeting in the YMCA Hall on the Prom of the Raith Rovers Supporters' Club.

Mr Adamson, the Chairman of the club, and Mr Bogie, the Treasurer, were both in attendance.

It was a fine night, and Rovers, relegated in 1926, had fought back and been promoted at the first attempt in 1927 under the managership of the dour and apparently unhappy George Wilson.

But promotion achieved, everything was hunky-dory and Mr Adamson stressed his admiration and gratitude for the strenuous efforts of the Supporters Club throughout the season to raise funds for the club.

Mr Gourlay, the Chairman of the Supporters Club, would be invited to take his seat on the Board of Raith Rovers.

While admitting the need to strengthen the playing squad, Mr Adamson regretted to say that no business had been done yet and that even some of last year's squad had not been re-signed because the "ridiculous" terms being asked for.

Mr Bogie had not yet prepared the financial statement but said that it would be "far from nice reading this year".

A lot of this, presumably, was the result of the general financial situation in the town, which had taken a long time to recover from the miners' strike of last year.

Mr Bogie said that the club intended to tackle the business community of the town. In spite of the discouraging financial news, the meeting ended harmoniously with questions asked politely and replied to in similar vein.

"We are all in this together. We want our club to do well" was the general tenor of the meeting.

Relations between Raith Rovers and their supporters were seldom so harmonious.

June 11 1945

The European war had now been over for a month, although the Far East war was still going strong.

A few soldiers had been demobbed already, although the authorities were reluctant to do everything all at once, lest it cause problems with unemployment.

In any case, troops were needed in Europe to help stabilise things. But today Tom Jennings was repatriated.

The Fife Free Press describes him as the "first to come ashore" when the ship docked in Greenock.

Tom had been working as a football coach in Holland in 1940 when the Germans invaded so quickly that he had no chance to escape, and he was captured and interned in Germany.

Internment probably wasn't desperately unpleasant, and certainly better than being a POW, but his family would have been concerned for him, not least for his chances of being bombed by the RAF, for the Germans were not above using internees as a "human shield".

He was able however to organise football games between other internees and German teams.

Tom was much loved by Raith Rovers supporters for his involvement in the T Duncan, J Duncan, Jennings, Bauld and Archibald forward line of 1922, and then the Bell, Miller, Jennings, James and Archibald side of 1924.

He then went on to play for Leeds United, then Bangor, and from 1934-1939 was the manager of Third Lanark.

In later years, he was well known in Kirkcaldy and attended a good few of Raith's games before his death in 1973.

June 12 1902

No Raith Rovers delegates seemed to attend the meeting of the East of Scotland League in Edinburgh.

Dan McMichael of Hibernian was in the chair and he was on a "high" in 1902, for Hibs were the winners of the Scottish Cup.

Various items of business were conducted, including the handing over of the McCrae Cup to Hibernian, but a letter had also been received from Raith Rovers objecting to the guarantee that had to be paid.

The "guarantee" was what had to be paid by the home team to the away team, if the takings at the pay boxes did not reach a certain level.

There seemed to be a certain anomaly that the guarantee which Raith Rovers had to pay to teams visiting Kirkcaldy was £20, whereas when Rovers went to, say, Hibs or Hearts, their guarantee was only £12.

This seemed to be a blatant piece of discrimination in favour of the city clubs, but the East of Scotland League's answer was the legalistic one that ten days' notice needed to be given so that delegates could consult their committees.

The East of Scotland League was now in any case losing its importance as far as Raith Rovers were concerned for they would now be playing from 1902 onwards in the Scottish League Division Two, and East of Scotland League fixtures would only be played on days when there were no Scottish League fixtures.

As far as Raith Rovers were concerned, the East of Scotland League would not last long, for season 1902/03 was their last season in it.

June 13 1930

At the Board Room of Stark's Park, at the AGM of shareholders, Raith Rovers were able to announce a profit for the season of £3,006, 16 shillings and 4 pence.

That was the good news.

It was, of course, very good news in 1930, the depth of the economic depression and a time of rocketing unemployment and businesses being compelled to close down.

The bad news was that the books had been balanced and the account was in the black rather than the red only because of the transfer of players, something which tended to alienate supporters, and was only short term benefit.

In addition, there was a profit only for this season.

Transfer fees reached a total of £5925 — Bruton and Turner to Blackburn Rovers, McAllister to Hearts, Pigg to Barnsley and Dorrans to Greenock Morton.

Incomes from "the gate" was down to £3361 now that the team was in the Second Division.

Although 1929/30 had shown a profit, the club was still in the red to the tune of £4288 following the disastrous years of the late 1920s.

Although brave noises were made about returning to "our rightful place" in Division One, it was now clear that full time football in Kirkcaldy was unsustainable, and there were even rumours that the club was to turn amateur.

The fault was not necessarily that of the club itself (although more than a few mistakes had been made in the running of the club) as the general economic situation.

Quite a few clubs — Bo'ness, Broxburn, Armadale, for example, had disappeared, or were in the process of doing so. It was a depressing time for everyone!

June 14 1999

Jimmy Nicholl's second spell in charge of Raith Rovers came to a sorry, but not entirely unpredicted end today.

Jimmy would have done well to listen to the advice of the Greek philosopher Heraclitus who said that "you can't jump into the same river" twice.

Why not?

Because it is not the same river! Things have changed.

Jimmy should of course never have gone to Millwall (Yes, Millwall! Why, Jimmy?) in 1996.

Nor should he have come back to Kirkcaldy in 1997, for two rather unproductive and financially ruinous seasons.

The problem was that Rovers had been bullied by the SPL into building a 10,000 all-seater stadium — but had been relegated, and were now unable to fill the stadium, which remains to this day a rather ugly pink elephant in Pratt Street.

Nicholl's remit was quite clearly to get Rovers back into the top tier. He had a near miss in 1998, but the team was woeful in 1999.

Their performances included a scarcely believable 0-4 defeat by Clyde in the Scottish Cup at Stark's Park.

Financial problems mounted inexorably, with Nicholl's expensive buys looking demotivated and generally giving the impression that they would rather be playing somewhere else.

In spite of all this, because of Nicholl's success in the past, he still retained a certain degree of popularity with the fans, and they were generally sad to see him go.

It is a pity that he came back, but even more of a pity that he went to Millwall in the first place.

After Jimmy's departure in 1999, the crazy days really started!

June 15 1828

The pre-history of Raith Rovers never had a more tragic day than this one.

Organised football (as distinct from street football) was still many years in the future, but there did not seem to be any problem persuading people to attend Churches.

The Old Kirk was thronged for its evening service this beautiful midsummer evening, the congregation all agog to see the Rev Edward Irving — a local boy made good who had now returned to preach in the Church of his father-in-law, the Rev John Martin (who would himself meet his death in tragic circumstances a decade later when his horse bolted in Pathhead).

The tower (still in existence in the 21st century) had been there for a few centuries, but the rebuilt Church was a mere 20 years old, and this was probably its biggest ever attendance.

As Irving came in the door of the Church from the Vestry, people leaned forward or stood up to get a better look at him, and the wooden gallery collapsed.

In the crush and the stampede to get out, 28 people perished in what was one of Kirkcaldy's saddest days, the bodies all laid out in the graveyard presenting a harrowing sight.

Fortunately Stark's Park has never seen such a tragedy, even though concern was often expressed about the rickety predecessors of the current Main Stand, but football generally was slow to learn lessons about crowds and wooden structures, notably the infamous Ibrox Disaster of 1902.

June 16 1925

The AGM was held this sunny Tuesday night in the Board Room of Stark's Park, and in keeping with the fine weather, the AGM was also serene and sunny.

(Not all AGMs either before or since were like that!)

A profit over the year of £1749 had cleared last year's deficit and Rovers were now comfortably in the black.

The League position was not as high as last year's nor that of 1922, but it was still comfortable.

All Kirkcaldy was still basking in the fact that it was a Raith Rovers player who had captained Scotland to a great treble against the other British nations, beating England at Hampden on April 4.

This was Davie Morris who was of course now in great demand from English teams notably Aston Villa.

This week, rumour had it, the Birmingham giants had offered £2000 to the club and £1000 to the player himself, but Davie had turned it down because he did not want to leave Scotland, and he loved Kirkcaldy.

George Barton had now bought himself a hairdresser's business and had settled in town, but manager James Logan had a disappointment this week when he tried to sign a young left back called Tommy Law from Bridgeton Waverley.

He travelled through to Glasgow to meet the boy's father only to be told that the boy had signed for Chelsea.

This was a shame; Law became one of the Wembley Wizards of 1928.

But in the meantime the summer was good and there was loads of cricket to watch at the Beveridge Park until the football season started again.

June 17 1953

Today saw the death of the man regarded as Scottish football's best ever player, Patsy Gallacher of Celtic and Falkirk.

He had been ill for some time.

Those who ever saw him on his visits to Stark's Park were enthralled with him, and of course, the attraction of a Raith Rovers v Celtic game in the 1920s was the prospect of Patsy Gallacher and Alec James on the same pitch.

By a macabre coincidence, James had died a few weeks earlier.

They were similar characters — both very small and almost puny looking, both skilful artists with the ball, and both more than a little capable of falling out with referees and officialdom.

Gallacher was born in Ireland in 1891, and so played for Ireland rather than Scotland.

He made his debut for Celtic in 1911, played throughout the Great War and was famous above all else for his goal in the 1925 Scottish Cup final against Dundee when, to avoid a tackle, he jumped or somersaulted into the back of the net with the ball firmly wedged between his feet.

He later moved to Falkirk and played with them for a few years before retiring to become a publican in Clydebank in the 1930s, narrowly missing the German bombs of 1941.

He was looked upon as the Lionel Messi of his day, and Raith Rovers, like every other Scottish team were well represented at his funeral in Arkleston Cemetery, Paisley, a few days later.

June 18 1931

It was the middle of the economic depression with unemployment at an unacceptable rate.

No politician or economist had any clue about how to solve the problem.

In these circumstances it was hardly surprising that Raith Rovers were also struggling economically. *The Fife Free Press* announced a loss of £1,049 over the past season, as distinct from a profit of £3000 in 1930.

The big difference was the money gained from transfer fees. To put it frankly and crudely, Raith Rovers had no-one worth selling, nor if they did, was there a club able to buy them.

Players' wages and bonuses had fallen slightly, but that was offset by a fall in gate drawings.

Even with the unemployed gate, there were times when fans simply could not afford football, if they did not have a job!

All this meant was that Raith Rovers had an overall deficit of over £5337.

It had not been all that bad a season on the playing side, for the team had finished fourth in the Second Division, and there had been some good games to interest the fans, but the problem was that Second Division teams were not well supported and brought few fans with them.

The Fife Free Press reports that the Directors "viewed this report with no little concern" and that an appeal would be made to business men and indeed the general public to rally round the club.

In the circumstances, however, the position was gloomy. Yet, Kirkcaldy remained a footballing centre with the unemployed men on the street corners talking about little else, and the younger ones playing the game at every opportunity.

Willie McNaught, Player of the Year awarded by the Supporters Club

June 19 1954

Willie McNaught was probably not a man to gloat, but he cannot but have felt that he might have done better for Scotland than the current incumbents in today's World Cup game in Switzerland.

Those few people in Kirkcaldy who had television (it had only really come to Scotland in 1952 but was becoming more and more common among the better off) were horrified to sit and watch Scotland lose 0-7 to a country that very few people had ever heard of called Uruguay.

It was Scotland's first venture in the World Cup, and the first time that the World Cup was televised.

It was by no means the last of Scotland's World Cup disgraces, but it was a collector's item in terms of tales of disorganisation and half-hearted approaches to the game.

The manager, Andy Beattie, resigned in the middle of the tournament!

The players had to wear their own tracksuits for training purposes, and the jerseys given were of the thick type that one would expect to use in November in Scotland rather than the very hot Switzerland of 1954.

One of the players, Neil Mochan, who would later play for Raith Rovers, told the story that no tactical talks were given and that the only words of encouragement he heard from the bench were "Get stuck in!"

Come to think about it, Willie McNaught probably did very well to avoid this calamity.

June 20 1960

This midsummer Monday brought the news that *The Fife Free Press* had been predicting for months, namely that Jim Baxter was being sold to Rangers.

The price was said to be £16,000, although later reports said £17,500, and *The Fife Free Press* stresses that for "domestic reasons" the transfer did not go through until several days after the end of Raith Rovers financial year.

What that meant we cannot be sure, but there can be no doubt that Rangers got a good deal here.

Baxter himself did not want to go to England, but there was little doubt that he would earn more money at Rangers, and no doubt, begin to be chosen for Scotland.

In any case, Raith Rovers needed the money to pay for the floodlights and other ground improvements.

There were also a few hints from those who knew a lot about the club that manager Bert Herdman and one or two Directors were not 100% upset at his departure, for he was no conformist to discipline, as later events would sadly confirm.

He had been with Raith Rovers since 1957 and those who saw him play would happily attest to his playing ability.

He would stay at Rangers for five seasons, winning the Scottish League three times, the Scottish Cup three times and the Scottish League Cup four times.

He would then go to Sunderland and Nottingham Forest where he would be less successful, although he was part of the Scotland team which famously beat England 3-2 at Wembley in 1967.

June 21 1902

The town was all decked in red, white and blue, not in honour of the visit of Rangers, but more to herald the imminent Coronation of King Edward VII and Queen Alexandra, something that had been the main topic of conversation for many months.

But the other thing that dominated the thoughts of football supporters in 1902 was the Ibrox Disaster of April 5.

26 people had been killed when a wooden stand collapsed at the Scotland v England game.

Rangers held themselves responsible and today came to Kirkcaldy to play a charity game for the disaster fund.

They had this midweek lost the Coronation Cup 3-2 to Celtic, and their players were still fit.

Although in the middle of the close season, Raith Rovers were able to get a team, agreeing to borrow a few players from other teams, as indeed did Rangers.

The game started in glorious sunshine, but by half time, as often happens in midsummer, torrential rain came on, rendering matters farcical.

In spite of all this, 1,500 turned up to see famous Glasgow Rangers, the League Champions for the past four years, and £23 was raised for the Ibrox Disaster Fund.

The Kirkcaldy Trades Band played at half time, and did so for free. Rangers won 3-1.

The Coronation was to be held the following Thursday, but the King took very ill with a form of appendicitis, and the event had to be postponed until August.

June 22 1974

Kirkcaldy High Street is normally on a sunny Saturday afternoon jam packed and busy with cars and pedestrians.

It was a quiet place this afternoon apart from clamour, shouting and general angst from pubs.

Those who were not in pubs were at home watching the TV with avid attention, for this was the afternoon in which Scotland might just have qualified for the quarter finals of the 1974 World Cup in West Germany.

The day had long passed — sadly — when any Raith Rovers player would have been even vaguely considered for selection to the Scotland squad, but this in no way diminished the passion in 1974 for Scotland, who, on the previous Wednesday night, had succeeded in earning a draw with Brazil and might even have beaten them.

However today meant that a win would qualify Scotland, and a draw might even do it, but it would then go down to goal difference.

Willie Ormond's side did well, but maybe Willie made a mistake in not playing his two talismanic, if unpredictable, geniuses of Denis Law and Jimmy Johnstone.

As it was, Yugoslavia scored late in the game, and Scotland, playing in all white, equalised just at the death, but a draw was not enough as Brazil had beaten Zaire and pipped Scotland on goal difference.

It was however Scotland's best ever World Cup, and everyone agreed that they deserved better.

It would be a lie, however, to say that this whipped up enthusiasm among Raith Rovers supporters for the new season.

Raith were at a low ebb in 1974, however well that the national team had done.

June 23 1956

This may be the summer (and a fine one it was as well) but Raith Rovers were still active.

Tonight at the Perth Ice Rink, they won a five-a-side tournament, beating East Fife 3-2 in the final, having disposed of Dunfermline and Falkirk on the way.

The five who represented Rovers were Andy Young, Willie McNaught, Andy Leigh, Jimmy McEwan and Ernie Copland.

They had won another five-a-side tournament, also in Perth, at Muirton Park a few weeks previously and clearly had some talent for this sort of competition, which *The Fife Free Press* states that it is an ideal way of keeping fit in the summer.

The idea was that one player would be the "backing in goalkeeper" i.e. he was expected to play "out" as well, there would be two defenders and two attackers. In a situation like this, a man of the versatility of Andy Young was ideal.

In the final Jimmy McEwan scored twice and Ernie Copland once, while Jimmy Bonthrone scored both goals for East Fife.

In the meantime it was becoming clearer that there was a major crisis developing in two parts of the world.

The Hungarians (much loved in western Europe because of their fine football players, notably Ferenc Puskas) were trying to shake off the Russian yoke.

In Egypt, President Nasser and the British Prime Minister Anthony Eden were spoiling for a fight with each other.

Both crises would deepen, but in the meantime there was some lovely weather to enjoy. And the Australians were in England playing for the Ashes.

458

June 24 1952

Midsummer has now passed, and already there are signs of Raith Rovers moving into gear for the start of the new season, looked forward to with a certain amount of hope and optimism.

But there was still a Cup final or two from last season to get out of the way.

For example tonight was the final of the Raith Rovers Supporters Club Cup between Raith Athletic and Prinlaws Albion, played at Coaltown of Balgonie.

Even as early as 1952 people asked the question of whether there should be summer football, but the idea had very few takers, not least because the summer gave opportunities for competitions like this, not to mention other sports like athletics, tennis and cricket. But even so, talk was mainly about football.

On Saturday Raith Athletic would be travelling to Kemback to play in another tournament.

In the meantime, Raith Rovers had signed a new outside left from Montrose called Ian Scott, and everyone was counting the weeks until the new football season would start.

Fans still talked about the great Scottish Cup games against Hibs last season, and there was great enthusiasm in the town with attendances still high.

But earlier this year, something called television had arrived in Scotland.

Was this going to make any sort of difference?

Or would it last?

There were already a few of these devices in Kirkcaldy, but apparently they did not always work well.

No, it would never take over football, in the opinion of most people.

June 25 1949

There was little wrong in Kirkcaldy at the moment.

The weather was absolutely glorious and had been for some time with cricket going strong.

Full employment had virtually returned to the town, and although some goods were still rationed as the country recovered from the war, more and more the controls were being relaxed.

The National Health Service had been up and running for almost a year now, and families were beginning to realise the benefits of being able to consult the doctor without having to pay for it.

Meanwhile football fans counted the weeks until the start of the season and Rovers' first post-war incursion into Division "A", now that promotion from Division "B" had been secured in April.

Manager Bert Herdman, resplendent in his double-breasted suit, was always willing to talk to the Press, if "talk" was the right word, given Bert's dreadful stammer.

He was trying to sign more players for the new season, aware that getting to Division "A" was one thing, but staying there was something quite different.

Last week, the team won a five-a-side tournament on the Isle of Bute at Rothesay, beating St Mirren 2-0 in the final.

This Saturday they took part in a slightly more prestigious tournament in Dunfermline to commemorate their Civic Week.

Sending six strong men in Andy Young, Willie Penman, Ernie Till, Bernie Kelly, Harry Colville and Johnny Maule, Rovers beat Falkirk by 3 corners to 1, then lost 0-2 to Rangers, the tournament being won by Partick Thistle.

June 26 1950

Life might have been a great deal different if today manager Bert Herdman had managed to sign Queen's Park's talented young goalkeeper Ronald Simpson.

Simpson had expressed a desire to turn professional on a part-time basis, but the snag was that Raith Rovers were unable to provide him with a day job in Kirkcaldy.

As a result the Glasgow-based youngster turned his attention to Third Lanark instead.

Simpson of course went on to play for Newcastle United, Hibs, Celtic and Scotland in a remarkable career.

Bert Herdman was having a frustrating time this close season. His main target was a centre forward, and he had been travelling all over the country to get one, but without any great success.

"Fifer" of *The Fife Free Press* was of the opinion that Willie Keith, one time of Dunfermline Athletic might fit the bill for that position, but there was better news of the full back position where David Condie of Markinch Victoria had been signed.

The club was also struggling with the bad news of the death of one of the Directors, Mr James Stein, a man who had been with the club since the Second World War and who had been responsible for ground improvements on the railway side of the ground.

And just to complete a fairly miserable picture for midsummer, yesterday the North Koreans had invaded the South, thereby instigating another war!

June 27 2007

History was made today when a Raith Rovers supporter became Prime Minister of Great Britain for the first ever time.

Gordon Brown's father John had been the Minister of St Brycedale Church, and Gordon had lived in the town since his earliest days, although he had been born in Giffnock in 1951.

He had grown up supporting Raith Rovers and had at one point been a programme seller.

He was probably just too young to have clear memories of the great days of the 1950s, but he would have remembered men like Gordon Wallace and Ian Porterfield, as well as the Scottish League Cup in 1994.

All this, of course, possibly did not form a major part of his conversation with the Queen today when he was asked to form a Government.

He had waited long enough for this opportunity, having served under Tony Blair and having been compelled to do certain things against his better judgement, like going along with the Iraq War, for example.

But he had been a good Chancellor of the Exchequer, no doubt having acquired his financial acumen in the selling of programmes at Stark's Park.

Some people, particularly in England, described him as "dour" and seemed to think that this was something to do with his Scottish Presbyterian background.

We knew better than that of course. A lifetime of watching some dreadful Raith Rovers teams would have been enough to make anyone a bit grumpy!

June 28 1923

Showing a certain amount of enterprise and initiative, (the early 1920s were great days for the Rovers, and prosperous ones!), a Raith Rovers party embarked on a ship called the *Highland Loch* to travel to Gran Canaria for a pre-season tour.

It was the habit in those days for Scottish teams to feel that they had some "missionary duty" to introduce football to parts of the world where the game was slightly less well developed because Scottish football was (rightly) very highly rated throughout the world.

Rovers themselves had made a successful tour of Denmark the year before, Celtic had had several tours to Germany (including a tour of the battlefields in France and Belgium) and Third Lanark went even further afield to South America.

When the Glasgow side returned (barely in time for the start of the season) their claim that Argentina had some good players and that Argentina might one day be better than Scotland at football was met with a certain amount of laughter and derision!

But Raith on their tour of the Canary Islands would have one unexpected adventure in the shape of a shipwreck!

They generally had a good time, although some of the conditions they found there were just a little primitive.

The weather was hot, but the players adapted, even though the locals did not really always understand the rules.

The predominant mood however as the players embarked was one of excitement at the idea of a new adventure, mingled with apprehension.

June 29 1920

Those familiar with the plot of "Trial By Jury" of Gilbert and Sullivan will know that it was all about a "breach of promise" case.

The gentleman concerned promised to marry a lady then reneged on it "doubly criminal to do so because the bride had bought her trousseau".

It is a harmless piece of Victorian musical melodrama, but it came as a bit of a shock for Raith Rovers supporters to discover that one of their players, James Bauldie was involved in a similar and real life case.

Bauldie, sometimes called Baldie (but he still had a good head of hair!) had joined the club in 1919 and had been a reasonable centre forward, scoring 7 goals including 3 against Scottish Cup finalists Albion Rovers.

Bauldie had apparently promised to marry a girl from Bowhill on February 20.

He failed to do so, and the following week a court order compelled him to pay the sum of £250 and £2 per week as long as he was playing professional football — something that says something about the wages paid to professional footballers in 1920, for the order specified that it would only be £1 per week if he gave up his football career!

The word "seduction" was used in the indictment, and it would not be unreasonable to suppose that the poor girl was pregnant.

Be that as it may, Bauldie failed to cough up, and even failed to appear today at the Court hearing. He also seems to have disappeared from Raith Rovers as well.

June 30 1939

Raith Rovers financial statement was released today and it showed a deficit of £883 15 shillings and 3 pence for what would prove to be the last peace-time season.

Relegation was of course a disappointment after the euphoria of 1938, but the problem was that Rovers probably did not quite have the resources for a prolonged stay in the First Division.

Gate receipts were up but that was because they had games with well-supported teams like Rangers and Celtic.

This was balanced by the fact that they had been obliged to run a reserve team which had been very poorly supported by the public particularly at the end of the season.

But *The Fife Free Press* remained upbeat, expressed the view that an early come back to the top tier was a possibility and exonerated manager Sandy Archibald who had done "some good work" during the season

He had been on several occasions this season pipped, sometimes at the last minute, when he tried to sign a player when another club had been able to offer more money.

But the bank overdraft was being steadily reduced over the past few years, and things looked optimistic.

But this was 1939, the summer in which many people stuck their heads in the sand and hoped that things would get better.

It did not really look as if Hitler was going to go away, however.

His verbal attacks on Great Britain were becoming more vitriolic, and he clearly had his eye on Poland for his next conquest.

A fine view of Stark's Park from the air

Index

Events by year appear at the end of this index

A

Abbotshall School 427
Abercorn 202, 420, 440
Aberdeen x, 2, 67, 74, 81, 98, 141, 144, 146, 178, 181, 192, 206, 227, 233, 247, 267, 295, 298, 319, 333, 339, 351, 355, 357, 363, 367, 388, 398, 417, 432, 440
Aberdeen Press and Journal 363
Adamson AG (Chairman) 13, 443
Adamson Bobby 146, 182, 227, 336, 379
Agathe, Didier 104
Agnew, Spiro 134
Agnew, Scott (Stranraer) 147, (Dumbarton) 394
Airdrie 4, 29, 70, 72, 75, 82, 97, 106, 109, 146, 152, 154, 162, 207, 214, 228, 249, 281, 311, 328, 336, 357, 381, 395, 405, 407, 420, 441
Airdrieonians 109, 207, 395
Airlie Arms Hotel 439
Aitken, Jimmy 163
Aitken, Mike (journalist) 83
Aitken, Morris 146,
Aitken, Samuel 67
Akranes 101, 116
Albion Rovers 2, 42, 57, 109, 158, 213, 219, 229, 376, 441, 464
Alexandria (Egypt) 150
Alexandria (Dunbartonshire) 235
Allan, Bob 153, 260
Allan, Scott 30,
Allison, Willie 73, 228
Alloa 26, 153, 204, 221, 222, 267, 314, 405, 441

Almondvale 104
Andersen, Soren 297
Anderson, George 103, 131
Anderson, George (Dundee) 327
Anderson, Grant 119
Anderson, Harry 111, 136, 224, 258, 313, 369, 383, 436
Anderson (Dunfermline) 253
Andrews, Marvin 104, 153, 198, 217, 293, 374, 425
Anelka, Claude 120
Arbroath 39, 44, 59, 88, 96, 106, 198, 208, 233, 246, 267, 339, 380, 385, 388, 441
Archibald, Bobby 3, 109, 175, 237, 261, 288, 321, 365, 415, 444
Archibald, David 24
Archibald, Jacky 93
Archibald, Sandy 11, 12, 21, 24, 135, 149, 153, 211, 226, 249, 282, 335, 424, 425, 427, 465
Armadale 376, 446
Armour (Ayr United) 362
Arsenal 112, 414, 431
Arthur, Gordon 43,
Arthurlie 125, 238, 250, 262, 420
Aston Villa, 117, 118, 423, 449
Auld (Celtic) 325, (Hibs) 375
Axford, David 382
Ayr 107, 121, 147, 175, 198, 217, 221, 246, 262, 332, 357, 362, 403, 405, 420, 440, 441

B

Bain, Ian 241, 348
Bainsford 65
Baird (Aberdeen) 178
Baird (Rangers) 209,
Baird, John 242, 359, 361

467

Baker, Gerry 257
Baker, Joe 52, 114, 134, 271
Ballantyne, Ian 186, 356
Balwearie 1, 270
Bangor 53, 444
Bankies 186
Bantams 34
Barr, Bobby 79
Barrhead 125, 238
Barry, John 428
Barton, George 341, 449
Batchelor, Tommy 93, 230
Bath City 59
Bathgate 416
Bauld, Bobby 3, 109, 175, 247, 254, 288, 321, 365, 444
Bauld (Hearts), 345
Bauldie, James 305, 464
Baxter, Bill 96
Baxter, Jim 5, 106, 185, 207, 257, 275, 312, 372, 421, 454
Bayern Munich 143, 160, 287, 423
Bayview 61, 63, 79, 93, 343, 376
"B" Division 168
Beath 93, 228, 230, 265
Beattie (Kilmarnock) 190,
Beattie (Scotland) 453
Bell, Andy 93, 230
Bell, Baillie Robert 291
Bell, John 238, 252, 314
Bell, Peter 371, 427, 444
Bellamy (Motherwell) 111, (Hibs) 137
Bellshill Athletic 414
Benedictus, Kyle 26
Bennett, (Albion Rovers) 229
Bennochy 32, 77, 179
Benvie, Willie 165
Berwick Rangers 60, 183, 254, 273
Beveridge Park ix, 1, 2, 18, 27, 28, 40, 42, 48, 65, 92, 132, 233, 246, 270, 293, 306, 310, 318, 325, 419, 437, 449
Beveridge Report 14
Bird (Dundee) 212

Birrell, Willie 57, 228, 274, 305, 376, 426
Black (Airdrie) 328
Black (Forfar) 126, 226
Blackburn Rovers 32, 418, 419, 446
Blackpool 23, 158
Blairgowrie 314
Blessington (Celtic) 428
Bloomer, Steve 135
Blue Brazil 77
Blyth, Andy 410, 428
Boden (Celtic) 124, 352
Boer War 65
Boghead 252, 356
Bogie, Alex 437
Bogie, James 13, 295, 443
Bolton, John 339
Boner, David 146
Bo'ness 125, 332, 373, 446
Bonthrone (East Fife) 457
Borland, Johnny 113
Borussia Dortmund 47
Bowie (Dumbarton) 252
Bowman, Dave 50
Boyd (Dundee) 417
Boyle (Airdrie) 328
Bradford City 34, 111
Brady, Tommy 159, 204, 329
Brand, Ralph 150, 162, 208
Brander, George 61, 319, 327, 352
Brechin 2, 21, 214, 279, 290, 297, 337, 346, 405, 412, 413
Bremner (Aston Villa) 423
Brewster, Craig 47, 54, 92, 133, 177, 366
Bristol 3
Brittle (referee) 114
Broddle, Julian 55, 193, 408
Brogan (Celtic) 370
Broomfield 70, 72, 109, 207
"Brown" 320
Brown, Gordon MP 367, 462
Brown, James 3, 68, 109, 175, 278, 288, 321, 365, 424

Brown, Willie 314
Brown (Arbroath) 106
Brown (Dundee) 211
Brown (Dunfermline) 91
Brown (Rangers) 329 (Scotland) 372
Browne, Paul 243
Broxburn 261, 446
Bruton, Leslie 418, 446
Buchanan, Liam 79, 441
Buchanan (Hibs) 141
Buckley (Aberdeen) 141, 192, 206
Buddies *see St Mirren*
Buist, Johnny 424
Burnley 383
Burns, Alex 243
Burns (Celtic) 53,
Burns (poet) 125, 179, 362
Burntisland Cricket 419
Burntisland Shipyard 84
Burrows, Frank 314

C

Cadete (Celtic) 396
Cairns (Rangers) 24, 103, 135, 150
Calderon, Antonio 120
Callaghan (Dumbarton) 252
Camelon 304
Cameron, Colin 5, 53, 54, 55, 92, 101, 193, 328, 408
Campbell, Mark 217, 242
Campbell (Celtic) 428
Campbell (Rev. John) 48, 415
Canary Islands 8, 18, 20, 68, 463
Candlish, Chris 354, 401
Cappielow 67, 271, 305, 380
Capuano (Queen's Park) 49
Carabine (Third Lanark) 255
Cardle, Joe 49, 119
Carlton Cricket 424
Carlyle (literary) 160
Carlyle (Dundee United) 317
Carr, Jimmy 253

Carrick (Karen) 33
Carroll (Bobby) 227
Carson, George 204
Carson, Tom 177
Cassidy (Celtic) 64, 237, 308
Cathkin Park 61, 95, 174, 207, 255
Caven, John 317
"C" Division 290
Celtic   2, 5, 17, 19, 20, 29, 43, 53, 60, 61, 64, 70, 72, 75, 78, 81, 86, 88, 93, 97, 105, 106, 113, 124, 125, 128, 138, 147, 154, 158, 163, 172, 182, 184, 191, 193, 207, 208, 209, 224, 227, 229, 230, 232, 237, 238, 247, 250, 251, 252, 254, 258, 267, 291, 306, 308, 309, 312, 313, 316, 322, 325, 328, 336, 337, 339, 340, 341, 342, 345, 347, 348, 349, 352, 357, 358, 365, 367, 369, 370, 372, 373, 376, 379, 383, 385, 386, 387, 388, 396, 399, 421, 428, 436, 440, 441, 450, 455, 461, 463, 465
Chalmers (Celtic) 227, 309, 370, 379
Chaplin (Charlie) 112
Chapman, George 332
Church 10, 31, 32, 261, 275, 426, 448, 462
Cikos (Ross County) 35
City Park 293
Clements (cricketer) 48
Cliftonhill 158, 213, 219
Clinton, Mike 182
Clunie, Henry 304
Clyde 82, 146, 184, 207, 261, 278, 283, 291, 312, 317, 322, 328, 337, 345, 350, 358, 395, 420, 447
Clydebank 73, 186, 261, 282, 321, 331, 366, 375, 436, 450
Coaltown of Balgonie 459
Coatbridge 57, 213, 376
Collier, Will 3, 19, 64, 68, 175, 212, 219, 237, 247, 254, 278, 282, 288, 316, 321, 365, 371, 377, 415, 436, 439

Collins, Alan 290, 329, 389, 390
Colville, Harry 291, 327, 329, 389, 390, 460
Condie, David 461
Conn, Alfie 257
Connor, Frank 43, 299, 300, 402, 403
Conway, 150
Cook (referee) 148
Cook (Kilmarnock) 337
Cooper (Airdrie) 152, 328
Cooper, Robert 267
Copland, Ernie 62, 154, 185, 209, 241, 253, 283, 294, 348, 457
Cousin, Alan 336
Cove Rangers 26
Cowan, Joe 93, 230
Cowan (Morton) 433
Cowan, William 437
Cowdenbeath 17, 21, 27, 77, 126, 144, 180, 222, 250, 254, 256, 303, 374, 382, 425, 427, 441
Cowie, Doug 59, 252, 314, 417
Cowper, John 428
Cox (Rangers) 138, 215, 329
Coyle, Ronnie 43, 47, 53, 116, 243
Crabbe, Scott 100
Craigie, Alex 260
Craigmyle (referee) 144
Cranston, Tom 136, 358, 369
Crawford, Steve 53, 55, 74, 116, 177, 193, 195, 276, 285, 349
Cringan (Celtic) 308
Croal (Dunfermline) 91, (Falkirk) 369
Crombie (referee) 152
Crossgates 21
Crosskey, Tom 126, 424
Cruickshank (Hearts) 162
Cullen (Celtic) 428
Cumming, Arthur 67, 201, 369
Cummings, Jason 302
Cunningham (Rangers) 24, 135
Cunningham (Falkirk) 165

Cup Winners' Cup 76, 385
Cuthbert, Jim 62
Cuthbertson (Third Lanark) 61
Czechoslovakia 115

D

Dackers (Stenhousemuir) 314
Daily Herald, The 282
Dair, Jason 5, 47, 50, 53, 55, 92, 116, 193, 408, 409
Dall, Willie 132, 304
Dallas (referee) 176
Dalrymple, George 201, 262
Dalziel, Gordon 43, 47, 54, 121, 152, 176, 177, 193, 194, 256, 265, 300, 301, 403, 408
Dargo, Craig 104
"Dark Blue" 68, 212
Dartford 377
Daun (Montrose) 347
Davidson, Ian 148, 395
Davidson (referee) 233, 370, 379
Dawson, Davie 247
Delaney (Aberdeen) 319
Dempsey, Jim 96, 346
Denbeath Star 17
Denholm, George 335
Dennis, Shaun 43, 54, 55, 116, 193, 328
Dens Park 30, 41, 44, 182, 197, 211, 290, 327, 354, 401
"Derwent" 129, 144, 164, 261, 342
Deuchar, Willie 341
Devine, Jimmy 233
Devon Loch 345, 375
Diack, Dougie 25
Dickson, Jimmy 305
Dickson (Dunfermline) 94, 253
Directors x, xi, 3, 4, 12, 13, 23, 29, 120, 216, 240, 281, 296, 307, 414, 420, 422, 430, 451, 454, 461
Divers (Celtic) 227, 370, 379, 428
Division "A" 389, 390, 460

Division "B" 168, 204, 290, 329, 389, 460
Division One 43, 67, 114, 167, 186, 212, 246, 401, 441, 446
Division Three 36, 416
Division Two 65, 134, 167, 202, 235, 260, 265, 317, 340, 416, 420, 421, 440, 445
Dobbie, George 78
Dolan (York City) 36
Donagher, Michael 67
Donaldson (Falkirk) 369
Doncaster 3
Don John v, 260, 376
Donnelly (Airdrie) 395
Dons *see Aberdeen* 192, 206, 295, 298, 355, 432
Doonhamers *see Queen of the South*
Dorrans, Owen 73, 373, 446
Douglas Park 108, 380, 408
Dowie, William 201
Doyle (Celtic) 428
Drain, George 40
Drummond, Charlie 141, 178, 185, 203, 263, 348
Dryburgh Cup 41
Duffield, Peter 36, 396
Dumbarton x, 4, 59, 222, 250, 252, 303, 310, 314, 337, 366, 394, 437, 440
Dunbar (Celtic) 428
Duncan, Davie 90, 141, 150, 241, 283
Duncan, John "Tokey" 3, 19, 64, 109, 175, 247, 258, 288, 321, 365, 439, 444
Duncan, Ronnie 167, 267
Duncan, Tom 3, 64, 109, 175, 288, 365, 444
Duncanson (Rangers) 329
Dundee 20, 30, 41, 44, 50, 54, 55, 59, 68, 92, 98, 108, 111, 121, 128, 131, 137, 146, 156, 168, 182, 196, 197, 211, 212, 227, 232, 242, 244, 245, 260, 261, 290, 314, 317, 319, 327, 333, 336, 341, 354, 358, 367, 370, 375, 401, 405, 407, 408, 417, 424, 433, 434, 440, 450

Dundee Courier, The 62, 65, 68, 73, 76, 103, 109, 126, 131, 136, 138, 156, 159, 163, 168, 173, 196, 197, 212, 214, 222, 230, 232, 241, 244, 245, 250, 254, 260, 283, 285, 303, 305, 316, 327, 329, 358, 365, 376, 407, 415, 417, 440
Dundee Hibernian 137
Dundee North End 244
Dundee United 30, 44, 50, 54, 55, 92, 98, 121, 137, 146, 168, 260, 317, 367, 370
Dundee Violet 211, 244
Dunedin Cup 67
Dunfermline 4, 17, 23, 32, 41, 44, 48, 52, 91, 94, 114, 146, 177, 196, 204, 222, 223, 230, 235, 242, 243, 250, 253, 268, 284, 302, 309, 337, 356, 381, 386, 389, 408, 413, 437, 441, 457, 460, 461
Dunn, John 184
Dunn, Willie 84, 184, 363
Dunnikier 17, 19, 25, 27, 153, 426, 427
Dunterlie Park 238

E

East End Park 91, 94, 177, 196, 230, 242, 243, 253, 284
Eastern League 63, 110, 137, 169, 295, 333, 387, 433
Easter Road 114, 129, 134, 141, 143, 170, 201, 244, 270, 294, 302, 345, 349, 361, 400, 406
East Fife 4, 17, 57, 59, 61, 62, 63, 73, 79, 93, 96, 153, 159, 172, 222, 241, 249, 254, 267, 273, 283, 318, 340, 343, 344, 373, 376, 382, 393, 399, 441, 457
East of Scotland League 77, 131, 445
East of Scotland Qualifying Cup 103, 406
East of Scotland Shield 132, 180, 406
East Stirlingshire 2, 65, 249, 300, 303, 305, 331, 373, 420

East Stirlingshire Clydebank 331
Eckford, John 103, 233, 410, 428
Edinburgh 18, 19, 27, 32, 83, 127, 141, 143, 175, 201, 213, 244, 262, 285, 307, 311, 316, 320, 345, 348, 350, 375, 406, 427, 439, 440, 445
Edinburgh City 293, 303
Edinburgh Evening News 2, 270
Edinburgh Saints 262
Edinburgh Shield 132
El Bakhtaoui (Dundee) 30
Elliot, Calum 49, 119
Ellis, Jimmy 168, 204
English Cup 23, 34, 36, 52, 105, 111, 127, 244, 383, 398, 414, 418, 425, 431, 435
European Cup 47, 76, 160, 185, 322, 340, 372, 385, 399, 421, 423
Evans, Bobby 88, 89, 105, 140, 183, 273, 380, 388, 423
Evening Times,The 165, 185, 188, 252, 275, 323, 345, 352
Ewen (Aberdeen) 178, (Dundee) 327
Ewing, James 67

F

Falkirk 65, 100, 112, 119, 128, 148, 156, 165, 173, 192, 208, 216, 232, 247, 249, 251, 258, 279, 297, 302, 333, 336, 339, 348, 350, 358, 369, 375, 387, 396, 400, 420, 427, 450, 457, 460
Falkland 426
Falkland Islands 356, 411,423
Farm, George 22, 23, 41, 52, 88, 115, 140, 158, 183, 216, 255, 337, 386, 388
Faroe 55, 74
Faulds, Kris 119
Ferguson, Alex
Ferguson (cricket) 25
Ferguson (Rev John) 76
Ferguson (politician) 285, 298, 398
Fernie (Celtic) 309
Fife Charity Cup 393, 437

Fife Cup 41, 97, 223, 320, 382, 399, 427
Fife Flyers 221
Fife Free Press, The v, 13, 18, 20, 21, 24, 27, 40, 48, 57, 67, 76, 82, 91, 108, 110, 111, 113, 127, 132, 136, 137, 144, 149, 153, 164, 173, 175, 180, 184, 219, 224, 226, 229, 232, 233, 235, 237, 244, 247, 261, 262, 263, 265, 278, 304, 320, 335, 342, 350, 369, 371, 373, 410, 417, 418, 420, 424, 427, 431, 444, 451, 454, 457, 461, 465
"Fifer" v, 138, 149, 461
Finlay (St Bernards) 201
Finnie (referee) 49
Firhill 224, 261, 276, 408
Fir Park 111, 172
Firs Park 249
First Division ix, 21, 23, 25, 31, 32, 44, 48, 50, 52, 57, 67, 73, 79, 80, 81, 83, 91, 92, 96, 106, 111, 145, 146, 154, 168, 178, 183, 201, 202, 203, 207, 241, 251, 253, 257, 266, 267, 271, 274, 275, 281, 284, 287, 293, 300, 303, 307, 311, 321, 323, 337, 351, 361, 367, 373, 375, 376, 379, 382, 383, 385, 388, 395, 398, 399, 408, 412, 435, 439, 440, 465
Fitzpatrick (referee) 190
Flanagan (Partick Thistle) 323
Folkestone 40
Footballers Battalion 29
Ford, Bobby 284
Forfar iii 2, 5, 21, 24, 26, 44, 49, 98, 126, 140, 214, 226, 246, 279, 356, 405, 416
Forsyth, Allan 251
Forthbank 149
Fraser, Cammy 43,
Fraser (Dundee United) 317
Fulton, George 226, 260, 335, 374

G

Gallacher (Airdrie) 228, 357
Gallacher (Celtic) 97, 316, 342, 365, 417, 450

Gallacher (Dundee) 417
Gardner, Pat ix, 88, 105, 140, 157, 158, 183, 213, 255, 266, 268, 273, 331, 372, 380, 385, 386, 388, 399
Gatherum (cricket) 42
Gayfield 88, 96, 106
Gemmell (Dundee) 41, 401 (Celtic) 191
General Strike 73, 125, 228, 393, 407
Georgeson, Roddy 322
Gibbons (Falkirk) 369
Gibson, Ian 43
Gibson, Fred 67, 136, 232, 369, 383
Gibson, William 284,
Gilchrist (Celtic) 237
Gilfillan, Bobby 336, 351, 370
Gillespie (Rev George) 160
Gillespie (Dundee United) 317
Gillick (Rangers) 329
Gilligan (Clyde) 82
Gilmour, Tommy 149, 219, 249, 293, 303, 311
Gilpin, James 252, 314
Gilzean (Dundee) 182
Glasgow Ashfield 414
Glasgow Charity Cup 428
Glasgow Herald, The 70, 109, 251, 349, 370, 375
Glasgow Rangers x, xi, 2, 12, 19, 20, 21, 24, 26, 43, 49, 60, 67, 72, 75, 76, 81, 86, 93, 95, 110, 125, 135, 138, 149, 153, 158, 162, 172, 176, 182, 183, 185, 203, 204, 207, 208, 209, 210, 215, 227, 229, 247, 250, 252, 254, 267, 268, 273, 290, 291, 300, 308, 312, 319, 323, 325, 329, 336, 337, 339, 341, 347, 356, 357, 359, 361, 363, 365, 370, 372, 376, 379, 385, 386, 394, 396, 399, 425, 428, 437, 454, 455, 460, 465
Glassey, Bob 432
Glebe Park 297, 405
Glen, Alex 293, 311
Glen (Aberdeen) 355
Glencraig Celtic 17

Goodfellow, George 32
Goodwillie (Dundee United) 367
Gorman (Montrose) 347
Gotu Itrotterfelag 55, 74
Gould, John 110
Gourlay, Jimmy 67, 163, 256, 265, 281, 350, 369, 443
Gracie (Morton) 67
Graham, Ally 53, 152, 176, 193
Graham, Bobby 267
Graham Harry 369
Graham (Hearts) 274
Graham (Ross County) 35
Grant (Celtic) 396
Grant (Inverness) 266
Grant (St Bernards) 311
Gray, Alex 105
Gray, Dave 340
Gray, John 202, 238, 262
Gray (Celtic) 396
Gray (Third Lanark) 255
Great War ix, 9, 126, 150, 170, 174, 261, 274, 308, 313, 316, 377, 416, 436, 450
Green (Albion Rovers) 158
Greenock 67, 254, 283, 313, 333, 417, 444, 446
"Grenadier" 245
Grierson, Sandy 201, 238
Grieve, Andrew 132, 428
Grove (Partick Thistle) 341
Gunners 414, 425
Gunnlaugsson (Akranes) 116

H

Haddock (Clyde) 146
Haffey (Celtic) 227, 370, 379
Halliday (Dundee) 197
Hallowe'en Ghost Walk 160
Hamilton Academical ix, 50, 71, 108, 115, 135, 163, 186, 196, 258, 314, 341, 363, 380, 408, 420

473

Hampden 81, 88, 118, 136, 154, 158, 215, 256, 258, 273, 275, 329, 340, 341, 348, 352, 357, 365, 367, 371, 373, 374, 379, 382, 383, 418, 449
Harris, Colin 186, 221
Harrow, Andy 167, 347
Harvey (Airdrie) 328
Harvey (Leeds) 398
Hateley (Rangers) 176
Hather (Aberdeen) 178
"Hawk-Eye" 247
Haywood, Norman 149, 222, 249, 293, 303, 311
Hearts x, 27, 32, 33, 52, 67, 83, 121, 131, 150, 162, 172, 175, 207, 247, 253, 265, 268, 274, 285, 286, 289, 316, 325, 326, 345, 349, 350, 376, 386, 394, 406, 421, 428, 435, 445, 446
Hearts of Beath 265
Heath (Prime Minister) 134, 271
Heath (referee) 326
Henderson, Darren 100
Henderson (Hibs) 400
Henderson (Rangers) 24
Henderson (Stenhousemuir) 314
Henderson (Third Lanark) 61
Hendry (Dundee) 30
Herd (Clyde) 312
Herd (East Fife) 343
Herdman, Bert ix, 37, 38, 145, 154, 165, 263, 275, 287, 327, 421, 454, 460, 461
Hetherston, Peter 100, 133, 177, 243
Hibernian (Hibs) 32, 33, 35, 50, 83, 108, 111, 114, 129, 131, 133, 134, 137, 141, 147, 156, 165, 169, 170, 177, 185, 186, 192, 208, 225, 251, 261, 270, 289, 290, 294, 302, 352, 357, 375, 400, 445, 459, 461
Hickman 150
Higgins (Hibs) 141
Highland Loch 8, 463
Hi-Hi-Hi 95
Hilland, Paul 107

Hilley (Third Lanark) 255
Hillhouse (Third Lanark) 174
Hislop, John 167, 216, 267
Hodge, Peter x, 32, 163, 280, 281
Hoeness (Bayern Munich) 423
Houston, Tommy 284
Houston (Falkirk) 148
Howie (Newcastle United) 127
Hubbard (M.P.) 14, 39, 291
Hubbard (Rangers) 86, 203, 209
Huddersfield Town 414
Hughes, John 302
Hughes (Celtic) 105, 191, 309, 322
Hunter, David 267
Hunter (Dundee) 245,
Hurrell, William 150
Hurricane Brian 147
Hutchison, Davie 25
Hutchison, Ronnie 105
Hutchison (M.P.) 174, 237
Hynd, Alex 65, 103

I

Ibrox 43, 65, 75, 83, 93, 95, 172, 176, 182, 185, 193, 203, 208, 209, 288, 350, 370, 448, 455
Iceland 74, 101, 116
Inglis, Bill 3, 18, 19, 42, 67, 68, 108, 173, 175, 201, 212, 238, 288, 321, 365
Inter Cities Fairs' Cup 385
Inverness 2, 266
Irvine (Dundee United) 317

J

Jablonski, Neil 107
Jackson (Hibs) 225
James, Alec ix, 2, 18, 68, 69, 97, 112, 113, 129, 144, 164, 173, 174, 197, 219, 228, 237, 245, 254, 261, 316, 332, 342, 357, 371, 414, 425, 431, 439, 450
Jardine (cricket) 25

Jennings, Tom 3, 18, 68, 109, 129, 144, 173, 175, 197, 288, 316, 321, 332, 365, 371, 427, 444
Jessop (cricket) 65
Johnston (Rangers) 208
Johnstone, George 206, 319, 352
Johnstone (Scotland) 456
Joyner, Francis 110, 159, 168, 204, 249, 293, 329, 374
Judge, Mike 162
"Junior" 90, 153, 275, 346

K

Kahn (Bayern Munich) 143
Kelly, Bernie 62, 95, 118, 141, 154, 172, 190, 209, 270, 348, 460
Kelly (Celtic) 428
Kelso 196
Kemback 459
Kennedy (Celtic) 379
Kennedy (M.P.) 144, 174, 321, 426
Kennedy (US President) 188
Kerr, Jimmy 84, 362
Kerr (Kilmarnock) 263
Kerray, Jim 70, 86, 185, 257
Kettering 377
Kichenbrand (Rangers) 86, 203
Kilbowie Park 186, 331
Kilmarnock 53, 113, 172, 190, 192, 263, 308, 337, 339, 346, 348, 366, 385, 407
King Cup 406
King's Park 73, 149, 374
King's Rifle Volunteers 180
Kinnell (Aberdeen) 355
Kirk, Steve 297
Kirkcaldy *passim*
Kirkcaldy Cottage Hospital Cup 410
Kirkcaldy Cricket Club 25, 42, 77, 426
Kirkcaldy High School 10, 19, 276
Kirkcaldy Times, The v, 129, 138, 184, 263
Kirkcaldy United 27, 108, 256, 262, 320
Kirkpatrick (Dumbarton) 394

Kirkwood, Davie 152
Kivlichan (Celtic) 306
Klinsmann (Bayern Munich) 143
Knowles (referee) 186

L

Laing, John 131
Laird (Forfar) 226
Lambert, John 223, 250, 428
Lambert (St Mirren) 47
Lassodie 132
Laurie, Ian 182, 188, 252, 314
Law (Scotland) 372, 456
Law (Chelsea) 449
Lawrence (Airdrie) 152
League Challenge Cup xi, 104, 107, 119, 359, 360, 361, 441
League Cup x, 2, 3, 26, 30, 33, 35, 41, 49, 59, 61, 70, 72, 75, 83, 86, 88, 95, 96, 100, 104, 105, 106, 107, 128, 133, 134, 145, 147, 152, 154, 156, 158, 159, 172, 176, 177, 178, 192, 193, 194, 195, 204, 241, 263, 287, 300, 328, 329, 361, 381, 389, 403, 417, 421, 423, 454, 462
League Division Two 65, 134, 202, 235, 265, 440, 445
League of Ireland 95
Ledgerwood (Partick Thistle) 276
Leeds United 332, 398, 444
Leicester City 129
Leigh, Andy x, 2, 25, 70, 95, 106, 172, 178, 182, 189, 190, 203, 207, 267, 275, 289, 294, 309, 329, 348, 355, 379, 389, 390, 417, 457
Leishman (East Fife) 62
Leitch, John 437
Leitch, Sam (BBC commentator) 388
Leith Athletic 110, 131, 153, 214, 311, 330, 406, 420
Leith Franklin 77, 426
Lennon, Danny 74, 101, 160
Lennon (Hibs) 302

Lennox (Celtic) 105, 372
Leslie Hearts 27
Levein, Craig 121
Lincoln City 427
Lindsay, Alec 211
Lindsay, Jimmy 340
Links Market 366, 370
Links Park 347, 385
Linlithgow 48
Lister, Ian 52, 96, 158, 380, 386, 388, 399
Little (Aberdeen) 178, 355
Little (Hamilton Academical) 258
Liverpool 383
Livingston 36, 104, 441
Livingstone (referee) 329
Livingstone (Montrose) 385
Lloyd George 127, 131, 211, 229, 247, 265, 321
Lochgelly 103, 127, 180, 254, 435
Locke, Gary 148
Locked Out Engineers 244
Logan, James ix, 2, 13, 15, 16, 42, 48, 97, 107, 111, 136, 163, 170, 171, 184, 196, 219, 224, 226, 229, 258, 287, 307, 369, 383, 407, 416, 427, 435, 439, 449
Longmuir (Celtic) 64
Love Street 153, 154,164
Low, Alec 150
Lunn (Dunfermline Athletic) 268
Lyall, George 88, 105, 331

Mac/Mc

McAinsh, Tom 382
McAllister, William 446
McAnespie, Stephen xi, 5, 55, 101, 143, 193, 328, 338, 408
McAtee (Celtic) 64
McAulay, Archie 67, 265
McBride (Celtic) 105, 242
McCalliog (Scotland) 372
McClure, Malcolm 389
McColl (Hibs) 129

McColl (Rangers) 329
McCrae Cup 445
McCrae's Batallion 196
McDermott, Murray x, 5, 96, 186, 187, 216, 251, 267, 354, 401
McDiarmid Park 152

MacDonald, John 201, 235, 238
McDonald, John 202
MacDonald (Prime Minister) 131, 144, 261
McDonald, Tommy 317, 370
McDonald (Dundee) 197, 245
McDonald (Falkirk) 369
McDonald (Hearts) 162
MacDonald (Rangers) 75, 208 (Airdrie) 328
McDougall (Aberdeen) 298
McEwan, JImmy 62, 86, 94, 118, 172, 178, 192, 241, 253, 294, 348, 349, 457
McFarlane, Tommy 267
McGarr (Aberdeen) 339
McGeachie, George 83
McGill (Airdrie) 207
McGillivray, Angus 198
McGinlay (Hibs) 225
McGinn (Hibs) 400
McGlynn, John x, 217, 218, 367, 395
McGowan (Dundee) 30
McGregor (Hibs) 400
McGrogan, Felix 188, 252, 314
McGrory (Celtic) 230
McGuire, Benny 162
McGurn, David 39
McInally, Jim 55
McInally (Celtic) 64, 365 (Third Lanark) 174
McInnes (Inverness Caley) 266
MacKay, Bob 424
MacKay (Celtic) 370
MacKay, (Queen's Park) 340
MacKay (Kilmarnock) 190,
McKenzie, Sandy 230

McKeown, Tommy 105
McKinlay (Dundee United) 92
McKinnon, Ray 400
McLaren, Jackie 57, 93, 376
McLaughlin, Joe 352
McLaughlin (Clyde) 312
McLay, George 48, 136, 196, 334
McLean, Davie 245
McLean, Tommy 98, 99
McLean, Willie 105, 410
McLean (Celtic) 308
McLean (Dundee United) 44, (Clyde) 146
McLean (Forfar) 126
McLeish (Hibs) 133
MacLeod (Edinburgh City) 293
McLure, Malcolm xi, 329, 345, 349, 390, 434
McMahon (Celtic) 428
McManus, Declan 35, 148, 405
McManus, Paul 107
McMenemy (Celtic) 306, 313
McMichael (Hibs) 445
McMillan, Hamish 203
McMillan (Falkirk) 369
McNamee, John 165
McNaught, Ken 423
McNaught, Willie ix, xi, 2, 5, 25, 85, 86, 95, 106, 110, 138, 154, 159, 172, 192, 203, 207, 215, 241, 270, 275, 283, 294, 295, 327, 329, 345, 348, 352, 355, 369, 389, 390, 417, 423, 452, 453, 457
McNeill (Celtic) 373
McNicoll, George x, 200, 201, 235 326
McPhail (Airdrie) 228
McPhail (Celtic) 352
McSeveney (Motherwell) 172
McStay, Jock 43
McStay (Celtic) 193, 357, 365
McTaggart (referee) 207
McVeigh, John 104
McWilliam (Newcastle United) 127, 313

M

Mackems 398
Mackie, Alex 131, 238
Mackie, Jimmy 111, 233
Mackle, Tommy 372
Madden (Celtic) 428
Main, Alex 335
Mair (Dumbarton) 250
Maley (Celtic) 237, 369, 440
Manchester City 300
Manning, John 32, 201, 419
Marchbanks, Walter 245
Marine Gardens 293
Markinch Victoria 461
Marshall, Jimmy 362
Marshall (Celtic) 193
Martin, Fred 48, 224, 232, 285, 358, 369
Martin (Aberdeen) 192
Martin (Rev John) 448
Mason (Third Lanark) 255
Masson, Willie 110
Mathieson, Jimmy 197, 245
Mathieson, Willie 76
Matthew, Andy 31, 62, 114, 167, 347
Maule, Johnny 5, 25, 61, 84, 90, 156, 159, 204, 270, 276, 290, 327, 329, 352, 390, 427, 460
Maxwell (Kilmarnock) 337
Mays (Kilmarnock) 190
Meiklejohn (Rangers) 276, 357
Melchior (Austria) 215
Mennie (Clyde) 291
Menzies, Brian 252
Mercer (Hibs) 33, 83
Merchant (Falkirk) 348
Meredith (Wales) 436
Methil 62, 382, 393
Michie (Dunfermline) 389
Midland League 304
Millar, Jimmy 75, 162, 208, 268, 325, 339
Miller, Allan 72

477

Miller, George 68, 144, 173, 225, 245, 298, 332, 341, 371, 427, 444
Miller (Aberdeen) 298
Miller (Hibs) 225
Miller (Celtic) 124
Miller (referee) 320
Milligan (Clyde) 291
Millwall 287, 396, 427, 447
Miners' Strike 60, 73, 125, 216, 271, 443
Mitchell, Henry 201, 202, 326
Mitchell, John 251
Mitchell, (Dundee United) 317
Mitchell Cup 432
Mochan, Denis 106, 421, 453
Mole, Jamie 367
Moller (Hearts) 162
Montgomery, Willie 387, 432
Montgomery (Sunderland) 398
Montrose 21, 26, 100, 140, 183, 244, 267, 296, 347, 380, 385, 388, 459
Moodie, Charlie 131, 201
Moody, John 90
Moran (Falkirk) 348
Morris, David 2, 3, 5, 64, 68, 109, 113, 129, 138, 144, 146, 159, 175, 197, 212, 219, 228, 229, 237, 245, 247, 254, 288, 307, 308, 316, 321, 332, 342, 357, 365, 371, 377, 415, 439, 449
Morrison, William 369
Morrison (Director) 414
Morrison (Stenhousemuir) 128
Morton 24, 67, 81, 104, 140, 183, 184, 254, 271, 283, 305, 308, 313, 314, 335, 357, 365, 380, 388, 407, 417, 433, 446
Motherwell 48, 55, 57, 104, 111, 156, 164, 172, 176, 253, 267, 273, 281, 316, 323, 352, 420, 441
Moyes, David 3, 175, 288, 308, 321, 365
Muir, Harry 198
Muirton Park 457
Munro "Geordie" 116
Munro, Iain 225, 297
Munro (politician) 285

Murray, Derek 43
Murray, Euan 441
Murray, Grant 361
Murray, Jimmy 331
Murray, Les 138, 276, 290, 352
Murray (Forfar) 98
Murray (politician) 144
Murray (referee) 281
M'Voto, Jean-Yves 413

N

Nairn (linoleum manufacturers) 19, 410, 426
Napier (Stenhousemuir) 128
Napier (Supporters Club) 214
Narey, David 193, 408
National Union of Miners 393
Neilson, John 238,
Neilson, Jimmy 410, 428
Neilson (St Mirren) 154
Neish, John 19
Nelson, Tommy 304
New Bayview 79
Newcastle United 34, 127, 158, 313, 435, 461
New Powderhall 293
Newto(w)n Park 410, 437
Nicholl, Jimmy ix, x, 28, 47, 50, 53, 83, 92, 116, 160, 177, 193, 195, 279, 287, 366, 396, 408, 447
North British Railway Company 175
North Eastern League 63, 110, 169, 295, 387, 433
North End Park 382
Northern Ireland 53, 72
Northern League 13, 233, 406, 420
Nottingham Forest ix, 51, 52, 454
Novar 221, 237, 251, 285, 426

O

Oag, Eck 180, 428
O'Boyle, George 36

Ochilview 128, 167
Ogston (Aberdeen) 351
O'Hara (Falkirk) 348
Old Kirk 32, 76, 160, 179, 415, 448
Ollerton Hotel 4
Omand (Queen's Park) 275
"Onlooker" v, 113, 219
Orion 233
Ormond (Hibs, Scotland) 114, 128, 141, 165, 294, 456
Orrock (Falkirk) 369
Orwell (author) 60, 362
Oswald (Dunnikier) 19, 25, 131
Owers (Clyde) 350

P

Paisley 138, 153, 154, 164, 202, 333, 440, 450
Panayiotou, Harry 400
Panther, Fred 40, 57, 376
Parkhead 72, 105, 106, 138, 182, 322
Pars 23, 177, 242, 253, 268, 284, 386, 389
Partick Thistle 55, 70, 100, 106, 154, 224, 232, 247, 261, 276, 279, 293, 300, 303, 306, 308, 312, 323, 336, 337, 340, 341, 357, 371, 396, 407, 408, 460
Pathé News 270
Paton, Bertie 216, 268
Paton (Rangers) 329
Pattillo (Aberdeen) 432
Penman, Willie x, 5, 61, 75, 124, 156, 159, 168, 204, 290, 319, 327, 329, 330, 352, 381, 387, 389, 390, 432, 433, 460
Penman (Dundee) 336
Perth 107, 141, 152, 168, 457
Peters (Forfar) 246
Petershill 29
Pettigrew (Ayr United) 121
Philip, David 67
Phillip, Alec 238,
Phillip (Aberdeen) 333

Phillips (referee) 348
Philp, Davie 111
Philp (referee) 235
Phinn (Dunfermline) 242
Phypers, Ernest 150
Pigg, Albert 228, 446
Pittodrie 2, 67, 110, 146, 178, 206, 319, 351, 355, 377, 432
Polland, Willie 348
Porter, Willie x, 125, 224, 232, 258, 259, 383
Porterfield, Ian xi, 88, 105, 183, 213, 273, 380, 397, 398, 462
Port Glasgow Athletic 440
Potter, Brian 152
Premier League xi, 2, 31, 44, 47, 53, 54, 60, 92, 104, 133, 150, 167, 176, 186, 297, 354, 364, 366, 375, 396, 401, 408, 411
Premiership 148, 242, 356, 361, 396, 400
Prest (Bradford City) 34
Preston (Forfar) 126
Preston North End 112, 357, 418, 431
Prinlaws Albion 459
Puskas, Ferenc 154, 457

Q

Queen of the South 23, 380, 385, 388, 399
Queen's Park 49, 88, 136, 163, 179, 256, 257, 258, 273, 294, 312, 340, 369, 383, 437, 461
Quinn (Celtic) 113, 175, 306

R

Raeburn, Jimmy 3, 64, 68, 175, 212, 219, 237, 247, 254, 288, 321, 342, 365, 371, 377
Raeside, Robbie 408
Rafferty (Airdrie) 281

Railway Stand 1, 92, 268
Raisbeck (Partick Thistle) 224
Raith Athletic 169, 459
Raith Rovers passim
Raith Rovers Sports 27
Ramsay, George 250
Rangers – *see Berwick Rangers, Glasgow Rangers*
Rankin (Airdrie) 207
Rankine, Simpson 103
Rattray, John 19, 229, 321
Ravenscraig Park 19, 116
Reay, George 73
Red Lichties 380
Reekie, Willie 29, 38, 63, 150, 295
Reid, Bobby 75, 105, 158, 191, 267, 272, 273, 296, 314, 323, 325
Reid (Clyde) 350
Reilly (Hibs) 141, 213, 294
Rennie (referee) 173
Renton 244
Reynolds (Celtic) 428
Richardson, John 48, 82, 274
Richardson, Jocky 105, 140, 213, 255, 273
Richardson, Jimmy 180
Rippon (Hamilton Academical) 163
Ritchie, Alex 341, 373
Robbie's Park 1, 437
Robertson, Malcolm 271, 346
Robertson (Clyde) 312
Robertson (Falkirk) 369
Robertson (Third Lanark) 95
Robinson, Jack 150
Ross County 26, 35, 367
Rougier, Tony 55, 225
"Rover" 175
Rowbotham, Jason 176, 193
Roxburgh (East Stirlingshire Clydebank) 331
Royal Scots 16, 17, 19, 29, 439
Rugby Park 113, 190
Rummenigge (Bayern Munich) 423
Rutherford (Rangers) 329

S

Schaedler (Hibs) 134
Scotland 2, 3, 14, 21, 23, 35, 39, 55, 60, 61, 65, 70, 77, 95, 101, 103, 108, 115, 118, 120, 121, 127, 131, 132, 138, 141, 144, 146, 154, 158, 165, 179, 180, 183, 185, 186, 190, 192, 198, 202, 206, 207, 209, 213, 215, 224, 228, 235, 245, 254, 258, 282, 297, 308, 311, 313, 316, 317, 326, 331, 332, 333, 341, 357, 358, 365, 371, 372, 374, 377, 383, 393, 399, 403, 406, 411, 414, 417, 418, 420, 421, 423, 426, 427, 431, 433, 435, 436, 445, 449, 450, 453, 454, 455, 456, 459, 461, 463
Scotsman, The 83, 201, 244, 311
Scott, Ian
Scott, Jimmy (1910s) 29, 232, 334, 335, 459
Scott, Jimmy (1930s) 335
Scott (Falkirk) 173
Scott (Hibs) 225
Scott (Rangers) 86, 185, 203
Scottish Challenge Cup 3
Scottish Consolation Cup 250, 256, 265
Scottish Cup xi, 4, 13, 16, 23, 38, 42, 48, 60, 73, 76, 82, 103, 111, 113, 125, 129, 131, 133, 137, 145, 153, 163, 179, 180, 206, 217, 219, 228, 229, 232, 235, 238, 244, 250, 252, 254, 255, 256, 257, 261, 263, 265, 266, 267, 268, 270, 271, 273, 275, 276, 278, 281, 282, 283, 285, 289, 290, 291, 293, 294, 297, 298, 300, 303, 307, 308, 309, 312, 313, 314, 316, 319, 322, 326, 327, 328, 332, 337, 339, 341, 342, 343, 344, 345, 348, 349, 350, 351, 352, 355, 356, 358, 367, 369, 370, 373, 376, 379, 382, 383, 386, 388, 400, 406, 407, 421, 427, 428, 435, 436, 437, 439, 445, 447, 450, 454, 459, 464

Scottish Football League 416
Scottish League ix, x, 2, 3, 13, 25, 26, 30, 32, 33, 35, 48, 49, 64, 65, 66, 67, 70, 75, 80, 81, 82, 83, 88, 91, 95, 97, 100, 104, 106, 107, 128, 131, 137, 147, 152, 156, 158, 159, 177, 182, 192, 193, 195, 201, 202, 204, 207, 209, 212, 235, 237, 241, 246, 250, 255, 265, 270, 287, 293, 298, 306, 331, 333, 337, 361, 365, 382, 389, 399, 406, 415, 417, 420, 421, 428, 437, 440, 445, 454, 462
Scottish League Cup x, 2, 3, 30, 33, 35, 49, 70, 75, 83, 88, 100, 104, 106, 107, 128, 147, 152, 156, 158, 159, 192, 193, 195, 204, 241, 287, 361, 389, 417, 421, 454, 462
Scottish Qualifying Cup x, 2, 13, 91, 103, 180, 200, 201, 326, 440
Scouller (Clyde) 82
Second Division ix, 21, 31, 32, 40, 59, 66, 73, 93, 125, 140, 149, 188, 201, 202, 266, 267, 271, 273, 275, 283, 293, 300, 303, 306, 307, 314, 322, 323, 331, 340, 343, 373, 374, 388, 398, 403, 407, 416, 435, 446, 451
Selkirk 103
Sharkey (Airdrie) 207
Shaw, Hugh 145, 146, 165, 182, 351, 379
Shaw (Celtic) 29, 237, 342, 365
Shaw (Kirkcaldy United) 320
Shaw (Motherwell) 172
Shaw (Rangers) 329
Shawfield 82, 207, 278, 283, 312
Sheffield Wednesday 377
Shyberry Excelsior 395
Simpson (Queen's Park, Third Lanark, Celtic) 61, 461
Simpson (Rangers) 203
Simpson, Hugh 67
Sinclair, Colin 72, 75
Sinclair, Davie xi, 55, 143, 193, 338, 408
Sinclair (Newcastle United) 127

Singapore 295, 432
Skacel, Rudi 35
Sligo Rovers 441
Sloan, Robert 217
Small (Hamilton Academical) 380
Smith, Barry 79, 441
Smith, Gordon 49
Smith, Jimmy 103, 146, 256
Smith Dr John 179
Smith, John 84
Smith, Paul 298, 363
Smith, Willie 416
Smith (Aberdeen) 339
Smith (Dundee) 182
Smith (Edinburgh City) 293
Smith (Hibs) 270
Smith (Rangers) 81
Sneddon (Hibs) 251
Sneddon (Kilmarnock) 339
Somme ix, 9, 16, 17, 29, 126, 150, 170, 174, 261, 274, 308, 313, 316, 377, 416, 436, 439, 450
Sons of the Rock 252, 394
Souness (Rangers) 43
Southern League Cup 128
Spence, Greig 49, 79, 246, 361, 441
Sporting Post, The 167, 222
Stair Park 147, 188, 403
Staite, Dick 337
Stamford Bridge 358
St Andrews United 374, 425
Stark's Park x, xi, 1, 17, 19, 20, 24, 27, 30, 31, 34, 42, 47, 50, 52, 53, 54, 55, 61, 62, 64, 68, 72, 73, 75, 81, 83, 84, 86, 90, 92, 95, 96, 100, 101, 103, 105, 106, 107, 116, 118, 121, 126, 133, 134, 136, 138, 144, 146, 159, 163, 165, 167, 169, 174, 175, 177, 180, 183, 184, 191, 196, 198, 202, 208, 209, 212, 214, 216, 221, 222, 224, 225, 226, 227, 228, 232, 233, 235, 236, 238, 241, 242, 247, 251, 254, 256, 258, 261, 264, 267, 271, 273, 278, 285, 290, 291, 293, 294,

295, 298, 300, 303, 304, 305, 309, 317,
321, 322, 325, 326, 336, 337, 339, 341,
342, 343, 346, 351, 362, 363, 366, 371,
373, 374, 375, 376, 377, 381, 383, 384,
385, 386, 387, 388, 389, 395, 399, 400,
407, 412, 413, 425, 428, 433, 434, 437,
440, 446, 447, 448, 449, 450, 462, 466
Station Park 24, 26, 49, 140, 226, 279
St Bernard's 19, 27, 131, 201, 214, 262,
  307, 311, 316, 342, 420
Steel (Dundee) 327, 433, 434
Steen, Ian 251
Stein, Bobby 140, 314
Stein, James 461
Stein, Jay 104
Stein (Celtic) 105, 191, 322, 325, 388
Stein (Rangers) 208
Stenhousemuir 77, 84, 90, 128, 167,
  314, 372, 441
Stephen (Inverness Caledonian) 266
Stevenson (referee) 164
Stevenson, Ryan 302
Stewart, George 238
Stewart, Jackie 63, 128, 198, 283, 295,
  345
Stewart, Mark 148, 394
Stewart (Falkirk) 369
Stirling Albion 2, 41, 88, 103, 149, 204,
  323, 336, 374, 381, 389, 390, 403
St John (Motherwell) 31, 32, 172
St Johnstone x, 53, 54, 107, 231, 256,
  322, 375, 381, 403, 411
St Mirren x, 47, 138, 153, 154, 164, 173,
  192, 227, 257, 313, 324, 366, 379,
  407, 436, 460
Stott (Partick Thistle) 276
Stranraer 147, 188, 403
Strathmore, Earl of 226
St Roch's 144
Stubbs (Hibs) 400
Sunderland 105, 398, 454
Sunday Post, The 135, 168, 198, 247, 433
Supporters Club xi, 12, 13, 38, 145,
  214, 329, 443, 452, 459

Suttie, Eck 132, 428
Sutton (Bradford City) 34
Swanson (Dundee United) 367
Sweeney, Paul 43
Syme (referee) 266

T

Tade, Gregory 242
Tannadice Park 137, 168, 260
Taylor, Alex 55
Taylor, James 267
Telford Street 266
Terris (Falkirk) 369
"The Judge" 222
Thiepval 29
Third Division 36, 100, 416
Third Lanark x, 61, 95, 138, 174, 196,
  255, 269, 291, 312, 313, 444, 461, 463
3rd Lanarkshire Rifle Volunteers 95, 255
Thoms, Jackie 59
Thomson, Jason 35
Thomson, Scott 55, 101, 116, 151, 152,
  193, 396, 408
Thomson (Celtic) 93
Thomson (Clyde) 278, 396
Thomson (Dundee) 137, 245
Thomson (referee) 213
Thorarinsson, Hjalmar 121
Thorburn, Alex 67
Thorburn, Jim 114, 336, 351
Thordursson (Akranes) 101
Thornton (Rangers) 329
Three-Day Week 271
Tighe (Dunfermline Athletic) 253
Till, Ernie x, 204, 205, 329, 363, 460
Todd, James 196, 334
Todd, Hugh 373
Tosh, Steve 243
"Townsend" 184, 229
Trades Fortnight 26
Trade Union Congress 393
Troup (Dundee) 68, 97, 212
TUC 393

Tully (Celtic) 352
Turnbull (Hibs, Aberdeen) 134, 141, 270, 294, 339
Turner, Tommy 144, 341, 418, 446
Twaddle, Kevin 225
Twin Towers 100
Tynecastle 62, 150, 162, 270, 271, 274, 289, 316, 326, 341, 348, 350, 358, 406

U

UEFA Cup 74, 101, 116, 143
Ure (Dundee) 336
Urquhart, Donald 186, 298, 356, 375, 401
Urquhart, John x, 70, 86, 114, 165, 178, 209, 210, 267, 348, 427
Uruguay 453

V

Vale of Leven 235
Vaughan, Lewis 26, 30, 35, 49, 79, 119, 147, 246, 394
Victoria United 233

W

Waddell (Rangers, Kilmarnock) 263, 329
Wagner (Austria) 215
Waite (George) 184, 229
Walker, Davie 132, 223, 410, 428
Walker, Tommy 52, 191, 268, 349
Walker (Celtic) 193
Walker (Hearts) 316, 326
Wallace, Gordon 44, 75, 96, 139, 140, 183, 186, 255, 267, 273, 325, 339, 346, 380, 388, 399, 401, 411, 462
Wallace, Joe 202, 238
Wallace, Willie 114, 118, 191, 257, 309, 312, 325, 355, 372, 386, 388, 421
Ward (Hibs) 141
Ward (referee) 282

Wardhaugh (Hearts) 349
Warriors 90, 128
Watson (Rangers) 208
Watt (Newcastle United) 127
Waugh (referee) 180
Webster (Dundee United) 367
Weir, Bobby 233
Weir, Graham 395
Weir (Aberdeen) 298
Weir (Celtic) 352
Welsh (referee) 126
Welsh, Fletcher 135
Welsh (Hearts) 274
Wembley Wizards 425, 431, 449
Wemyss Cup 406
West Bromwich Albion 244, 418
Westland, Doug 329, 381, 389, 390
Whalley, George 110
Wharton (referee) 94
White, Tommy 70
White (Rangers) 75
White (Hamilton Academical) 258
Whitelaw, Johnnie 149, 249, 293, 303
Wightman, John 137
Wilkie, James 201, 235
Williamson, Johnny 95, 209, 348
Willis, Dave 112
Wilson, Barry 101, 408
Wilson, Billy 314, 351
Wilson, Bobby 221
Wilson, George 73, 127, 435, 443
Wilson, Jimmy 335
Wilson, Pat 323
Wilson (Hearts)
Wilson (Rangers) 185
Wilton (Rangers) 81
Windass (Bradford City) 34
Withe (Aston Villa) 423
Wood (Hibs) 170
Woodburn (Rangers) 329
World Cup 10, 115, 213, 372, 411, 418, 423, 453, 456
Wright, Keith 60, 362

Y

Yacamini (referee) 141
Yoker 282
York City 36
Young, Andy 2, 5, 62, 70, 95 98, 106, 128, 138, 141, 155, 156, 172, 198, 203, 207, 241, 253, 270, 275, 276, 289, 294, 329, 345, 348, 349, 355, 381, 387, 389, 390, 417, 432, 457, 460
Young (Celtic) 97, 306
Young (St Bernards) 307
Young (politician) 14

Z

Zanatta, Dario 246

Events by Year

1828 448
1856 25
1883 1, 260, 287
1884 179, 250
1888 244
1890s 112, 135, 250, 428
1891 1, 250, 437, 450
1892 132, 179, 250, 304
1894 180
1896 223, 369
1897 238, 244, 250
1898 2, 244, 410
1901 131, 233, 406
1902 ix, 65, 66, 103, 201, 237, 400, 420, 445, 448, 455
1904 xi, 27, 238, 435, 442
1905 x, 202, 234, 320
1906 201, 235, 262, 285, 435
1907 32, 326, 349, 419
1908 32, 306, 419
1909 93, 113, 127, 137, 382, 435
1910 ix, 48, 67, 80, 81, 82, 91, 111, 137, 256, 265, 350, 435, 440
1912 82, 111, 136, 163, 281, 350, 450
1913 x, 16, 29, 224, 232, 252, 290, 324, 350, 358, 369, 427, 436, 439
1914 x, 48, 196, 285, 286, 313, 383, 424, 436
1915 19, 29, 48, 82, 108
1916 15, 16, 29, 211, 274
1917 17, 137, 333, 393
1919 135, 170, 313, 436, 439, 464
1920 42, 64, 113, 184, 219, 229, 258, 305, 308, 377, 436, 464
1920s x, 2, 4, 5, 13, 16, 20, 39, 97, 113, 179, 197, 219, 228, 236, 287, 332, 418, 446, 450, 463
1921 x, 19, 64, 109, 175, 212, 288, 321, 365
1922 x, xi, 1, 3, 20, 97, 113, 174, 219, 236, 237, 247, 254, 278, 282, 283, 371, 377, 378, 393, 404, 415, 427, 431, 439, 444, 449
1923 8, 18, 20, 68, 129, 137, 164, 173, 254, 261, 308, 371, 377, 463
1924 v, 4, 144, 197, 228, 261, 307, 316, 342, 377, 393, 439, 444
1925 112, 245, 332, 341, 357, 431, 449, 450
1926 73, 125, 228, 393, 407, 416, 435, 439, 443
1927 13, 228, 373, 376, 435, 443
1929 40, 376, 418, 426, 446
1930 57, 376, 414, 439, 446, 451
1930s 2, 4, 12, 39, 450
1931 93, 230, 451
1932 ix, 58, 425
1932-33 ix, 58
1934 179, 226, 444
1935 12, 14, 24, 153, 335
1936 21, 126, 214, 225, 260, 427
1937 x, 149, 222, 249, 292, 374
1938 249, 293, 303, 311, 343, 344, 424, 465
1939 84, 90, 110, 363, 424, 444, 465
1940s 39, 204
1941 100, 110, 450
1942 150, 169, 295

1943 63
1944 14, 105, 388, 433
1945 14, 38, 39, 145, 387, 432, 444
1946 14, 128, 198, 241
1948 5, 159, 168, 204, 283
1949 xi, 62, 88, 124, 145, 152, 204, 317, 329, 330, 381, 389, 390, 460
1950 x, 61, 138, 156, 215, 269, 291, 461
1950s x, 2, 3, 31, 36, 105, 178, 207, 240, 287, 345, 401, 417, 462
1951 276, 290, 319, 327, 352, 462
1952 270, 289, 453, 459
1953 ix, x, 23, 102, 206, 318, 431, 450
1954 10, 141, 377, 418, 453
1955 62, 178, 192, 203, 241, 283, 423
1956 25, 118, 154, 190, 209, 294, 345, 349, 375, 457
1957 86, 95, 172, 253, 348, 454
1958 10, 94, 178, 207, 224, 229
1959 52, 70, 106, 185, 376, 421
1960 ix, 105, 114, 117, 118, 257, 263, 275, 312, 355, 421, 454
1960s v, x, 3, 31, 94, 98, 264, 284, 401
1961 145, 165, 182, 227, 263, 309, 439
1962 146, 336, 379, 417, 421
1963 59, 188, 252, 317, 351, 367, 370, 388, 417
1964 252, 314, 398
1965 88, 105, 213, 266, 331, 372
1966 44, 140, 158, 183, 213, 421
1966/67 44
1967 ix, 23, 51, 52, 191, 255, 273, 322, 372, 380, 385, 388, 398, 399, 421, 454
1968 ix, 23, 139, 145, 208, 386
1969 44, 72, 75, 162, 268, 325, 339, 372
1970 31, 92, 216, 323, 340, 366
1970s 23, 229, 347
1971 5, 96, 322, 340
1972 3, 4, 76, 158, 337, 346
1973 41, 76, 105, 115, 134, 398, 444
1974 216, 271, 456
1975 31
1976 4, 76, 267, 296

1977 ix, 166, 167, 347, 423
1977-78 ix, 166
1979 44, 401
1980 44, 186
1980s 1, 2, 298
1981 4, 44, 60, 221, 241, 251, 287, 300, 354, 356, 366, 375, 411, 423
1982 284, 356, 411, 423
1983 44, 221
1984 60, 77, 103, 362
1985 ix, 34, 56, 298
1987 43, 300, 403
1988 x, 43, 310
1990 83
1990s xi, 2, 4, 5, 384
1991 279
1992 33, 47, 177
1993 ix, x, xi, 28, 46, 54, 92, 176, 231, 287, 300, 364, 366
1994 ix, 46, 53, 71, 152, 193, 287, 300, 361, 403, 462
1995 ix, x, 55, 74, 78, 101, 116, 142, 143, 160, 181, 328, 408
1996 98, 225, 287, 396, 447
1997 43, 50, 76, 287, 297, 447
1998 50, 447
1999 104, 287, 447
2000 243
2000s xi, 2, 392
2001 36, 100, 133
2003 xi, 34, 120, 422, 458
2004 xi, 120, 458
2005 107
2006 ix, 121, 122
2008 395
2010 367
2011 242
2013 49, 119
2015 394
2016 9, 26, 35, 148, 400, 413
2017 30, 79, 147, 148, 302, 405, 412, 413, 441
2018 v, 246, 321, 412

Lightning Source UK Ltd.
Milton Keynes UK
UKHW021432191118
332600UK00012B/1308/P

9 781849 211727